Northern Ireland after the troubles

MANCHESTER
1824

Manchester University Press

Northern Ireland after the troubles

A society in transition

Edited by
COLIN COULTER AND MICHAEL MURRAY

Manchester University Press

Manchester and New York

distributed exclusively in the USA by Palgrave Macmillan

Published by Manchester University Press
Oxford Road, Manchester M13 9NR, UK
and Room 400, 175 Fifth Avenue, New York, NY 10010, USA
www.manchesteruniversitypress.co.uk

Distributed exclusively in the USA by
Palgrave, 175 Fifth Avenue, New York NY 10010, USA

Distributed exclusively in Canada by
UBC Press, University of British Columbia, 2029 West Mall,
Vancouver, BC, Canada V6T 1Z2

British Library Cataloguing-in-Publication Data
A catalogue record for this book is available from the British Library

Library of Congress Cataloging-in-Publication Data
A catalog record for this book is available from the Library of Congress

ISBN: 978 07190 7440 0 hardback

ISBN: 978 07190 7441 7 paperback

First published 2008 by Manchester University Press

First digital edition produced by Lightning Source 2010

Belfast, Northern Ireland, 7 September 2005, 21:19 BST

Contents

Tables

Figures

Notes on contributors

Fidelma Ashe is Lecturer in Politics in the School of Economics and Politics, the University of Ulster at Jordanstown. She has written widely on issues of gender in Northern Ireland and is the author of *The New Politics of Masculinity: Men, Power and Resistance* (Routledge, 2007).

Alan Bairner is Professor of Sport and Social Theory in the School of Sport and Exercise Sciences, Loughborough University. He is the author of *Sport, Nationalism and Globalization: European and North American Perspectives* (SUNY Press, 2001) and the editor of *Sport and the Irish: Histories, Identities, Issues* (UCD Press, 2004).

Stephen Baker is Lecturer in Film and Television Studies in the School of Media, Film and Journalism, the University of Ulster at Coleraine. He has published widely on media representations of the conflict in Northern Ireland.

Sean Campbell is Senior Lecturer in the Department of English and Media at Anglia Ruskin University, Cambridge. He is the co-author (with Gerry Smyth) of *Beautiful Day: Forty Years of Irish Rock* (Cork University Press, 2005) and the author of a forthcoming study of second-generation Irish musicians in Britain.

Andreas Cebulla is Research Director at the National Centre for Social Research, London. He has published widely on economic and regeneration policy in Northern Ireland and is the co-author (with David Greenberg, Karl Ashworth, and Robert Walker) of *Welfare to Work: New Labour and the US Experience* (Ashgate, 2005).

Paul Connolly is Professor in the School of Education, Queen's University, Belfast. He has published extensively on issues of race and racism in Britain and Northern Ireland and is co-author (with Alan Smith

& Berni Kelly) of *Too Young to Notice? The Cultural and Political Awareness of 3–6 Year Olds in Northern Ireland* (2002, Belfast: Community Relations Council).

Colin Coulter is Senior Lecturer in the Department of Sociology, the National University of Ireland, Maynooth, He is the author of *Contemporary Northern Irish Society: An Introduction* (Pluto, 1999).

Geraint Ellis is Senior Lecturer in the School of Planning, Architecture and Civil Engineering, Queen's University, Belfast. He has written widely on issues of spatial planning and sustainable development in a Northern Irish context.

Romana Khaoury is completing a doctorate in the School of Sociology, Social Policy & Social Work, Queen's University, Belfast. Her research is focused upon the experience of ethnic minorities in Northern Irish schools.

Patricia Lundy is Senior Lecturer in the School of Sociology and Applied Social Sciences, the University of Ulster at Jordanstown. She has published widely on issues of victimhood and memory in Northern Ireland is the co-author (with Mark McGovern) of *Ardoyne: The Untold Truth* (Beyond the Pale, 2002).

Claire Mitchell is Senior Lecturer in Sociology in the School of Sociology, Social Policy & Social Work, Queen's University, Belfast. She has written widely on religious and political identities in Northern Ireland and is the author of *Religion, Identity and Politics in Northern Ireland: Boundaries of Belonging and Belief* (Ashgate, 2005).

Michael Murray is Lecturer in Sociology in the Department of Adult and Community Education, the National University of Ireland, Maynooth. He has written extensively on the politics of waste management on both sides of the Irish border.

Mark McGovern is Reader in Social Sciences at Edge Hill University. He has published widely on issues of victimhood and memory in Northern Ireland and is the co-author (with Patricia Lundy) of *Ardoyne: The Untold Truth* (Beyond the Pale, 2002).

Greg McLaughlin is Senior Lecturer in Media Studies in the School of Media, Film & Journalism, the University of Ulster at Coleraine. He is the author of *The War Correspondent* (Pluto, 2002).

William J. V. Neill is Professor of Spatial Planning in the Department of Geography and Environment, the University of Aberdeen. He has written extensively on urban change. His publications include *Urban Planning and Cultural Identity* (Routledge, 2003).

Mary O'Rawe is Senior Lecturer in the Transitional Justice Institute, the University of Ulster at Jordanstown. She has written widely on issues of policing and human rights in a Northern Irish context and is the co-author with Linda Moore of *Human Rights on Duty–Principles for Better Policing: International Lessons for Northern Ireland* (Belfast: Committee for the Administration of Justice, 1997).

Peter Shirlow is Senior Lecturer in the School of Law, Queen's University, Belfast. He is the co-author (with Brendan Murtagh) of *Belfast: Segregation, Violence and the City* and the co-author (with Kieran McEvoy) of *Beyond the Wire: Former Prisoners and Conflict Transformation in Northern Ireland* (Pluto, 2008).

Gerry Smyth is Reader in Cultural History in the department of English at Liverpool John Moores University. Among his books is *Noisy Island: A Short History of Irish Popular Music* (Cork University Press, 2005).

Jim Smyth is Lecturer in Sociology in the School of Sociology, Social Policy & Social Work, Queen's University, Belfast. He has written widely about issues of political economy in Northern Ireland and is the co-author (with Graham Ellison) of *The Crowned Harp: Policing Northern Ireland* (Pluto, 1999).

Jonathan Tonge is Professor of Politics in the School of Politics and Communications Studies, the University of Liverpool. He has written extensively about Northern Irish political life and is the author of *Northern Ireland* (Polity, 2006).

Acknowledgement

The editors and contributors wish to acknowledge the generous support of the National University of Ireland in the form of a grant in aid of publication. Thanks also to Martin Hargreaves for compiling the index.

1

Introduction

Colin Coulter and Michael Murray

While the recent turbulent political history of Northern Ireland has produced countless moments that will be difficult to forget, most of those that remain longest in the memory do so for the most harrowing of reasons. The particular day in question here, however, marks a stunning exception to that miserable general rule. Even the invariably doleful Northern Irish weather appeared to have read the script. At midday on 31 August 1994, as the region basked in glorious sunshine, the Provisional IRA declared that from midnight it would embark upon a 'complete cessation of military operations'. Within six weeks, this seemingly historic move would be echoed in a cease-fire called by the principal paramilitary organisations on the loyalist side. The biggest-selling local newspaper sought to capture the sense of relief and perhaps even euphoria that many – though not, of course, all – felt that sumptuous late summer day when republicans committed themselves to laying down their arms. In its evening edition the banner headline of the *Belfast Telegraph* declared simply and boldly, 'It's over!'

It was always entirely predictable of course that the rhetorical optimism that greeted the republican cease-fire – in some quarters, at least – would transpire to be rather ill judged. The era of the troubles had produced a few false dawns, and hard experience had counselled that there would be many twists in the plot before the conflict could genuinely be said to be over. It was widely expected, therefore, that the path to political reconciliation would be a long and arduous one. There were few who would have anticipated, however, that the peace process would be beset by quite so many reversals. As the crises have accumulated the optimism once harboured by many ordinary people in the region has been largely displaced by disillusionment at – and even uninterest in – the prospect of real political progress. While the unlikely and possibly historic developments that unfolded in the spring and early summer of 2007 would seem to herald a genuinely progressive turn in the political life of the six counties, it is entirely likely that there will be further twists to come in this complex narrative. More than a dozen years on from those heady days signalled by the original paramilitary cease-fires, it still remains less than entirely clear what precisely will be the fate of Northern Ireland after the troubles.

The Good Friday Agreement

The era of the peace process has witnessed an at times bewildering sequence of political initiatives. The most significant political development of the period has of course been the agreement that eventually emerged from the tortuous negotiations that began in the autumn of 1997 in the wake of the decision of republicans to reinstall their cease-fire. On Good Friday 10 April 1998 the various parties to the talks announced that, against all odds, they had finally come to an agreement on the political future of Northern Ireland. Not for the first time, and certainly not for the last, it appeared for a while that the political fortunes of the region might just have taken a turn for the better.

The document that emerged from the multi-party negotiations at Stormont inevitably was detailed, multi-faceted and wide-ranging. The Belfast Agreement seeks to address and resolve a series of relationships – those between people living either side of the Irish border and either side of the Irish sea – that are understood to be at the heart of the 'Northern Ireland problem'. The principal concern of the document is inevitably, however, to mend the often troubled relations between unionists and nationalists living in the region. In essence, the deal struck at Stormont represents an attempt to reach an honourable compromise between the ambitions and identities that often appear to divide the 'two communities' in Northern Ireland. The text of the document seeks to allay the enduring fears of the unionist community that they might be forced or duped into a united Ireland. It is stated quite categorically that 'Northern Ireland in its entirety remains part of the United Kingdom'.[1] Furthermore, the text affirms that any change to the constitutional status of the region can happen only with the concurrent electoral consent of people living in both jurisdictions on the island. While the agreement clearly seeks to accord with unionists' ambition to remain citizens of the United Kingdom, it also sets out to accommodate nationalists' aspiration that they might in the future become citizens of a united Ireland. The text clearly acknowledges as legitimate both the political objectives and the cultural practices that are associated with the tradition of Irish nationalism. In addition, it is stated that if in the future a majority of people living either side of the border give their simultaneous support to the unification of Ireland, it would be a 'binding obligation' upon both the British and Irish governments to ensure that this came to pass.

While the Belfast Agreement clearly envisages that nationalists will remain *de facto* British citizens for some time to come, it also seeks to assure that they will do so on rather more favourable terms than has often been the case in the past. The historical experience of the minority community in the region has been marred by discrimination and disenfranchisement. The text agreed in the multi-party talks marks an attempt to resolve these historical grievances through the implementation of a sweeping programme of political and institutional reform. The 108 seat Assembly devised under the deal is obliged to operate in a manner that empowers both communities more or less equally. Those matters that come before the legislature that are deemed to be 'key' can be endorsed only on a cross-community basis. Furthermore, the two most senior positions in the proposed Executive – the First and Deputy First Ministers – have to attract the support of both nationalist and unionist Members of the Legislative Assembly (MLAs). The remainder of those holding Ministerial posts are to be assigned on the basis of party strengths and according to the d'Hondt system, which in effect means that the positions of executive power are in the hands of equal numbers of nationalist and unionist politicians.

The consociational mode of government envisaged by those who framed the Belfast Agreement proves to be emblematic of a broader concern to build an equitable and inclusive social order in Northern Ireland. In effect, the agreement reached at Stormont represents a new deal for nationalists living in the region. One of the most alienating aspects of the nationalist experience in Northern Ireland was dealing with a police force that was drawn almost exclusively from the unionist community and that often conducted itself in a discriminatory and draconian manner. The Belfast Agreement seeks to redress the grievances of nationalists by promising a 'new beginning to policing' in the region. The text of the deal provides for the creation of an independent commission charged with beginning the arduous task of creating a police force that both reflects the composition and enjoys the trust of Northern Irish society as a whole. The commitment to a programme of reform is expressed further in the provisions for a review of the criminal justice system and for the establishment of a Human Rights Commission as well as an Equality Commission. Finally, the terms of the agreement seek to underline the need for greater respect for cultural and linguistic diversity. While Ulster-Scots is mentioned in passing, it is of some significance perhaps that it is the Irish language that is discussed at greater length as a cultural practice that deserves attention and funding.

Moving on?

In the early days after the deal was struck, it seemed that the Belfast Agreement might just be that hitherto elusive settlement that might mark a new and more progressive phase in the political life of Northern Ireland. The document that had emerged from months of painstaking negotiation was both comprehensive and clever – a little too clever, some critics would say, but more of that later. The accord enjoyed the backing of the British, Irish and US administrations as well as of all the main-stream local parties, with the ominous exception of the Democratic Unionist Party (DUP). More important, perhaps, the agreement had gained favour among the ranks of those paramilitary groupings on both sides of the divide whose opposition would have made it untenable. While the deal negotiated at Stormont had the blessing of most of the political classes, its broader popular appeal would be tested in the dual referenda scheduled for 22 May 1998. In the Irish Republic the Belfast Agreement had evidently struck a chord, with 95 per cent of the votes cast being in favour. On the other side of the border, predictably, the outcome of the ballot was rather less clear-cut. In the Northern Irish poll some 71 per cent of the electorate that exercised their right to vote said 'yes' to the Belfast Agreement. In most electoral circumstances, of course, such a proportion would be considered a ringing endorsement. A closer examination of voting patterns, however, revealed a marked and poten-tially dangerous trend. While the overwhelming majority of the nation-alist community had cast their votes in favour of the proposed deal, only a very slim majority of unionists had also voted 'yes'.[2] What were the reasons for the very different responses that the agreement elicited within the 'two communities'?

In a sense, it was always fairly inevitable that most nationalists would find the Belfast Agreement to their liking. The influence of certain nation-alist thinkers was, after all, clearly apparent in the terms of the deal.[3] The notion of the three strands of relationships, the emphasis upon power sharing and the conviction that the problems of Northern Ireland could be resolved only through political arrangements that both acknowledge and, more importantly, transcend that particular territorial space, all bear the hallmark of the SDLP. The popularity of the Belfast Agreement among constitutional nationalists was always, therefore, more or less guaranteed. In principle, however, the response of republicans to the deal should perhaps have been rather different.

Over the preceding three decades the republican movement had waged a brutal military campaign designed to take Northern Ireland out of the Union. The Belfast Agreement, however, quite clearly recognises and guarantees the constitutional status of the region as part of the United Kingdom. While a minority expressed their opposition to the deal, the republican movement *en masse* chose to endorse it. In so doing, republicans would seem to have violated the most central and cherished ideal of their political tradition.[4] Quite conscious perhaps of the betrayal entailed in accepting the Belfast Agreement, the upper echelons of Sinn Féin have sought to shift attention away from the constitutional provisions of the accord. The leadership of Sinn Féin has sought consistently to cast the agreement as a process rather than an outcome. It is argued that the new political arrangements – and in particular the North/South bodies established under the deal – have a latent 'dynamic' that will gradually and inevitably nudge the six counties into a united Ireland.[5] While this 'inevitability thesis' is on balance a matter of pure political fantasy, that has not prevented it from becoming a comforting mantra regularly rehearsed by the Sinn Féin leadership.

The second, and rather more convincing, strategy that republicans have adopted to obscure their blatant betrayal of their own ideals is to focus upon the benefits that will arise from the programme of reform sketched out in the Belfast Agreement.[6] The Sinn Féin leadership has sought to underline those elements of the deal that appear to promise nationalists fairness and equality within Northern Ireland.[7] While this strategic shift of focus from the 'national question' to the 'democratic question' raises questions about the legitimacy and utility of the IRA campaign over the previous three decades, the emphasis that republicans have placed upon a reform agenda that seems to offer genuine cultural and material parity would appear to have struck a chord within an increasingly pragmatic but confident nationalist community.[8]

In principle, there were elements of the Belfast Agreement that had the potential to appeal greatly to most of the unionist community.[9] After all, the signatories to the accord had agreed that the constitutional status of Northern Ireland was to be respected and could not change without the voluntary consent of the majority of people living there. In effect, therefore, the deal hammered out at Stormont explicitly endorsed the principal ideal and ambition of the unionist tradition. While the constitutional guarantees enshrined within the Belfast Agreement were attractive to a great many unionists, their appeal was somewhat diminished by two further considerations. Firstly, the fairly generalised sense of mistrust that defines and deforms their political imagination ensured that unionists were unwilling to take at their word a whole range of other political actors and in particular the British state.[10] Quite simply, the unionist community was from the outset never entirely convinced that the constitutional guarantees within the Belfast Agreement were in fact worth the paper they were written on. Secondly, those aspects of the deal that were attractive to unionists were from the beginning finely balanced against other elements that they found deeply troubling. While the unionist community hoped that the Belfast Agreement might be a final settlement, they also feared that it would in fact prove to be a process that would undermine their interests and perhaps ultimately sweep them into a united Ireland.[11]

Hence, when unionists went to the polls in May 1998, they were torn between an ambition to strike a deal that would finally signal an end to the troubles and an anxiety to avoid being duped into arrangements that would ultimately undermine their position. The ambivalence and tension that defined the response of the unionist community to the new political circumstances were all too apparent in the way they cast their votes. While more unionists voted for the Belfast Agreement than against, this was the product more of rational calculation than principled or emotional attachment to the deal itself.[12] There were clearly many within the unionist community who had severe misgivings about the agreement but who took a leap of faith in the hope that a 'yes' vote might finally bring peace and stability to the region. The precise balance of forces within unionism in the future would hinge largely upon how this particular group of pragmatists who supported the deal in principle would respond to the specific manner in which it was implemented in practice – whether they felt that it was fair, whether they considered that promises had been honoured, whether measures that might have appeared just about tolerable in prospect turned out to be entirely intolerable in reality, and so forth.[13] It would soon become apparent, however, that many of the developments initiated under the auspices of the Belfast Agreement were deeply alienating even for those unionists who had made the pragmatic decision to give the deal a chance. The early release of paramilitary prisoners and the reform of the police were particularly crucial in nurturing a sense even among relatively liberal unionists that the new political dispensation was heavily loaded against them. As the terms of the Belfast Agreement were gradually implemented the widespread and growing alienation of the unionist community would become the most palpable cause and symptom of the crisis that would engulf the entire peace process.

Guns and government

The actual substance and prospective success of the Belfast Agreement often appeared to assume the existence of a crucial symmetry in the interests and experiences of unionists and nationalists respectively. The advocates of the new political dispensation were from the outset keen to insist that it made more or less equal demands upon, and offered more or less equal benefits to, both the principal ethnopolitical traditions in Northern Ireland. The new deal was held to signal an honourable and historic compromise that would in time usher in an era of peace and prosperity for all. It would soon become apparent, however, that the particular balance presumed by the proponents of the Belfast Agreement did not in fact exist. While the implementation of the deal would of course require compromise across the board, it would in practice make rather more onerous demands of one community than the other. The ramifications of this critical imbalance within the peace process would become readily apparent when it came time to initiate the principal institutions conceived under the terms of the Good Friday Agreement.

The centrepiece of the political arrangements agreed at the multi-party negotiations was of course a consociational mode of government for Northern Ireland in which unionists and nationalists would exercise authority more or less equally. While agreeing to share power necessarily required uncomfortable decisions on all sides, these would transpire to be rather more unpalatable for some than for others. The formation of an Executive required that politicians agree to co-operate with others whose views and actions in many cases they regarded as odious. The practice of power sharing demanded that nationalists accept that they will in part be subject to the decisions of unionist political figures, some of whom they considered to be indelibly sectarian. With the unedifying image of his victory jig along the lower stretches of the Garvaghy Road fresh in the mind, the prospect as the millennium turned of having David Trimble as First Minister cannot have been one that appealed greatly to the nationalist community. Crucially perhaps, however, the devolution of power to Northern Ireland did not actually require nationalists to enter government with individuals who had been directly involved in politically motivated violence against them.

Since the beginning of the troubles there has existed relatively little support or respect for paramilitarism within unionist communities. In the main, unionists have turned their backs on the unofficial violence of the loyalist paramilitaries and preferred the role of advocates and agents of the official violence of the British state. The poor esteem in which paramilitarism is held within the unionist community finds critical expression in electoral trends. Those parties that are associated with the loyalist paramilitaries have only a miniscule presence in the Assembly and stand no chance whatsoever of securing Ministerial positions. When the new executive was eventually formed for the first time in December 1999 nationalist politicians were, therefore, spared the anguish of having to sit across a table from people who had been closely associated with the campaign of violence against their community.

The same cannot of course be said of those unionist politicians who were selected for Ministerial positions. Over the period of the peace process the republican movement has made considerable ground at successive elections. Their growing electoral strength meant that, when the first ill starred power sharing executive was formed at Stormont, Sinn Féin secured the two key Ministries of Health and Education, thereby placing the party in charge of half the devolved governmental budget. The composition of the new cabinet inevitably alienated a great many unionists who were appalled at the prospect of crucial decisions concerning their lives being taken by individuals who had orchestrated and rationalised the campaign of violence they considered the IRA to have waged against their community. The outrage that many unionists felt at the advent of republicans in government was embodied in the figure appointed to the position of Minister of Education in the initial ill fated Executive. That Martin McGuinness – widely regarded at the time as a long-standing chief of staff of the IRA – would now be in charge of their children's schooling struck many within an already sceptical unionist community as emblematic of the insidious and intolerable nature of the entire peace process.

In the referendum held to ratify the Belfast Agreement a majority – albeit a slim one – of unionists had of course voted to endorse a deal that they knew would inevitably lead to republicans holding positions of government. The decision of unionists to lend their support to the settlement was, however, a largely pragmatic one that assumed that the unpalatable inclusion of Sinn Féin within the Executive would be paired with the disarming and disbanding of the IRA. This issue of the 'decommissioning' of paramilitary weapons has of course represented the principal stumbling block that the peace process has faced from the very beginning. The enduring disputes surrounding the fate of the IRA's arsenal and that of other groupings owe their origins to a particular trait of the Belfast Agreement that may be considered both its greatest strength and its principal weakness.

The potential success of any prospective political settlement in Northern Ireland would crucially hinge upon its ability to appear to be able to square the circle of what are in some cases the mutually exclusive demands of the nationalist and unionist communities respectively. Those who framed the Belfast Agreement sought to create such an impression through a 'constructive ambiguity' designed to create the impression that the deal signalled a 'loserless' conclusion to the troubles.[14] Some of the provisions of the text are worded in a manner that both enables and encourages unionists and nationalists to interpret them differently. This characteristic is particularly, and possibly fatally, apparent in section 7, which deals with the issue of decommissioning.[15] The relevant section of the Belfast Agreement[16] states that all the participants to the talks:

> reaffirm their commitment to the total disarmament of all paramilitary organisations. They also confirm their intention to continue to work constructively and in good faith with the Independent Commission [the official body established to oversee the decommissioning process], and to use any influence they may have, to achieve the decommissioning of all paramilitary arms within two years . . .

While the text that faced them was of course exactly the same, unionists and nationalists almost inevitably chose to read the provisions for decommissioning in ideologically convenient and, therefore, starkly different ways. In the eyes of the unionist community, the Belfast Agreement simply signalled that the IRA and other paramilitary organisations would disarm and disband during the two-year period in which their prisoners would be released. The reading to which the republican movement chose to adhere was predictably rather different. The view consistently offered by the Sinn Féin leadership was that decommissioning would be a long and arduous process that could work only within the context of the wider demilitarisation of Northern Irish society. While republicans acknowledged that the Belfast Agreement required them to use their influence to bring about disarmament, they did not appear to regard the deal as necessarily obliging them actually to bring about this particular outcome.

The coincidence of unionist expectations that the IRA should disband quickly and verifiably and the refusal of republicans to do so repeatedly thwarted the development of the peace process in Northern Ireland.[17] The various attempts to break the deadlock over decommissioning typically assumed the increasingly predictable form of the following cycle.[18] In the hope of making progress, the then Ulster Unionist Party (UUP) leader David Trimble would take a leap of faith and agree to go into government on the proviso that republicans would disarm during a specified period of time.[19] During this window of opportunity the IRA would then either fail to dismantle its armoury or would do so in a manner that unionists found accountable and acceptable.[20] The resultant crisis in confidence would see the institutions of government suspended and the whole cycle of negotiation and recrimination would begin anew. The final performance of this particular farce came to a conclusion in October 2002 when allegations concerning continuing activity on the part of the IRA – in particular that republicans were gathering illicit information on their supposed partners in government – led to the Executive collapsing for a fourth time.[21] In total, the power sharing government conceived within the Belfast Agreement had operated for a mere nineteen months and would remain in cold storage for a further four and a half years.

While the stalemate over decommissioning of itself represented a fundamental crisis of and for the Northern Irish peace process, it also unleashed forces that appeared to threaten further the prospect of genuine political progress in the region. The dispute over 'guns and government' inexorably served to harden and polarise political opinion in Northern Ireland.[22] In the minds of many nationalists, the refusal of unionist politicians to engage in sustained co-operation with Sinn Féin represented a violation of their rights and bespoke an abiding sectarian aversion among unionists to actually share power with the nationalist community. This reading served to nurture an alienation that has seen a growing body of nationalists switch their allegiance to Sinn Féin, whom they regard as the party more willing and able to face unionists down and assert their interests. In the 2001 Westminster elections Sinn Féin overtook the SDLP for the first time, and the polls held since have merely confirmed and indeed amplified the status of the party as the principal voice of contemporary Northern Irish nationalism.

The hardening of nationalist opinion sparked largely by the issue of decommissioning has inevitably found its double within the unionist community. The seeming refusal of republicans to fulfil their presumed obligation to disarm inevitably alienated many within the unionist community. In the summer of 2005 the IRA would of course complete an independently verified process of decommissioning that signalled its apparent demise as an organisation. But by then, unfortunately, the damage to unionist confidence had already been done. The nagging conviction that republicans were not to be trusted, and that their decision to disarm was merely a pragmatic move designed to enable the pursuit of their goals through other means, hardened the outlook of the unionist community. This would find electoral expression in the emergence of the DUP as the strongest voice within unionism. In the Westminster elections of 2005 the party secured twice as many votes as the erstwhile pre-eminent UUP, which suffered the humiliation of being able to retain only a single seat, in affluent North Down.

The polarisation of political opinion that has unfolded during the present decade had the potential of course to fatally undermine the political settlement codified in the provisions of the Belfast Agreement. As opinion divided and hardened the prospect of the principal players in Northern Irish political life having the appetite or freedom to make real compromise and progress appeared to recede. If the relative moderates of the UUP and the SDLP had been unable to sustain a power sharing government, what then were the chances of the more fundamentalist voices of the DUP and Sinn Féin coming to agreement? While the widespread pessimism induced by the polarisation of political opinion in Northern Ireland was not of course entirely without reason, it failed to acknowledge at least one crucial, if admittedly perverse, facet of political reality, both here and elsewhere. While the fundamentalists in any political environment often appear to be the ones least willing or able to make compromises, they are also at certain times and under certain circumstances the best placed to do so. And so it would prove in the particular context of Northern Ireland.

In October 2006 yet another instalment in the seemingly endless series of talks designed to get the peace process back on track convened in the picturesque setting of St Andrews. After three days of intensive negotiations in the Scottish town it appeared that perhaps some progress had finally been made. With the now customary fanfare, the British and Irish governments unveiled a series of measures that they agreed would enable the political logjam to be resolved. The provisions of the 'St Andrews Agreement' made substantial demands upon all the principal players in the peace process. Sinn Féin would be required to recognise the legitimacy of the police, the DUP would be expected to enter into government with republicans and the British state would have to introduce measures to advance equality and human rights.

While the St Andrews Agreement was heralded in official circles as a potentially historic breakthrough, previous harsh experience ensured that many people in Northern Ireland remained somewhat less than optimistic about the prospects of genuine political progress. For once, however, this scepticism would prove perhaps to be ill founded. While the early months of 2007 would feature more squabbles and histrionics, it would gradually become apparent that beneath the surface there had possibly been some fairly seismic shifts in the political landscape of Northern Ireland. Seemingly against all odds, the DUP and Sinn Féin had finally come to terms with the substantial compromises that were required if they were ever to hold and share power together. The fresh Assembly elections held in March 2007 offered both parties renewed and strengthened mandates to enter into government with one another. The prospect that the new version of power sharing might actually work this time round was enhanced not only by the status of the DUP and Sinn Féin as the most popular forces within unionism and nationalism respectively but also, and perhaps ultimately more crucially, by the fact that they represent the most radical mainstream voices within their different communities. The fundamentalist credentials of the two parties ensure that they will be able to make the compromises that power sharing demands without the constant pressure of influential and dissenting voices seeking to outflank them. It is unlikely, for instance, that there will be a repeat of the scenario in which David Trimble was hounded at every turn by more extreme voices within unionism appalled by what they considered as intolerable concessions to nationalists.

The newfound position of virtual hegemony that Sinn Féin and the DUP have come to enjoy within their communities served, therefore, to prepare the ground for an unlikely political deal between the two former implacable opponents. On 8 May 2007 the global media gathered at Stormont to witness the peculiar sight of Ian Paisley and Martin McGuinness sharing smiles and jokes as they were installed as the First Minister and Deputy First Minister respectively. It is of course rather too early to gauge the fortunes of these particularly unlikely bedfellows but the perilous course that political developments have taken in Northern Ireland over the last generation tends to counsel caution. While the complex narrative of the peace process may appear to have found a happy resolution, the various reversals that occurred along the way have inevitably taken their toll on ordinary people living in the region. With every initiative that transpired to be another dead end, and with every institution that collapsed acrimoniously, the faith and perhaps even interest of the general public in the peace process have been undermined.[23] While undoubtedly there is a great deal of relief that a deal has finally been done, there does not appear to be genuinely popular enthusiasm for this new political dispensation. It all feels a very long way indeed from the excitement of that glorious day in the late summer of 1994.

New dawn fades

When discussing the perilous course of the peace process in Northern Ireland we tend routinely to refer to the Belfast Agreement when perhaps we should in fact be talking in the plural. There are, depending on how you look at it, quite a few Belfast Agreements. When simultaneous referenda were held in May 1998, for instance, people living either side of the Irish border were asked for their opinions on texts whose contents were identical but which were, crucially, physically presented in rather different ways. In the Irish Republic, the version of the agreement that was made available to the electorate assumed the form of a rather drab A5 size legal script. The formal appearance of the text ensured that it made no recommendation one way or the other to its readers, who were in effect entrusted to make up their own minds on its contents. In light of the rather more substantial objections that the agreement had generated in Northern Ireland, however, those official agencies that sought to sell the deal in the region were rather less prepared to leave matters to take their own course.

The version of the Belfast Agreement that was widely distributed north of the border inevitably bore a close resemblance to those simulations of corporate portfolios through which New Labour routinely chooses to affect communication with those it governs.[24] The electorate in the region was greeted with a glossy A4 document that contained the same text as the southern Irish version but which prefaced it with a striking and comforting cover image. The photograph chosen to frame the script of the deal was the entirely predictable but nonetheless powerful one of the four members of a classic nuclear family, embracing one another and gazing across an idyllic bay towards the sumptuous vista on the horizon of what is in all likelihood a sunset but which presumably acts metaphorically here as a sunrise. While the text on the cover of the brochure declared in large font that the outcome of the forthcoming referendum was 'your decision', it was quite clearly intended to sway the minds of those less than entirely convinced by its contents. The bucolic image that greeted the Northern Irish electorate before they turned to consider the detail of the proposed deal evidently inferred that the Belfast Agreement offered an altogether sunnier political future for the region and that the only reasonable course of action was to vote 'yes'.

The decision to package as something akin to a holiday brochure what was after all a legally binding document with enormous political ramifications was from the outset distinctly questionable. What made the practice more objectionable still, though, was that it would subsequently emerge that the particular image used on the cover of the agreement distributed to Northern Irish homes was in fact, in a certain sense at least, a fraud. One particularly sharp-eyed photographer noticed that in the relevant shot the sun appeared to be setting/rising on the opposite side of the sky to what one would expect in Northern Ireland. After some investigative research it was discovered that the photograph employed to imagine the political future of the region was taken not along the Northern Irish coastline as was implied but rather in the somewhat more cheery climes of Cape Town in South Africa.[25] The deception employed here is of course entirely typical of the seeming addiction to spin that formed one of the more insidious traits of the Blair administration. The sleight of hand involved in packaging and selling the Belfast Agreement may also be considered emblematic of the deeply problematic manner in which official discourse routinely operates in relation to Northern Ireland.

Over the period of the peace process those operating within the orbit of the British and Irish states have sought, predictably, to place an unequivocally positive slant on the course that Northern Ireland has taken since the cease-fires. While the political life of the region has stumbled from one crisis to the next, the response of the agents of official discourse has been to remain valiantly on message. The speeches of British and Irish politicians persist with references to new dawns and historic developments. The Northern Ireland Tourist Board[26] seeks to entice visitors to the region with the reassurance that '[m]uch has happened in the past few years and old perceptions of the North have had to be rewritten'. And infomercials in the southern Irish press strive to depict the regional capital, Belfast, as a 'thriving' city in which 'new investments are helping to sustain growth at levels unimaginable a decade ago'.[27]

The official narrative that seeks to recount the peace process as an era marked overwhelmingly by progress contains, it must be said, a substantial kernel of truth.[28] In the dozen years since the first IRA cease-fire many things have changed for the better in Northern Ireland, and these should not be dismissed lightly. In particular, the number of fatalities arising from politically motivated violence has fallen considerably. While there were 857 deaths arising out of the conflict in the eleven years that preceded the initial cessations, in the same period afterwards there were 225. The advent of the peace process has, therefore, ensured that there are several hundred people in Northern Ireland – most of them young working-class men – who are alive and well who might otherwise be prematurely in their graves.[29]

Furthermore, over the period of the peace process, there has arguably been rather greater progress on the issue of policing than would once have been considered possible. The independent commission conceived under the Belfast Agreement and chaired by the former Governor of Hong Kong, Chris Patten, made a series of broadly progressive recommendations that laid the ground for the dissolution of the Royal Ulster Constabulary (RUC) and its replacement in November 2001 by the Police Service of Northern Ireland (PSNI). The latter has a new badge which more fully reflects the range of cultural identities within the region, a revised oath that commits officers respect for human rights and a provision that half of all new recruits to the force should be from Catholic backgrounds.[30] Moreover, unlike its predecessor, the PSNI is subject to greater scrutiny and accountability in the guise principally of the Policing Board and the Office of the Police Ombudsman. The latter, in particular, displayed willingness to ruffle feathers within the police establishment with its damning report that highlighted the incompetence of the RUC investigation of the bombing of Omagh that claimed twenty-nine lives and those of two unborn children in August 1998.[31] The reputation of the Office of the Police Ombudsman as being willing to shine light in some very dark corners was enhanced yet further in January 2007 with the disclosure of widespread collusion in the recent past between police officers and loyalist paramilitaries in north Belfast.[32] While most unionists roundly condemned the dissolution of the RUC as the betrayal of an honourable force that had held the line against 'terrorism' and most nationalists have criticised the pace and extent of change,[33] it would seem that nonetheless we may well be entering into a new era of policing in Northern Ireland. After a great deal of soul searching, Sinn Féin finally agreed at a special *ard fheis* convened in January 2007 to participate in the administration and oversight of policing in Northern Ireland. The presence of three republicans on the Policing Board represents a remarkable turn of events that raises the prospect that the PSNI may in the near future become a body broadly acceptable within the nationalist community.[34]

While the official narrative of the peace process has then some basis in truth, it is important as ever to assume a little critical distance here. As the tale of the misleading cover of the Belfast Agreement testifies, all may not necessarily be quite as the sophists of New Labour would have us believe.[35] Although a great deal of progress has admittedly been made in Northern Ireland, closer examination reveals a sequence of troubling trends. Although the level of fatalities arising out of the conflict has fallen substantially, the number of incidents of certain non-fatal forms of political violence has in fact grown since the 1990s.[36] The inadequate attention afforded to 'punishment beatings' in particular suggests willingness in official circles to overlook certain versions of violent paramilitarism in the interests of political expediency.

The 'narratives of progress' that often inform official discourse on Northern Ireland are undermined further when we turn to consider the state of communal relations in the region after more than a decade of the peace process. When it was signed, the Belfast Agreement was heralded as an historic compromise that would enable and encourage the 'two communities' in the region to transcend their differences and enter a new era of mutual appreciation and co-operation. It has become increasingly apparent, however, that the effect of the deal may have been to nurture rather less progressive political dispositions. In the main, the Belfast Agreement presumes and prescribes those very ethnopolitical interests and inclinations that it ostensibly seeks to overcome. The institutions and processes initiated under the deal presuppose that people in Northern Ireland can mobilise politically only as unionists and nationalists respectively and insist that they compete for resources accordingly. The effect of the Belfast Agreement has, therefore, been to reproduce and legitimate many of those forms of ethno-political feeling and competition that sparked the Northern Irish conflict in the first place.[37]

The ethno-religious prejudice that insinuates its way into the institutions of the Belfast Agreement on those occasions when they are actually working, finds rather starker expression in the everyday life of Northern Ireland. While the peace process has often been depicted as facilitating an era of enhanced intercommunal relations, it has become apparent that sectarian feeling has not only failed to dissipate but may even have hardened in some districts. In recent years, research has indicated that reactionary ethno-political stereotypes are part of the outlook even of infants and central to the mind-set of many teenagers in the region. In the particular context of Belfast, these sectarian prejudices both articulate and are articulated through the organisation of physical space. Since the advent of the Belfast Agreement six new 'peace lines' have been constructed and eleven existing ones heightened and/or extended in the regional capital.[38] The growing spatial segregation of Belfast offers a further dramatic reminder that the peace process has failed to stem the tide of communal polarisation in Northern Ireland.[39]

Indeed, it may well be the case that the recent period of alleged progress in Northern Ireland has been one that has seen not only the persistence of established versions of social prejudice but also the growth of other, historically less significant forms of intolerance. The research that has been conducted to date suggests that the various ethnic minorities living in the region routinely encounter hostility and abuse from some sections of what remains an overwhelmingly homogeneous, white society. As elsewhere, this ranges from commonplace verbal assaults through to less frequent but more serious physical violence.[40] In recent years there has been a spate of attacks upon both new and existing ethnic minorities in various parts of the six counties but especially in deprived loyalist neighbourhoods in south Belfast.[41] This violence has prompted commentators both at home and abroad to ask whether Northern Ireland is in the process of becoming a markedly racist society.[42]

There is a further worrying social trend at work within Northern Ireland that needs to be acknowledged but which is often overlooked in mainstream discussions of the region. One of the assumptions that have often informed official discourse is that the resolution of the Northern Irish conflict would usher in an era of greater prosperity that would serve the interests of all.[43] It has become increasingly evident, however, that, in so far as there can actually be said to have been a peace dividend, its benefits have not been evenly distributed. The middle classes in the region continue to enjoy an affluence that, for the time being at least, continues to be underwritten by enormous subsidies from the British taxpayer.[44] While there are clear cultural and political differences between the unionist and nationalist middle classes respectively, these are typically overridden by a shared and substantial interest in the prevailing order of things. As time passes, the concerns of middle-class unionists and nationalists alike drift ever further away from the disputed realm of the political and converge upon a common preoccupation with that most potent of all contemporary bourgeois totems, spiralling house prices.[45]

The manner in which the poorer sections of Northern Irish society have experienced the peace process has been rather less beneficial. In reality, there has been little discernible peace dividend for working-class people living in the region. The ongoing underdevelopment of the local economy has ensured that the less advantaged within Northern Ireland still have relatively few opportunities for material advancement. While unemployment has admittedly declined, working-class communities in the six counties continue to endure high levels of impoverishment. The multiple social problems that are rife within many working-class neighbourhoods have predictably provided a fertile breeding ground for the production and reproduction of ethno-political hatred. It is in the marginalised districts of north and west Belfast rather than the leafy avenues that grace the south of the city that the most virulent forms of sectarian enmity continue to fester.[46] The intimate association between poverty and prejudice suggests that the cause of progress in Northern Ireland demands not merely the creation of sustainable political arrangements but also the radical redistribution of wealth and opportunity. If there is to be a genuine and lasting peace in the region, those marginalised communities that invariably give voice to the most vehement forms of sectarianism will require the material and cultural resources that are necessary to persuade them that they are valued members of the society in which they live.

During the period of the troubles the gnawing disaffection of working-class nationalists was evidently the most palpable source and emblem of the political instability prevalent within Northern Irish society. The alienation that defines the outlook and experience of republican communities has during the peace process been mirrored in the growing disenchantment increasingly apparent within poorer unionist districts. In the period since the cease-fires were called it has become painfully apparent that working-class unionists have derived little benefit from the supposedly historic political developments unfolding around them. While rates of poverty in nationalist areas appear to be slowly declining, those in loyalist neighbourhoods are in fact on the rise. The problems that poorer unionists face are expressed most keenly perhaps in their educational underattainment. Of the fifteen districts in Northern Ireland where academic performance is worst, no fewer than thirteen are predominantly unionist.[47]

The substantial and multiple disadvantage which they face has inevitably served to alienate many working-class unionists from a peace process which they consider to have conferred benefit upon others but not upon them. The disenchantment rife within loyalist communities has given rise both to stern opposition to the Belfast Agreement and to various troubling forms of political violence. The widespread rioting that ignited in north and west Belfast in September 2005 and in which members of the PSNI came under sustained assault represents possibly the most dramatic manifestation to date of the political alienation common among the less advantaged sections of unionism. It might perhaps be suggested that the mood of sullen disaffection that has descended upon working-class unionist districts constitutes the single most significant threat to the entire peace process. If there is to be meaningful political progress in Northern Ireland then the poorer sections of unionism will have to be able to see that there are benefits that accrue from the compromises that any truly durable settlement will inevitably demand. In the dozen years or so since the cease-fires were called, however, there has been little tangible peace dividend that might encourage working-class unionists to feel that they are among the beneficiaries of the substantial political changes afoot in the six counties. Until such time as they do Northern Ireland will continue to represent a society that, while no longer at war, is not quite yet truly at peace with itself.[48]

The structure of the book

In many respects, therefore, Northern Ireland may be best understood as a society in the throes of transition. The process of social change that has overtaken the region in the last generation has inevitably been complex and at times contradictory. While there are numerous ways in which Northern Ireland has progressed during the peace process, there are also of course various other senses in which it has not. The purpose of this particular book is to relate and explain this dense narrative of social change in a place emerging from three decades of violent conflict – to ascertain what has been transformed and what has not, what has got better and what has not, who has benefited and who has not.

The chapters that follow are written by individuals who come from different backgrounds and work within different academic disciplines. While the collection is, therefore, rather diverse, there is at least one common thread that runs through the entire text. The era of the peace process has seen the formulation of a specific orthodoxy among elements of the political and media establishments in both London and Dublin. At the heart of official discourse has been the contention that the people of

Northern Ireland have turned their backs on their historical differences and are moving inexorably towards a brighter future. A central concern that embroiders the contributions to this volume is to challenge this comforting but ultimately misleading 'narrative of progress'. While all the contributors acknowledge that advances have been made since the cease-fires were brokered, they are also keen to identify the various difficulties – some new, others of rather older vintage – that continue to plague the six counties. In so doing, it is hoped, this collection will offer a rather more nuanced and critical understanding of contemporary Northern Irish society than that which often emanates from the centres of cultural and political power.

The essays that follow are gathered into three broad categories. In Part I we examine those political developments and divisions that are essential to a critical understanding of the nature of Northern Irish society. The collection opens with a chapter by Patricia Lundy and Mark McGovern that considers the significance of historical memory in the six counties. The issue of whether there should be a truth commission to address the events of the troubles in particular has drawn rather different reactions from unionists and nationalists respectively. While acknowledging that memory has become yet another site of dispute in Northern Ireland, Lundy and McGovern suggest that an adequate recall of the past remains essential if people living in the region are to move on and share a better future.

Jonathan Tonge turns our attention towards the disputed political present of Northern Ireland. Chapter 3 documents the process of political polarisation that has defined the period since the initial cease-fires were declared. The collapse of the middle ground, coupled with the growing appeal of competing fundamentalist positions, ensures, Tonge argues, that the creation of a durable political settlement remains far from inevitable. The persistence of political division in Northern Ireland is a theme that is taken up in Chapter 4 by Pete Shirlow. Drawing upon research conducted in some of the most divided and dangerous districts of Belfast, Shirlow argues that sectarian hatred remains undiminished in many of the more deprived neighbourhoods of the city. The 'peace lines' that have been constructed or extended since the cease-fires were called offer a striking material reminder that the peace process has been rather less of a success than some politicians and pundits would have us believe.

The significance of physical space is underlined in the contribution of William Neill and Geraint Ellis. The authors provide a searing critique of the inadequacies that continue to characterise spatial planning in Northern Ireland. While Neill and Ellis are critical of the policies that have defaced the rural landscape, they are especially damning of the decisions and interests that are (mis)shaping the region's principal city. The sequence of chapters devoted to the political life of Northern Ireland concludes with an examination by Mary O'Rawe of one of the most crucial issues of the peace process, that of police reform. Chapter 6 acknowledges that a great deal of progress has been made since the 1990s. It is the conclusion of O'Rawe, however, that the resistance to change coming from some politicians and police officers has thwarted the possibility of creating a genuinely transformed force that is acceptable to all sections of Northern Irish society.

In Part II we shift focus towards the various social identities that shape the lives of people in Northern Ireland. Claire Mitchell addresses the particular source of identity that perhaps springs most readily to mind when thinking about Northern Ireland. Chapter 7 challenges the view that religion is a mere signifier of other, more significant forms of social being. While formal observance may have waned somewhat, religious identity remains, Mitchell asserts, deeply important to how Northern Irish people see themselves and one another. Chapter 8 by Fidelma Ashe sets out to challenge the manner in which the issue of gender is approached in most accounts of Northern Irish society – and not least in this particular book. Ashe analyses the multiple ways in which the experience of war and peace has been gendered in the six counties. The essay concludes with the contention that a more fruitful examination of contemporary Northern Irish society demands the more systematic employment of feminist theory and perspectives.

Jim Smyth and Andreas Cebulla deal with a form of social being and division that is often understated in relation to Northern Ireland, not least at the level of political practice. In Chapter 9 they examine the various ways in which social class defines and deforms the lives of people living in the six counties. While the reconfiguration of global capitalism may have altered the precise formation of Northern Irish society, Smyth and Cebulla illustrate that class remains an essential source of status and identity in the region. Part II concludes with an analysis of what appears to be an increasingly substantial issue – and possible problem – in Northern Ireland. Paul Connolly and Romana Khaoury illustrate in Chapter 10 that race represents an important source of identity and division in the six counties. They provide a range of evidence to suggest that, lamentably, racism appears to be a growing feature of everyday life in Northern Ireland.

Part III focuses upon a number of those elements of (popular) cultural practice that are often overlooked when social scientists address Northern Ireland. In Chapter 11 Alan Bairner examines the important though often dispiriting role that sport plays in Northern Irish society.

Particular attention is paid to the heated debate that centres upon the proposed construction of a new stadium catering for a range of sports on the site of the former Maze/Long Kesh prison. While it is often suggested that sport has the power to heal communal relations, Bairner concludes that it remains principally a source of division in the specific context of Northern Ireland.

Sean Campbell and Gerry Smyth examine the ways in which popular music enables a better understanding of how Northern Irish society has evolved over recent generations. Chapter 12 illustrates that the traumatic events of the troubles were often variously disputed and avoided within the medium of popular song. The work of those Northern Irish artists who have emerged in the last generation leads Smyth and Campbell to suggest, however, that popular musicians have begun largely to leave the preoccupations of the past behind. In the final chapter Stephen Baker and Greg McLaughlin draw our attention to a range of visual cultures in the guise of movies, state-sponsored advertisements and television sitcoms. It is their contention that these media have provided the means through which the British state in particular has sought to rehabilitate paramilitaries whom it had previously demonised in the pursuit of a resolution to the Northern Irish conflict. Chapter 12 concludes with a damning depiction of a cultural establishment in Northern Ireland that has promoted visual cultures that articulate a smug conception of the social world that bears little resemblance to the everyday experience of most people who actually live in the region.

After the troubles?

One of the multiple difficulties associated with commenting on Northern Ireland in the period since the cease-fires is deciding precisely in which tense to speak or write. In spite of the various setbacks that have overtaken the peace process it remains, thankfully, unlikely that the region will return to the level of violence that defined the era of the troubles. While Northern Ireland may no longer be at war with itself, neither can it be said to be genuinely at peace. Those hatreds that were in part the source of the conflict remain clearly evident and may even in fact have grown. The persistence of ethno-political prejudice in particular suggests the need to exercise a little caution before speaking of Northern Ireland as a place that exists 'after the troubles'.

The perilous course that the political process has taken in Northern Ireland inevitably articulates the problems that afflict the broader social context in which it has evolved. The distrust and competition that often define relations between different communities in the region necessarily circumscribe the desire and opportunity of the principal political players to make those leaps of faith that have the potential to enable the region to genuinely move beyond the conflict. It has to be acknowledged, however, that the poverty of political discourse and practice in Northern Ireland is not merely the symptom of a wider dislocated social environment but also its cause.

One of the presumptions upon which the Belfast Agreement rests is that unionism and nationalism are innately valuable political identities, worthy of equal respect and representation. The experience of making peace in Northern Ireland over the last generation, however, has fatally wounded many of the assumptions that inform the ideal of 'parity of esteem'. As the political process has staggered from one crisis to the next it has become increasingly and painfully apparent that unionism and nationalism have really very little to offer the people of Northern Ireland. The principal players within both political traditions evidently possess neither the ability to understand how the social life of the region works in the present nor the facility to imagine how it might be transformed in the future. The intellectual poverty of unionism and nationalism largely reflects a blind spot within their field of vision which they share both with each other and with a great many contemporary political dispositions.

The demise of Stalinism invited and enabled a whole range of social scientists and political commentators to assert that the ways of thinking and talking about capitalism that prevailed hitherto had been rendered obsolete. In particular, it was claimed that the notion of class had ceased to have any real meaning either as an analytical category or as a source of social experience.[49] The essential shortcoming of this influential reading is of course that it simply fails to accord with how real social actors live their lives. While social theorists have sought to pronounce the 'death of class' a substantial body of social research has accumulated that suggests precisely the opposite interpretation.[50] The enduring salience of social class is no more evident than in a region where it has often been assumed to have relatively little. While the social formation that obtains within Northern Ireland may well be rather particular, it remains far from unique. The region exhibits all of those inequalities and injustices that are the essential trait of all capitalist societies. Once we move beyond surface appearances it becomes immediately apparent that the fundamental line of fissure within Northern Ireland primarily reflects socio-economic origins. While the divisions prevalent within the region may often find expression in the form of ethno-religious feeling their substance is principally that of social class.

An acknowledgement of the persistence and prevalence of class divisions is essential if we are to appreciate both the limits to and possibilities for real social transformation in Northern Ireland. A genuine resolution of the conflict will necessarily entail a massive redistribution of both resources and opportunities. If there is truly to be peace in Northern Ireland, those working-class communities that have endured most during the war will have to feel that their interests are being served and their voices heard. The essential failing of the peace process is that it remains defined by political dispositions and discourses that cannot even imagine, let along enable, such a progressive turn. While the principal players in the political process may well sincerely desire an end to conflict, they appear unable or unwilling to conceive of the radical social transformation that peace will demand. We are faced then with the gnawing contradiction of a political settlement that both aspires to heal the divisions within Northern Ireland and intends to allow to remain intact the social forms and interests that gave rise to those divisions in the first place. It is scarcely surprising then that the peace process should have run aground time and again.

The poverty of imagination that characterises both contemporary unionism and nationalism suggests that the causes of peace and progress will ultimately have to be pursued elsewhere. The transformation of the political fortunes of Northern Ireland will inevitably require rather more radical social change than the architects of the peace process are able or willing to acknowledge. If there is to be a genuine and lasting peace, then ordinary people in the region will have to come to recognise that which they share in common and mobilise to redefine the social order in the interests of the many rather than the few. It is only in that historic moment of epiphany that it will become possible, or indeed meaningful, to talk of Northern Ireland as a place that exists 'after the troubles'.

Notes

1 Agreement reached in the multi-party negotiations, 1998, Annex A, Part 1 (1).
2 A. Aughey, 'The 1998 Agreement: three unionist anxieties', in M. Cox, A. Guelke and F. Stephen (eds), *A Farewell to Arms? Beyond the Good Friday Agreement* (Manchester: Manchester University Press, 2006), pp. 89–108, p. 92.
3 A. Aughey, *The Politics of Northern Ireland: Beyond the Belfast Agreement* (Abingdon: Routledge, 2006), p. 30; C. McCall, 'From "long war" to the "war of the lilies": "post-conflict" territorial compromise and the return of cultural politics', in M. Cox *et al.*, *A Farewell to Arms?*, pp. 302–16, p. 303; J. Tonge, 'Polarisation or new moderation? Party politics since the GFA', in M. Cox *et al.*, *A Farewell to Arms?*, pp. 70–88, p. 79.

4 J. Tonge, *Northern Ireland* (Cambridge: Polity Press, 2006), pp. 6, 23, 27, 37.

5 Aughey, *The Politics of Northern Ireland*, pp. 54, 98, 100–2.

6 *Ibid.*, p. 126.

7 J. Tonge, *The New Northern Irish Politics?* (Basingstoke: Palgrave Macmillan, 2005), p. 6; Tonge, *Northern Ireland*, pp. 8, 27.

8 Aughey, *The Politics of Northern Ireland*, pp. 13, 140; C. Mitchell, 'From victims to equals? Catholic responses to political change in Northern Ireland', *Irish Political Studies* 18 (2003), pp. 51–71.

9 Tonge, *The New Northern Irish Politics*, p. 4.

10 Aughey, 'The 1998 Agreement: three unionist anxieties', pp. 92, 97; Tonge, *Northern Ireland*, p. 158.

11 Aughey, *The Politics of Northern Ireland*, pp. 34, 51.

12 Aughey, 'The 1998 Agreement: three unionist anxieties', p. 93.

13 A. Guelke, M. Cox and F. Stephen, 2006, 'Conclusion. Peace beyond the GFA', in M. Cox *et al.*, *A Farewell to Arms?*, p. 444.

14 Aughey, *The Politics of Northern Ireland*, pp. 3, 44–5, 55, 87.

15 P. Shirlow and B. Murtagh, *Belfast: Segregation, Violence and the City*, London: Pluto, p. 47; Tonge, *Northern Ireland*, pp. 191–3.

16 Agreement reached in the multi-party negotiations, 1998, section 7 (3).

17 J. Darby, 'A truce rather than a treaty? The effects of violence on the Irish peace process', in M. Cox, A. Guelke and F. Stephen (eds), *A Farewell to Arms? Beyond the Good Friday Agreement* (Manchester: Manchester University Press, 2006), p. 221.

18 Guelke *et al.*, 'Conclusion. Peace beyond the GFA', pp. 444–9.

19 Aughey, *The Politics of Northern Ireland*, pp. 129–30; 'The 1998 Agreement: three unionist anxieties', pp. 99–101.

20 Shirlow and Murtagh, *Belfast*, p. 43.

21 Tonge, *Northern Ireland*, p. 200.

22 *Ibid.*, pp. 173–81; Tonge, 'Polarisation or new moderation?', p. 70.

23 Aughey, *The Politics of Northern Ireland*, p. 179.

24 T. Nairn, 'Ukania under Blair', *New Left Review* 2:1 (January–February 2000).

25 J. Mullin, 'Picture of a perfect family not quite what it seemed', *Irish Times*, 16 June 1998.

26 Northern Ireland Tourist Board, *Visitor Guide 2006*, p. 4, available at www.discovernorthernireland.com.

27 *Irish Times*, 'Investment in Belfast: a special report', 24 April 2006.

28 Aughey, *The Politics of Northern Ireland*, pp. 161–6.

29 Shirlow and Murtagh, *Belfast*, p. 53.

30 B. Dickson, 'New beginnings? Policing and human rights after the conflict', in M. Cox *et al.*, *A Farewell to Arms?*, pp. 173–5.

31 See Chapter 6 by Mary O'Rawe in this volume.

32 G. Moriarty, D. Keenan, F. Millar and A. Cochrane, 'RUC special branch had "serial killer on books" ', *Irish Times*, 23 January 2007.

33 Dickson, 'New beginnings? Policing and human rights after the conflict', p. 171.
34 McCall, 'From "long war" to the "war of the lilies"', p. 305; Tonge, *Northern Ireland*, p. 196.
35 Aughey, *The Politics of Northern Ireland*, p. 142.
36 Shirlow and Murtagh, *Belfast*, p. 52.
37 R. Wilford and R. Wilson, *The Trouble with Northern Ireland: The Belfast Agreement and Democratic Governance* (Dublin: TASC, 2006).
38 Tonge, *Northern Ireland*, p. 212.
39 O. Bowcott and M. Oliver, 'Another brick on the wall', *Guardian*, 4 July 2007.
40 N. Jarman and R. Monaghan, *Racist Harassment in Northern Ireland* (Belfast, Institute for Conflict Research, 2004); J. Betts and J. Hamilton, *The Nature, Extent and Effects of Racist Behaviours Experienced by Northern Ireland's Ethnic Minority Health Staff* (Belfast, Institute for Conflict Research, 2006). *See also* Connolly and Khaoury in this volume.
41 H. McDonald, 'Loyalists linked to 90 per cent of race crime', *Observer*, 22 October 2006.
42 S. Breen, 'Has peace made us the race hate capital of the world?', *Sunday Tribune*, 17 July 2006.
43 These narratives of progress that have traditionally emanated from London and Dublin have inevitably been parroted by the newly installed power sharing government in Belfast. In the glossy promotional brochure *Your Government – Making a Difference* Ian Paisley and Martin McGuinness assert that their political stewardship provides 'an unprecedented opportunity to deliver a better future for everyone' and that '[t]ogether we can build a new society at ease with itself, where everyone shares and enjoys the benefits of this new opportunity and where no one is left behind'. The document is available at www.northernireland.gov.uk/devolution.pdf.
44 A. Ruddock, 'Addicted to state subvention, north will suffer when it's gone', *Sunday Times*, 8 January 2006.
45 Shirlow and Murtagh, *Belfast*, pp. 101–23.
46 M. Leonard, 'Sectarian childhoods in north Belfast', in M. P. Corcoran and M. Peillon (eds), *Uncertain Ireland: A Sociological Chronicle, 2003–2004*, Dublin: Institute of Public Administration, pp. 195–208.
47 See Smyth and Cebulla, Chapter 9 in this volume.
48 There is of course the further difficulty that any public funds that may be channelled into the most deprived unionist neighbourhoods may in effect be directed towards loyalist paramilitaries as an inducement to turn permanently away from violence. In this not entirely unlikely scenario it is probable that the wider community would derive relatively little benefit from what might appear on paper to be substantial government funding. See for instance H. McDonald, 'UDA wants £30m to disband', *Observer*, 16 July 2006.

49 U. Beck, *Risk Society: Towards a new Modernity* (London: Sage, 1992); A. Giddens, *Modernity and Self-identity: Self and Society in the late Modern Age* (Oxford: Polity Press, 1991); J. Pakulski and M. Waters, *The Death of Class* (London: Sage, 1995).
50 B. Skeggs, *Class, Self, Culture* (London: Routledge, 2003).

Part I

Political developments and divisions

2

Telling stories, facing truths: memory, justice and post-conflict transition

Patricia Lundy and Mark McGovern

How should a society emerging from conflict remember and deal with the violence and injustice of the past? This is a question peoples and states around the world, as well as international non-governmental organisations (NGOs) and institutions of global governance, have come to ask themselves more and more in recent decades, often leading to very different answers. However, what is perhaps most distinctive about Northern Ireland's approach to dealing with thirty years of violent conflict is that, as often as not, it has raised another *a priori* question: should we be remembering the past at all? There have been moves recently that appear to represent tacit acknowledgement on the part of policy makers that simply forgetting the conflict is not really an option. Understood another way, however, what we may be seeing is a new strategy in the management of truth recovery directed primarily at damage limitation. Any developments have also largely been the result of the long-term campaign work of a wide range of human rights and victims' organisations. In addition, moves toward a co-ordinated past-focused truth and justice mechanism have been halting and the subject of bitterly contested political debate. Fundamentally at stake has been whether or not remembering a past, scarred as it is by violent division, is good for the future. Why this has been the case, what form that debate has taken and what it says about the nature of transition in Northern Ireland is the subject of this chapter.

First, however, these questions need to be placed into a wider theoretical and geographical context. The place of the past in the present and future has become a growing concern for thinkers in a range of disciplines.[1] For some, we now live in an 'Age of Memory' in which the conditions of late modernity have given rise to a very specific need for 'making history'. Barbara Mistzal has gone so far as to argue that 'coming to terms with the past has emerged as the grand narrative of our times'.[2] Nowhere is this more apparent than in societies riven by the divisive impact of war, conflict and violence. Dealing with these issues is the

prime concern of the emergent field of 'transitional justice'.[3] To understand the debate on memory and post-conflict truth and justice in
Northern Ireland requires some grasp of how these questions have come
to be conceptualised elsewhere. These will be explored in relation to
what might be called the therapeutic, judicial and archival imperatives of
post-conflict transitional justice work.[4]

If international comparisons show anything it is that the single greatest determinant of the role and nature of truth recovery processes in any
specific instance of post-conflict transition is the political circumstances
of that transition. What, then, have been the political forces framing the
debate on truth recovery in Northern Ireland? How, too, have such forces
impacted upon the attitudes and actions of various state and non-state
actors towards truth recovery? Post-conflict transition in Northern
Ireland has invariably been defined by the terms and conditions of the
Good Friday Agreement (GFA). Significantly, the Agreement made no
more than passing reference to truth recovery mechanisms. Indeed, in the
negotiations leading up to the Agreement discussion of such questions
was conspicuous by its absence. Yet, even as the GFA was being formu-
lated, varying, sometimes directly contradictory, voices were being raised
on truth, justice and victims issues. Often fractious debates emerged over
the early release of conflict-related prisoners, the fate of the 'disappeared', the creation of the Bloody Sunday inquiry and calls for further
investigations into state killings and allegations of collusion between the
security forces and the loyalists. Each evidenced the extent to which
various elements of Northern Irish society had unfinished business as far
as the conflict was concerned. Most remain so up to the present. We will,
therefore, examine the way such issues have shaped contemporary perspectives on memory work and post-conflict justice.

Finally, we will look at some of the problems and ways forward for
transitional justice and memory work in Northern Ireland today. There
have been some important official and civil society initiatives, but by far
the most contentious are concerned with the conduct of investigations,
inquiries and possible prosecutions for conflict-related offences. This is
particularly, but not exclusively, so where state agencies were allegedly
involved. Debate on such developments has also largely been framed by
traditional political and communal divisions. This has certainly informed
official responses in this area. For example, in 2004 the House of
Commons Northern Ireland affairs committee published a report into
'ways of dealing with Northern Ireland's past'. The time was not right
for the establishment of an official 'truth recovery process', the committee members argued, because of the political impasse in the peace process
and the problems with 'initiating truth processes that do not appear to

enjoy firm, cross-community support'.[5] The chapter will therefore conclude by exploring contemporary attitudes to 'ways of dealing with the past' (conducted as part of the Northern Ireland Life and Times in early 2005) particularly in terms of strategies designed to meet the 'judicial imperative' of transitional justice work.[6]

Transitional justice and the 'Age of Memory'

The social and political dilemma of how to remember or forget the past in the wake of violent conflict is far from new. Citing the example of the ancient Athenian state in the wake of civil war, Jon Elster suggests that the roots of 'democratic transitional justice [are] almost as old as democracy itself'.[7] Nor is it coincidental that the etymological origins of both 'amnesty' and 'amnesia' owe something to a period when law makers 'preferred the forward-looking goal of social reconciliation over the backward-looking goal of retribution'.[8] Indeed, forgetting, as well as the 'creative use of past events' as a means to engender future social cohesion, may be seen historically as the predominant response to past division and conflict – particularly when directed at the 'creation and reproduction of the nation'.[9]

However, the second half of the twentieth century witnessed a significant shift. The end of the Second World War saw the first real attempt to develop international jurisprudence in order to deal with 'war crimes' and past human rights abuses. This also gave memory a new social role. The attempt to universalise human rights through international law and a new regime of global governance in this post-Holocaust 'epoch of trauma' brought what the French philosopher Paul Ricoeur has called a 'duty to remember' to the centre of the stage.[10] Post-conflict traumatic memories came to be seen as having 'exemplary value' not simply in themselves but when turned into a 'project . . . directed toward the future'.[11]

The idea that memory has a future-focused social role is one that has emerged all the more strongly in recent decades. There are a number of reasons for this. First, the post-Cold War era saw a rash of former repressive regimes pass into history – most obviously in Eastern Europe and Latin America – that had pursued their own versions of a 'war on memory'.[12] In such circumstances, memory, accessed through testimony, often proved to be the only means to address past human rights abuses and so foster accountable future governance. This helped inspire the wave of truth commissions held, with differing degrees of success, in various Latin American countries during the 1980s, 1990s and beyond.[13] Since then, truth commissions have become the most familiar mechanism of non-judicial transitional justice.[14] Indeed, since the 1970s there have been around forty such truth recovery processes held in countries emerging from armed conflict and/or authoritarian rule.

The second major reason for the rise of post-conflict memory work is the changing nature of conflict itself. As Mary Kaldor has argued, one thing the diverse 'new wars' of our times tend to have in common is the 'indiscriminate suffering of civilians'.[15] Up to 80 per cent of victims in the conflicts of the late twentieth and early twenty-first centuries have been civilians.[16] In addition, conflicts today are far less likely to be fought between states, and far more likely to be characterised by violent, intra-state division. Civil conflicts raise particular issues for the forging of future political arrangements, and these have been a growing concern for transitional policy makers and practitioners. This has been paralleled by the rise of international law, human rights discourse, institutions of global governance such as the UN and an emergent 'global civil society'. The result has been that truth recovery processes have come to the fore as a means of opening up public space in which the legacies of internal divisions can be addressed.[17]

However, that political violence has more and more directly impacted on civilians has also led to growing concern with the way that societies emerging from conflict deal with its associated traumas. The form strategies to deal with trauma should take, and the wider potentially pervasive influence of a therapeutic paradigm on transitional mechanisms, have been the subject of much debate.[18] Indeed, for many analysts a growing focus on the psychological and emotional legacies of conflict (rather than, for example, issues of poverty and equality) is due primarily to the rise of 'therapeutic societies' in the Western world. Nevertheless, there is no doubt that conflict and human rights abuses do leave profound psychological consequences in their wake. Nor can there be any doubt that strategies to deal with such traumatic memories should invariably form part of the process of post-conflict transition. In this regard, it could be argued that the question as to whether or not to remember the past is a false one: for those individuals, families and communities directly or pervasively affected by the conflict, remembering is often not a choice. However, the role that personal traumatic narratives should play in the public sphere is a more difficult issue. Certainly, what might be called the therapeutic imperative, the idea that there may be beneficial psychological consequences for the giver of such testimony, has been an important determinant of the form and nature of memory work, and the place of traumatic testimony, in the making of post-conflict societies.

If post-conflict memory work today is concerned with anything it is with the relationship between testimony, truth and justice. As noted earlier, those who carry out systematic mass human rights abuses tend to go to great lengths to ensure that there is little or no record of their actions. In such circumstances, testimony, for all its problems and limitations, often forms 'an essential source of information' upon which a truth claim about such a past can be made.[19] In similar vein, Paul Ricoeur has argued that testimony constitutes the 'fundamental transition structure between memory and history'.[20] In everyday life, testimony, Ricoeur suggests, performs two roles that become even more significant in the work of post-conflict transition, meeting what might be termed the archival and judicial imperatives of 'truth telling'.[21] In the first sense, post-conflict memory work is in part concerned with 'historical justice', which can take both legalistic and non-legalistic forms.[22] The second role of testimony, designed to meet the judicial imperative, is more directly concerned with seeking some form of legal redress for a past injustice. Primarily rooted as it is within the world of legal theory and practice, it is this aspect of testimony which was been to the fore within theories of transitional justice.

Two key dilemmas arise as a result. First, what is the best way of accessing testimony to meet the ends of justice and, second, what form should justice then take? Competing models of truth recovery mechanisms are largely concerned with the first of these issues. Tensions arise because of the competing ends of truth recovery processes. For example, concern for the impact on victims of providing testimony is often set against the desire to garner the evidence required to initiate institutional reform. While states, practitioners, even the UN, can advocate a 'victim-centred' approach, what precisely does that mean, and how much of a priority is it likely to be?[23] The second dilemma is, if anything, even more difficult. At the heart of truth recovery is a restorative, rather than a retributive, conception of justice. Generally speaking, rather than being focused primarily on confronting or holding accountable the predecessor regime, a restorative model aims to incorporate a diverse range of values, including 'peace', 'stability' and 'nation building' into the idea of justice.[24] However, such social and political goals can raise a range of difficult and painful outcomes for those seeking other forms of justice and particularly for those most directly touched by political violence.

The therapeutic, archival and judicial imperatives can be taken as defining the logic of post-conflict memory work today. They also establish the, at times contradictory, ends of truth recovery processes: to find 'healing' for victims by giving them a public voice; to re-write the record of the conflict and establish a new, potentially shared narrative of the past; and to revisit past injustice in order to establish an accountable, rights-based regime in the future. In theory, the aim is the re-constitution of the social and political sphere to ensure, if not the end of conflict and division as such, then at least that conflict and division will cease to take a violent form.

Truth, justice and memory: developments in Northern Ireland

If this international and theoretical context is important for understanding the debate on dealing with the past in Northern Ireland, that was not initially apparent in the early years of the peace process. The Good Friday Agreement was a complex, multi-faceted document dealing with a wide range of issues that had both caused and arisen as a result of thirty years of conflict. However, nowhere did it make mention of a mechanism for dealing with the past. It did set out some broad principles and policy goals for dealing with the rights and issues facing conflict victims. These included the recognition that victims 'had a right to remember [as part of the] wider promotion of a culture of tolerance at every level of society'.[25] The Agreement also noted that a 'necessary element of reconciliation' was the need to 'acknowledge and address the suffering of the victims of violence'. But it made no recommendations as to the form such recognition and acknowledgement might take.

Indeed, 'truth recovery' was never a core concern in the talks leading up to the Agreement, if it was discussed at all. It was not an issue high on the agenda of any of the major actors in the conflict. In addition, the 'constructive ambiguity' that defined the peace process placed a premium on avoiding broaching anything as contentious and potentially divisive as a mechanism for 'dealing with the past'.[26] Indeed, the opposite of an overarching past-focused mechanism was the order of the day. Issues that, in other circumstances, might have fallen under the remit of a truth commission (reform of the police force, a review of the criminal justice system, prisoner releases, and so forth) were disaggregated from each other and dealt with in a 'piecemeal' fashion.[27] Victims' issues had already been partially addressed in a 1997 report produced by retired senior civil servant Kenneth Bloomfield and led to the creation of a governmental infrastructure focused on practical service delivery.[28] Bloomfield's report did note that there might be a 'cathartic effect of putting one's experience on record' and examined a number of suggestions for 'non-physical memorial schemes'.[29] But this therapeutic strain in the document was not paralleled by a concern for 'truth and justice' issues, which were all but absent. This was an approach repeated in the key policy document *Reshape, Rebuild, Achieve* produced by the Victims Unit of the Office of the First Minister and Deputy First Minister (OFMDFM) in 2002.[30] 'Practical help and services' were its self-declared primary concern. Recommendations on the questions of truth, justice and past-focused mechanisms were to be deferred to the non-governmental 'Healing through Remembering' project.[31]

By then there had been some official steps toward past-focused judicial processes. In 1997, under pressure from both the Irish government and an ongoing campaign organised by the Bloody Sunday Trust, the new Labour government established the Saville Inquiry to re-examine the deaths of fourteen civilians in Derry at the hands of the Parachute Regiment in January 1972. Yet to report its findings, this has proved to be the longest and most expensive inquiry of its kind. It has also become something of a touchstone for attitudes toward post-conflict truth and justice issues in the North. It was followed by inquiries into both general and specific allegations of state collusion in (mainly loyalist) killings: in the first instance under Sir John Stevens and in the second under retired Canadian judge Peter Cory. Both found grounds for further investigations and inquiries.

The Bloody Sunday campaign also proved something of a model for others to follow. If collusion became such an issue in the wake of the GFA, this was largely because of campaigns drawing attention to the issue, for example in the cases of the murdered solicitors Pat Finucane and Rosemary Nelson. Unsurprisingly, most have emerged from within, and gained their support from, the nationalist community. In addition, long-standing, mainly nationalist, human rights and victims' organisations were joined by a raft of other groups in the wake of the GFA.[32] Together these have come to form a locally based network, increasingly collaborating among themselves and with other well established human rights groups both at home and abroad, to engage in a wide range of truth recovery activities. Justice campaigns have been combined with providing support for victims' families. For some, such as the Ardoyne Commemoration Project (ACP), a community-based approach to archiving and publishing testimonies emerged as the prime focus.[33] Many of these are involved in Eolas ('Information'), a loose group of nationalist/republican victim and other community-based groups that launched a consultation document on truth and justice issues in 2003.[34] Taken together, such initiatives constitute a substantive civil society response to the imperatives of post-conflict truth recovery. It is clear that for many involved in such groups, and the wider nationalist/republican community, some form of overarching past-focused mechanism would help deliver justice, provide the basis for a shared historical narrative and address the social and psychological needs of victims. However, there is a great deal less enthusiasm for the idea that this should take the form of a truth commission as such.

There have been, it needs to be said, a range of organisations working on human rights and victims issues that are essentially politically
unaligned and have promoted debate on dealing with the past. Chief
among these has been the Healing through Remembering project (HTRP)
set up in 2001 following the visit to Northern Ireland of Alex Boraine,
former deputy chair of the South African TRC. Healing through
Remembering is an innovative civil society initiative specifically designed
to open up a public space to develop an inclusive strategy for post-conflict
truth and justice issues with cross-community support. Following years of
consultations with a wide range of relevant groups and agencies it published a series of options for possible ways to advance truth recovery.[35] In
addition, a range of victims' groups, faith-based reconciliation organisations and semi-statutory bodies have made significant contributions to the
debate. International experience of mechanisms for dealing with the past
have been deeply influential among such groups. Many are similarly linked
into the sort of transnational human rights networks that constitute the
contemporary face of the emerging global civil society.[36]

However, attitudes on truth recovery appear largely to have divided
along traditional community and political lines. The terms of the GFA,
and in particular the early release of conflict-related prisoners, did lead
directly to the creation of a number of mainly unionist victims groups.[37]
Most campaigned vigorously against the early release scheme and have
formed an important lobby on victims' concerns since. While certain
truth recovery issues have had broad backing within the unionist community – the most obvious instance being the fate of the 'disappeared' –
calls for further inquiries have been met with open hostility, particularly
at the political level. Both the main unionist political parties, the
Democratic Unionist party (DUP) and Ulster Unionist party (UUP), have
voiced ardent opposition to the idea of a truth commission, and representatives of fringe loyalist groups have largely followed suit. Certain
common themes have emerged in such views.[38] Truth recovery is conceived and, therefore, distrusted as part of a 'republican agenda'. The
welfare of victims would be better served by providing practical services
and 'letting sleeping dogs lie'. All victims are not equally so. Further rev-
elations are only likely to 'undermine communal confidence' and foster
future discord. Remembering the past is, in other words, a bad idea.

Yet it has become clear that the past will not go away all that easily.
Opinion, as we shall see, may well be divided on many issues, but by no
means on all. While truth recovery processes are not perhaps a major
policy priority for most, ongoing debate and initiatives emerging within
civil society have also kept past-related justice issues to the fore. Tacit
recognition of a need for policy development in this area may have been

evident in the separate consultation initiatives launched by the Secretary of State and the Northern Ireland Committee of the House of Commons in 2004, and more recently the Eames/Bradley initiative. Yet there is clearly still a great deal of official reluctance to envisage an inclusive mechanism, such as a truth commission, as the way forward. This is generally argued for on the basis of the sort of political divisions outlined above and the slow progress of the peace process. However, something of a coherent strategy seems to be taking shape, although still characterised by segmentation of the means and ends of truth recovery, and geared primarily to those past-focused areas seen to enjoy a larger degree of consensus. This strategy may also be critically assessed as to whether key elements of its implementation are designed to open up or delimit the horizons of truth recovery.

What are the developments taking shape? First, the implementation of policy and services to meet the practical needs of victims was placed under the authority of an Interim Commissioner for Victims and Survivors. While providing services for victims has tended to be the least contentious aspect of the debate on dealing with the past, and largely remains so, some clear underlying divisions have also emerged. This became most obvious following the appointment to the new post of Interim Commissioner for Victims and Survivors of Mrs Bertha McDougall, the widow of a member of the RUC reserve, killed by the INLA in 1981.[39] Victims' groups representing mainly nationalist relatives, and particularly victims of state violence, opposed the move and have been critical of aspects of her final report, published in January 2007.[40] Such groups also supported the widow of a man shot dead by an RUC reservist in 1984 who successfully challenged the Secretary of State in court over the lawfulness of Mrs McDougall's appointment.[41]

There is also a growing impetus towards the creation of a 'storytelling' process in Northern Ireland. There have been numerous such initiatives, usually at a local or community level, in recent years, as illustrated by a study undertaken by the Healing through Remembering project.[42] Whatever the wide range of aims and rationales that underpinned such civil society projects, the growing official interest in 'storytelling' seems primarily defended on two interrelated grounds. First, that there is some need for victims and wider Northern Ireland society to 'come to terms' with the past, and that 'storytelling' may offer a suitable and safe 'cathartic' opportunity. Placing personal experiences of the past 'on record', developing an enriched shared narrative of the conflict as a result, and using that process as an occasion for 'healing', emerge as key to the logic of such approaches to post-conflict truth recovery. In other words, storytelling is a means to meet a fusion of the archival and therapeutic imperatives. The second grounds on which storytelling is defended is less positive, focusing rather on the negatives of possible alternatives. A new consensus on how to deal with the past could be established, it is implied, if the judicial imperative is removed from the scene. Any other approach, it is suggested, will do more harm than good. This logic, driven by a conception of 'reconciliation' as the social goal at the heart of truth recovery, has underpinned the perspective of government Ministers and officials as well as the House of Commons report on 'dealing with the past'. It was also exemplified by Mitchell Reiss (the US President's special envoy for Northern Ireland), who argued that Northern Ireland should have a storytelling process, modelled on Stephen Spielberg's Shoah Project, on the grounds that 'if participants are allowed to do more than simply tell their stories, the result may be greater resentment rather than reconciliation'.[43]

In other words, that attention has increasingly been drawn towards storytelling reveals how much more problematic investigative and judicial approaches to dealing with the legacy of the conflict remain. The question of justice is that much more contentious than the therapeutic or 'putting on record' experiences as an end in itself. This was, for example, evidenced in the widespread public criticism that forced the hasty withdrawal of the British government's Northern Ireland Offences Bill (or so-called 'on-the-run' legislation) in early 2005.[44] Ostensibly designed to allow 'on-the-runs' to avoid possible future prosecution, the Bill virtually amounted to a blanket amnesty for any unsolved conflict-related acts that occurred before the signing of the Good Friday Agreement. Vociferous criticism came from a wide range of quarters, including many of the victims' and human rights groups who have often differed widely on other issues.

Divided over memory and justice? Investigations and the future for transition in Northern Ireland

The debates over public inquiries in high-profile cases, on the one hand, and the 'on-the-run' legislation on the other, have revealed that, whether investigative and judicial approaches to dealing with the past are pursued or excluded, the outcome is invariably contentious. These tensions over investigative approaches to truth recovery are even more clearly illustrated in two other truth-and-justice areas. The first concerns the possible reopening of conflict-related cases under the provision of Article 2 of the European Convention on Human Rights, the second the 'Historical Enquiries Team' (HET) within the Police Service of Northern Ireland (PSNI). Each of these is a development in which the most potentially divisive and difficult truth-and-justice issues, those involving allegations against the state and its agencies, have been very much involved. They are also the key areas, alongside public inquiries, where an investigative dimension of truth recovery is likely to emerge. As the most contentious questions for the future of truth and transition, it may be worth dealing with these two areas in more depth and trying to place them in the context of community attitudes to such questions.

As has already been noted, relatives of victims, communities and campaign groups have attempted for some time to use the law to challenge the official management of truth recovery and wrest information and acknowledgement from a reluctant state. This is particularly pertinent where the victim was either killed directly by the state or amid allegations of collusion between the state and non-state armed groups. European human rights law has become a key arena in which this challenge to truth management, and the attempt to establish a past precedent for future state accountability, have been posed. In this, Article 2 of the European Convention on Human Rights has been key. Article 2 imposes a positive obligation on the state to protect the life of everyone within its jurisdiction. It means, for example, that where lethal force has been used by the state there is a 'procedural obligation', as the European Court of Human Rights has called it, for an effective official investigation. In a landmark judgement in 2002 in four cases involving the killing of eleven people by state forces, the European Court found that the British state had failed to meet this obligation to investigate the deaths and had therefore breached Article 2 and the right to life of the victims. This was a highly significant development because it presented the very real possibility that the floodgates could be opened to other similar cases, including some of the most contentious involving allegations of collusion and a state 'shoot to kill' policy. This also may have had a profound impact on the British government's strategy with regard to how it deals with the past. The state's apparent willingness to consider a truth commission as an alternative way forward on truth recovery at around the same time may be read in light of the challenge posed by this initial Article 2 judgement.

However, a House of Lords judgement in 2004 changed the complexion of the debate once again. The European Convention on Human Rights has been written into domestic British law via the 1998 Human Rights Act. In 2004 the Law Lords decided, with regard to one of the four Article 2 cases, that the 1998 Act could not be invoked retrospectively, so that the obligation to investigate prior to the date of the Act's implementation in 2000 was invalid. That said, in two other English-based retrospective cases (Middleton and Sacker), the judgement of a differently constituted House of Lords arrived at exactly the opposite conclusion. While the Law Lords are due to revisit and clarify the issue in the near future, the situation has massive implications for the way in which the state may decide to deal with the past. Certainly, it has direct relevance to any possible investigations likely to be carried out into conflict-related deaths in which lethal force was used by agents of the state.

If such investigations are going to be carried out, it is likely, at present, that they would occur under the auspices of the Historical Enquiries Team. Announced in March 2005 and officially launched in January 2006, the HET is the primary investigative mechanism for dealing with the past in Northern Ireland.[45] It is in many ways an innovative and unique development in post-conflict truth recovery. Interestingly, the immediate impetus to the foundation of the HET may have come from the police themselves. The debate on how to deal with the legacy of truth and justice issues has emerged as a key site of post-conflict struggle and has had significant ramifications for various institutions in society. For the newly constituted successor to the Royal Ulster Constabulary (RUC), the Police Service of Northern Ireland, that legacy has represented an ongoing challenge to its legitimacy, most obviously among nationalists. The RUC has itself been the focus of serious allegations of human rights abuses, collusion and cover-ups. Research suggests that there has also been a great deal of resistance within the PSNI to structural change, with the clear implication that the past may reassert itself in a new guise.[46] For the Chief Inspector of the PSNI, Hugh Orde, these problems for future policing and the need to win 'hearts and minds' have defined the logic of the HET: 'the past has the potential to destroy all the effort and real change policing has delivered in the post-Patten world . . . in order to deliver twenty-first-century policing, we require a radical solution to the past. The HET is the Police contribution to dealing with the past'.[47]

Including a mix of personnel recruited from within the RUC/PSNI and external police forces, the HET is led by two officers (from the Metropolitan Police force) formerly involved in the Stevens inquiries into collusion. One team, made up solely of officers from outside Northern Ireland, will deal with 'controversial' cases. The HET has two stated objectives. The first is to re-examine all deaths attributable to the 'security situation' in Northern Ireland during the period 1968–98 (currently estimated at some 3,268 cases). Case reviews would lead to re-investigation where there are felt to be 'evidential opportunities'. The second explicit aim is to instil confidence among those directly concerned and the wider public that all cases have been dealt with thoroughly and professionally and that all possible avenues for accumulating evidence will be actively pursued.[48] While the HET has stated that it is essentially a policing initiative, and not part of any 'political or truth and reconciliation process', there is a clear cathartic vein to its *modus operandi*.[49] It wants to 'help bring a measure of resolution where possible to these [victims'] families' and will therefore develop a process in which 'families sit at the heart'.[50] The goal, it is claimed, is therefore to provide as much information to relatives as possible, to adopt a policy of 'maximum permissible disclosure' to families.

Given its remit, it is fair to say that the HET is not only a unique development in Northern Ireland's approach to transitional justice but also unprecedented in policing internationally. The initiative is, nevertheless, controversial and to date it has not garnered cross-community support. Perhaps not surprisingly, it has generated considerable suspicion and debate within the nationalist/republican community, and a number of NGOs have raised concerns with regard to transparency, independence and accountability. In particular, it has been argued that there must be openness in any review of unresolved deaths, otherwise it will not have credibility and public confidence.[51] Moreover, there may be forces at work beyond the HET's control to prevent disclosure of information. The passing of the Public Inquiries Act, criticised by one commentator as having the potential to undermine the 'independence and impartiality of future inquiries', has demonstrated the capacity of the state to continue a truth management strategy by potentially concealing and protecting those who have perpetrated abuses in its name.[52] With its potential to erode rather than to reinvigorate two of the fundamental tenets of democratic governance, transparency and accountability, the concern must be that the imposition of an official 'regime of truth' is unlikely to be challenged by state structures when the authority and legitimacy of the state itself are ultimately called into question.[53] In many ways the HET is a journey into uncharted waters. It appears to have the potential to make a massive contribution to peace building. Conversely, it may ultimately end up only casting doubt on the ability of the PSNI to deliver accountable and open policing. The ramifications of this initiative for peace building, democracy and transition are highly significant, particularly in a context where divisions over approaches to truth recovery are often cited as the major stumbling block.

But are views on how to deal with the past, particularly in terms of investigations, as divided as sometimes appears to be the case in the political arena? Evidence from the 2004 Northern Ireland Life and Times survey shows a complex picture of attitudes to truth recovery processes.[54] While there may be only limited enthusiasm for a truth commission as such, and knowledge of such processes is more limited than many may have imagined, there is clearly a significant swathe of opinion that does feel some form of mechanism or mechanisms for dealing with the legacy of the past would be a good thing. Nor is this solely restricted to one community rather than another. For example, just under 50 per cent of those surveyed felt that a truth commission (or, at least, a process where people would 'have to tell the truth') was either important or very important for Northern Ireland's future, while only one in five said it was not. True, more Catholics (58.6 per cent) than Protestants (42.9 per cent) were in favour, but even among the latter there were more who thought a truth commission was important than thought it unimportant.[55] People were highly sceptical that any truth recovery process would actually get to the truth, but this did not manifest itself in an expressed view that leaving the past to be forgotten was either a possible or a desirable option. Therapeutic approaches (i.e. in terms of support for victims) were clearly well supported, and the desire of 'getting to the truth' was, for many, combined with the hope that truth recovery would result in 'healing and reconciliation'.[56] So too was the idea that there should be community-based initiatives to help people come to terms with the past and potentially a process whereby people could have the opportunity to 'tell their stories', more so for example than there was for the creation of memorials or centres of remembrance.[57]

Most interesting of all perhaps was that there was also apparent agreement that further conflict-related investigations should not be discounted, two-thirds of those asked thought that investigations, possibly leading to prosecutions, were important for future ways of dealing with the legacy of the conflict. That rose to around 70 per cent of Protestants but was still the view of over 60 per cent of Catholics.[58] Although the survey was carried out prior to the creation of the HET, a clear majority also supported the idea that a special unit should be set up to look at unresolved cases.[59] At one level, therefore, it would appear that the judicial imperative and investigative approaches are not as great a point of contention as is often assumed. However, looked at more comprehensively, there are clearly potential issues at stake. This is perhaps best illustrated in attitudes to future public inquiries, which (perhaps with Bloody Sunday and the Cory inquiries in mind) were much less well supported by Protestants (32 per cent) than Catholics (56 per cent). Similarly, when asked about fears that a truth commission might be 'just an excuse to attack the government', roughly a third of nationalist party supporters agreed, but over half of Ulster Unionist and two-thirds of Democratic Unionist Party voters felt this would be the case. Among the latter there was also a clearly discernible body of opinion in particular that any past-focused process should end in criminal prosecutions. While a significant number of both Catholics and nationalists felt that holding institutions accountable was an important aspect of truth recovery, this was far less likely to be the case among either Protestants or unionists.

What one might take from this is that while investigations and possible prosecutions are far from unwanted, who it is that should be investigated and prosecuted, and what the purpose of an investigative focus might be, are likely to be far more contentious. This is of course not really very surprising and reflects long-term, deeply ingrained and very different attitudes to the state and its agencies, on the one hand, and contending narratives of who and what was responsible for the conflict in the first place. If past experience is anything to go by, as issues such as those surrounding Article 2 decisions or HET investigations enter more into the public sphere, attitudes are also likely to harden. This may be a critical means by which the public debate on the extent and nature of these developments, particularly as they relate to the potential of holding the state to account, will be framed. The concern must be that differences are deployed politically, particularly by the state, as a way of preventing processes that would otherwise be considered essential to the inculcation of a rights-based future. If in public discussion the therapeutic and archival are privileged over – or indeed come to be presented as the necessary alternative to – the judicial and/or investigative, in whatever form that might take, it may act as little more than a flag of convenience for a more insidious and problematic desire to continuing to deny the truth.

Conclusion

There are still many voices suggesting that what might be called a 'duty to forget' may be the best way forward for Northern Ireland and that only in putting aside a divisive, conflict-ridden past can a consensus for positive social and political change emerge. However, advocates of forgetting have to ask whether or not, as popular parlance would have it, 'sleeping dogs' should (or can) be left to lie, or the 'can of worms' that is the past will remain unopened for long. A great deal of evidence from societies emerging from conflict in many other parts of the world would suggest otherwise. If the 'duty to remember' has superseded Renan's maxim it is, in part at least, because the seeds of future conflict have too often been found in failed attempts at amnesia. Histories of hurt and victimhood (whether imagined or real) have a habit of reasserting themselves despite efforts to bury them. However, this may be far less a 'therapeutic' matter than a question of practical politics and past-focused but future-oriented justice making. While there is undoubtedly a need to deal with the real psychological consequences of conflict (particularly for those who have been its direct victims), there is a danger of the metaphors of catharsis, healing and emotionality overtaking and overshadowing the social and the political. A cohesive democratic society is built upon the capacity to achieve consensus on structures of governance and a shared faith in the equity and accountability of its institutions. This is, of course, what has precisely been largely absent in Northern Ireland since the state's inception and has certainly also been a residual consequence of the long years of conflict. It is also what the debate on truth recovery in Northern Ireland may sometimes need to refocus upon.

Prioritising the therapeutic and archival ends of post-conflict memory work at the expense of the investigative and the judicial may sometimes appear to open up an easier road, but it brings with it real costs. The latter does not necessarily imply a retributive conception of justice by which investigation necessarily results in prosecution and punishment. This may be an outcome but it is not inevitable, nor is it invariably required in order to meet the ends of truth recovery. However, if such ends are understood as including the instigation and nurturing of a human rights-based social and political culture, then there are real limits for these to be achieved purely through processes which deal with the needs of victims and 'storytelling'. In the end, that is because neither of the latter addresses ultimately issues of power and how to hold those who wield it accountable. This may very well be why such approaches can appear the more attractive option to those in power. However, as has been identified by critics elsewhere, there are problems for the long-term social and political order when truth recovery processes become mere window dressing, part of a state truth management strategy, as well as evidence of lack of generosity towards all those who have been the victims of conflict.[60] The issues raised by investigations undertaken as part, for example, of the work of the Historical Enquiries Team or the Article 2 cases may be contentious and difficult. However, ignoring them may still mean failure to meaningfully fulfil, and benefit from, the duty to remember.

Notes

1 For example, there is a substantial literature by historians and historical sociologists considering the relationship between memory, conflict and history. See, for example; Timothy Ashplant, Graham Dawson and Michael Roper (eds), *The Politics of War Memory and Commemoration* (London: Routledge, 2000); Duncan Bell, *Memory, Trauma and World Politics: Reflections on the Relationship between Past and Present* (London: Palgrave, 2006); Jeffrey Olick and Joyce Robbins, 'Social memory studies: from "collective memory" to the historical sociology of mnemonic practices', *Annual Review of Sociology* 24 (1998), pp. 105–40; Pierre Nora,

Realms of Memory: Construction of the French Past I–III (New York: Columbia University Press, 1996); Peter Novick, *The Holocaust and Collective Memory* (London: Bloomsbury, 2001); Alessandro Portelli, 'The order has been carried out': *History, Memory and Meaning of a Nazi Massacre in Rome* (London: Palgrave, 2004); Jeff Winter, *Remembering War: The Great War and Historical Memory in the Twentieth Century* (New Haven CT: Yale University Press, 2006); Jeff Winter and Emanuel Sivian (eds), *War and Remembrance in the Twentieth Century* (Cambridge: Cambridge University Press, 2000).

2 Barbara Misztal, *Theories of Social Remembering* (Manchester: Manchester University Press, 2003), p. 147.

3 Transitional justice can be understood as a distinct body of enquiry and practice concerned with the 'the various judicial and non-judicial approaches to dealing with . . . a legacy of human rights violations' in societies emerging from conflict and/or an era of authoritarian rule; see www.grc-exchange.org/g_themes/ssaj_transitionaljustice.html (accessed 10 January 2005).

4 Louis Bickford, 'The archival imperative', *Human Rights Quarterly* 21:4 (1999), pp. 1108–22.

5 Northern Ireland Affairs Committee, *Ways of Dealing with Northern Ireland's Past. Interim Report: Victims and Survivors* (London: HMSO, 2004), p. 14.

6 Patricia Lundy and Mark McGovern, *Attitudes towards a Truth Commission for Northern Ireland* (Belfast: Community Relations Council, 2006).

7 Jon Elster, *Closing the Books: Transitional Justice in Historical Perspective* (Cambridge: Cambridge University Press, 2004), p. 3.

8 *Ibid.*, pp. 3–4.

9 Misztal, *Theories of Social Remembering*, p. 145.

10 Paul Ricoeur, 'Memory and forgetting', in Richard Kearney and Mark Dooley (eds), *Questioning Ethics* (London: Routledge, 1999), pp. 12–17.

11 Paul Ricoeur, *Memory, History, Forgetting* (London: University of Chicago Press, 2004), p. 86.

12 Primo Levi, cited in Tzvetan Todorov, *Hope and Memory: Reflections on the Twentieth Century* (London: Atlantic Books, 2005), p. 114.

13 Priscilla Hayner, *Unspeakable Truths: Confronting State Terror and Atrocity* (London: Routledge, 2002).

14 A truth commission can be understood as an 'official body set up to investigate a past period of human rights abuses or violations of international humanitarian law'. Differing significantly in terms of their remit, powers and goals, those held thus far have also tended to have certain characteristics in common. They are 'officially sanctioned', 'past-focused', concerned with patterns of human rights abuses and exist only for a set period of time. They are, in other words, the primary means today by which violently divided societies deal with the past.

15 Mary Kaldor, *Global Civil Society: An Answer to War* (London: Polity Press, 2003), p. 127.

16 Rama Mani, *Beyond Retribution: Seeking Justice in the Shadows of War* (London: Polity Press, 2002), p. 3.

17 Richard A. Wilson, *The Politics of Truth and Reconciliation in South Africa: Legitimising the post-Apartheid State* (Cambridge: Cambridge University Press, 2001).

18 For example, David Becker has been deeply critical of approaches that separate out trauma 'treatment' as a primarily medical concern rather than being part and parcel of wider, socially based strategies toward post-conflict reconstruction. Similarly, Vanessa Pupavac has argued that what she terms 'therapeutic governance' can pathologise whole populations as dysfunctional and 'legitimate' the ongoing denial of self-government. See David Becker, 'Dealing with the consequences of organised violence in trauma work', in *Berghof Handbook for Conflict Transformation*, Berlin: Berghof Research Centre for Constructive Conflict Management, 2001); Vanessa Pupavac, 'War on the couch: the emotionology of the new international security paradigm', *European Journal of Social Theory* 7:2 (2004), pp. 149–70.

19 Elizabeth Jelin, *State Repression and the Struggle for Memory* (London: Latin American Bureau, 2003).

20 Ricoeur, *Memory, History, Forgetting*, p. 21.

21 Bickford, 'The archival imperative'.

22 'Historical justice' refers to the way in which legalistic concepts, perspectives and mechanisms impact upon history-telling during periods of transition and the re-constitution of shared narratives of the past. However, it can take other, non-legalistic forms. As the French historian Pierre Nora has argued, the 'worldwide upsurge in memory' is evidenced not only through public criticism of 'official history' and attempts to recover repressed aspects of the past but also in the rise in commemorative events and museums. If this is partly to do with the growing cultural and economic significance of heritage, it also symbolises that the global 'tidal wave of memorial concerns' has heightened the relationship between memory, collective consciousness and identity. See, for example, Ruti Teitel, *Transitional Justice* (Oxford: Oxford University Press, 2001); Pierre Nora, 'Reasons for the upsurge in memory', *Eurozine*, 2002, www.eurozine.com/articles/2002-04-19-nora-en.html, p. 1 (accessed 12 August 2005).

23 United Nations Secretary General, *Report of the Secretary General on the Rule of Law and Transitional Justice in Conflict and Post-conflict Societies*, 2004, www.un.org/Docs/sc/sgrep04.html (accessed 31 January 2006).

24 Ruti Teitel, 'Transitional justice genealogy', *Harvard Human Rights Journal* 69 (2003), p. 16.

25 *Agreement reached in the Multi-party Negotiations, April 10, 1998.*

26 Arthur Aughey, 'The art and effect of political lying in Northern Ireland', *Irish Political Studies* 17:2 (2002), pp. 1–16; Paul Dixon, 'Political skills or

lying and manipulation? The choreography of the peace process', *Political Studies* 50:4 (2002), pp. 725–41.

27 Christine Bell, 'Dealing with the past in Northern Ireland', *Fordham International Law Journal* 26:4 (2003), pp. 1095–147.

28 See Patricia Lundy and Mark McGovern, *Community, 'Truth-telling' and Conflict Resolution: A Critical Evaluation of the Role of Community-based 'Truth-telling' Processes for Post-conflict Transition* (Belfast: Community Relations Council, 2005); Patricia Lundy and Mark McGovern, 'The politics of memory in post-conflict Northern Ireland', *Peace Review* 13:1 (2001), pp. 27–34.

29 Kenneth Bloomfield, *We Will Remember Them: Report of the Northern Ireland Victims Commissioner* (Belfast: Northern Ireland Office, 1997) p. 20.

30 Victims Unit (OFMDFM), *Reshape, Rebuild, Achieve: Delivering Practical Help and Services to Victims of the Conflict in Northern Ireland* (Belfast, OFMDFM/VU, 2002).

31 Healing through Remembering, *The Report of the Healing through Remembering Project* (Belfast: HTRP, 2002).

32 Well established groups include, for example, the Pat Finucane Centre and Relatives for Justice. More recently created organisations include Firinne, Cunamh, Duchas.

33 The authors were both members of the Ardoyne Commemoration Project. See ACP, *Ardoyne: The Untold Truth* (Belfast: Beyond the Pale Publications, 2002); Patricia Lundy and Mark McGovern, 'Participation, truth and partiality: participatory action research, community-based truth-telling and post-conflict transition in Northern Ireland', *Sociology* 40:1 (2005), pp. 71–88; Lundy and McGovern, *Community, 'Truth-telling' and Conflict Resolution*; Patricia Lundy and Mark McGovern, 'The politics of memory in post-conflict Northern Ireland', *Peace Review* 13:1 (2001), pp. 27–34.

34 Eolas, *Truth and Justice: A Discussion Document* (Belfast: Eolas, 2004).

35 Healing through Remembering, *Making Peace with the Past: Options for Truth Recovery regarding the Conflict in and about Northern Ireland* (Belfast: Healing through Remembering, 2006).

36 Kaldor, *Global Civil Society*; John Keane, *Global Civil Society* (Cambridge: Cambridge University Press, 2003).

37 For example, Fear Encouraged Abandoning Roots (FEAR), Families Acting for Innocent Victims (FAIR) and Families Achieving Change Together (FACT).

38 Lundy and McGovern, *Community, 'Truth-telling' and Conflict Resolution*.

39 Northern Ireland Office Media Centre, 24 October 2005, www.nio.gov.uk/media-detail.htm?newsID=12419.

40 Bertha McDougall, *Support for Victims and Survivors: Addressing the Human Legacy* (Belfast: Office of the Interim Commissioner for Victims and Survivors, 2007).

41 See www.belfasttelegraph.co.uk/news/story.jsp?story=671917 (accessed 26 June 2006).

42 Gráinne Kelly, *Storytelling Audit: An Audit of Personal Story, Narrative and Testimony Initiatives related to the Conflict in and about Northern Ireland* (Belfast: Healing through Remembering, 2005).

43 Mitchell B. Reiss and Eric Green, 'Lessons of the Northern Ireland peace process', *American Foreign Policy Interests* 27 (2005), p. 475.

44 See www.ireland.com/newspaper/special/2006/hain_statement/index.htm (accessed 26 June 2006).

45 At the time of writing this chapter one of the authors, Patricia Lundy, is engaged in ongoing and extensive research on the Historical Enquiries Team.

46 Mary O'Rawe, 'Transitional policing arrangements in Northern Ireland: the can't and the won't of the change dialectic', *Fordham International Law Journal* 23:4 (2003), pp. 1015–73.

47 Hugh Orde, 'War is Easy to Declare, Peace is an Elusive Prize', paper presented at School of Religious and Theology and the Irish School of Ecumenics at Trinity College Dublin (2005).

48 Historical Enquiries Team, *Policing the Past: Introducing the Work of the Historical Enquiries Team* (2006).

49 *Ibid.*

50 *Ibid.*

51 Open letter to Chief Constable Hugh Orde from the Pat Finucane Centre, 19 April 2005, www.patfinucanecentre.org; see also www.relativesforjustice.com for details of a conference 'State violence: state the truth'.

52 The Committee on the International Human Rights of the Association of the Bar of the City of New York, *An Analysis of the UK Inquiries Bill and US Provision for Investigating Matters of Urgent Public Concern*, 25 January 2005, p. 12.

53 Bill Rolston and Phil Scraton, 'In the full glare of English politics: Ireland, inquiries and the British state', *British Journal of Criminology* 45 (2005), p. 550.

54 Lundy and McGovern, *Attitudes towards a Truth Commission*.

55 *Ibid.*, p. 5.

56 *Ibid.*, pp. 6–8.

57 *Ibid.*, pp. 15–16.

58 *Ibid.*, p. 16.

59 *Ibid.*, p. 17.

60 See, for example, Elizabeth Stanley, 'What next? The aftermath of organised truth telling', *Race and Class* 44:1 (2002), pp. 1–16.

3

From conflict to communal politics: the politics of peace

Jonathan Tonge

The end of armed conflict and arrival of devolved power sharing in Northern Ireland does not appear to have lessened the communal divisions that mark the political life of the region. The link between religious affiliation and political preference remains the strongest in Western Europe. The supporters of each of the principal parties continue to be drawn almost exclusively from rival ethno-religious blocs, a pattern unlikely to be altered by the pinnacle of the peace process, the 1998 Good Friday Agreement (GFA) and its renegotiated successor, the 2006 St Andrews Agreement. According to critics of both its theoretical principles[1] and its institutional arrangements,[2] the GFA has legitimised sectarian division by replicating existing fault lines in the main political institutions it created in Northern Ireland, namely the Executive and Assembly.

Consociational political agreements, such as the one introduced in Northern Ireland in 1998, try to create power sharing between political elites in divided societies. Such enterprises bear considerable risks, as they accept the existing segmentation of politics and society and merely try and manage division, at least in the short term. Consociational deals provide four key elements by which each ethnic group has a stake in a reconstructed polity: power sharing; representation of each ethnic bloc in government institutions according to its proportional size; rights of veto for each ethnic bloc in respect of legislation and a degree of communal autonomy for each ethnic bloc.[3] Applied in Northern Ireland, the consociational ideas of the GFA assume the willingness of the political leaders of each ethnic bloc to share power whilst maintaining their community identity. Consociation assumes co-operation in government despite either bloc having the power of veto over proposals emanating from the 'other' community. As such, the GFA is predicated upon the notion of a frozen communal politics becoming sufficiently thawed to allow a degree of 'mutually suspicious co-operation' in a devolved Northern Ireland government.

Drawing upon electoral survey data, party membership surveys, existing literature and contemporary analysis, this chapter addresses several questions in an attempt to assess the potential for enduring political agreement, based upon some form of co-operative power sharing, in Northern Ireland. Firstly, has a new, less mistrustful political context emerged at elite level in Northern Ireland? Secondly, will polarisation in the region be diminished or consolidated by the revival of a consociational power sharing agreement? Thirdly, will parties in Northern Ireland continue to seek support within their traditional ethno-religious blocs rather than set out to appeal to a cross-community constituency? Fourthly, is there any sign of an electoral thaw in the province, indicated by a greater propensity of voters to transfer at least lower preference support to historic 'enemies'? Finally, the chapter assesses whether the politics of apathy are beginning to creep into Northern Irish political culture as turnout begins to fall within communities that are no longer mobilised by the 'war' and that are perhaps less animated than hitherto by traditional constitutional issues.

The end of conflict and the new political context

The paramilitary ceasefires of the 1990s, followed by the formal ending of the Provisional IRA's armed campaign and decommissioning of its weapons in 2005, created a new political context in Northern Ireland. The temporary collapse, in 2002, of the political institutions established under the GFA nonetheless indicated the vulnerability of the embryonic new politics. This was followed, in 2007, by a far-reaching accommodation between the DUP and Sinn Féin, ensconced as principal representatives of their ethnic blocs.

The GFA was followed by attempts to 'win the peace' by political parties and their ethno-religious blocs. Consequently a shared strategic vision of the political direction that might secure the greater communal good failed to materialise in the immediate aftermath. The early post-GFA period contained rows over the pace and transparency of the decommissioning of paramilitary weapons and unionist disillusionment with political change, especially on issues such as policing and parades. Only when unionists within the DUP felt sufficiently sure that they had won the peace was inclusive devolved power sharing placed securely on the political agenda.

The GFA was in many ways an 'old-new' agreement, containing ideas first attempted in the Sunningdale Agreement of 1973. Those political arrangements were deemed an 'agreement too far',[4] due to the highly unpromising circumstances in which they were negotiated. Although reached against a rather more favourable backdrop, the 1998 GFA should also be acknowledged as a highly ambitious political enterprise.

The GFA was as an elite deal constructed upon sectarian foundations of continuing communal mistrust and division, which political accommodation offered only to manage rather than to end. The endorsement of the deal by both communities in the referendum on the agreement served only to partially obscure the obstacles that the peace process was destined to face. A 57 per cent 'yes' vote among Protestants was hardly a ringing endorsement and was an affirmative based more upon a desire for peace than upon support for the Agreement's mechanics, whilst the extensive (99 per cent) enthusiasm among Northern Ireland's Catholics merely heightened unionist suspicion of the accord.[5] One month later, unionists began to turn to anti-GFA candidates in elections, a process which would result in the installation of the DUP as the primary representatives of unionism by 2003.

Nonetheless, the movement from armed peace towards disarmed republicanism recreated space for a revived political deal. In the past, the cessation of armed republican campaigns had led merely to the dumping of arms and a return to sullen abstention. The changed tactics adopted by republicanism in recent times, in contrast, have offered a vista of participatory politics, co-operation with the institutions of the state and tacit acceptance of the legitimacy of Northern Ireland as a political entity, at least in the short and medium terms. Although it remained difficult to envisage Northern Ireland as a polity in which a 'normal' system of government and opposition might emerge, the vacation of the main stage by paramilitaries offered the potential for the nurturing of fully constitutional politics. This optimistic scenario was nonetheless countered by the concern that any sharing of authority would amount to a division of power along the sectarian fault line. Politics would be less a collective building of the state than an ongoing ethnic struggle for a better deal for the ethno-religious bloc represented by a particular party, amid rhetorical electoral appeals to the ethnic gallery. Such appeals would be animated by the presumed self-interest of given parties, regardless of the implications for effective governance or the greater collective good.

Consociational power sharing: solution or problem?

The GFA rested upon three of the four core consociational principles outlined over two decades earlier by Lijphart and supported, albeit with important modifications, by some specialist experts on Northern Ireland.[6] It contained power sharing, proportionality in government and mutual veto rights for representatives of both communities. The fourth principle, of community autonomy, by which the culture, religion and political approach of each ethnic group were respected, was also evident in the deal, but most of the protections for the unionist and nationalist traditions already existed prior to the GFA.

The GFA operated as an 'all or nothing' agreement which failed to distinguish between principle and mechanism and as such was implemented on a basis which overlooked problems of 'mechanics'.[7] Whilst the presentation of the GFA as a package which parties would have to accept in its totality appeared to be one of its strengths, the failure of the Northern Ireland Executive from 1999 to 2002 to act as a cohesive collective highlighted institutional, in addition to party leadership, deficiencies. The GFA was the product of multi-party negotiations based upon 'least unacceptable' scenarios for rival ethnic blocs, rather than common approaches to political progress and societal reconciliation. The absence of the DUP from the negotiating process ensured that a significant section of unionism remained hostile and the initial hopes that the deal might marginalise Ian Paisley's party proved utterly ill founded. Sinn Féin remained largely in denial of the deal's implications – most crucially, acceptance of Northern Ireland as an entity and entry into a local Assembly under British sovereignty – until the end of the process. Thus the operation of the first post-GFA Assembly and Executive 'represented a deal hammered out between the UUP and the SDLP in the final days of the talks', producing 'an unusual form of compulsory power sharing, one that owed little to notions of executive efficiency or even credibility but much to notions of political expediency'.[8]

Operating as a set of party fiefdoms, the ruling Executive indicated how 'imposed' consociation may not necessarily mitigate ethnic polarisation. The 1999–2002 Executive was aptly described as 'more like a holding company for a collection of ministers with different party affiliations than a collective decision-making body'.[9] The application of the D'Hondt system in the allocation of ministerial portfolios exacerbates the association of Ministries with particular parties rather than with the broader government. Under the D'Hondt system the number of seats held in the Assembly determines the number of Ministerial portfolios available to each party and the order in which these jobs could be chosen.[10] This form of political lottery, whilst ensuring cross-community representation, allows selections based upon perceived party advantage rather than available talent or consensus around a policy programme. Sinn Féin's decision to choose the education Ministry, for example, while sensible for the party, contributed to heightened unionist opposition to aspects of policy in those areas. Individual Ministerial performance was often creditable, even though there was little sense of collective cabinet government.

Designed as a means of facilitating political progress in ethnically divided societies, consociational agreements are charged by critics as freezers of ethnic identity.[11] This sceptical view suggests that consociation, with its dim view that enshrined competitive identities tend to prevail over appeals to a common humanity, can at best act as a partial means of conflict management and, at worse, a contributor to greater polarisation. The means of transition from communal division to societal transformation and the unlocking of ethnic identity are often unclear in consociational theory. It is *assumed* that elite accommodation will have a beneficial impact upon societal ethnic rigidities, allowing differences to be managed peacefully and contributing to their possible eventual erosion. The precise means through which such a benign outcome will be arrived at often, however, remain unclear. Palpably, elite-level devolved power sharing will not in itself achieve the dismantling of supposed institutional apartheid, nor will it fully address polarisation within society at large.

The pessimistic reading of consociation, both generally and in its application to Northern Ireland, has been challenged. Firstly, consociational adherents suggest it offers a realistic appraisal of 'where we are at' in Northern Ireland and that consociation acts as a means to an end, namely the management of difference in the short term, leading to its amelioration in the longer run.[12] Secondly, whilst it is easy to criticise politics in Northern Ireland as sectarian, the symbolic and actual importance of the border in maintaining division cannot be overlooked. The state was founded upon, and remains in existence due to, a sectarian head count. That communal politics exist within the state should hardly come as a surprise. Finally, opponents of consociationalism offer few alternatives beyond the vague hope of building reconciliation from below. Other political solutions, such as integration within the United Kingdom or the creation of a united Ireland, risk the alienation of a substantial section of the population. A shift towards joint authority remains the coercive alternative to power sharing, although it would be unlikely to diminish political polarisation.

The question begged here is whether institutional tinkering would ameliorate the problems supposedly engendered by consociational ethnic 'freezing' and institutional apartheid. Yet the revamped Executive and Assembly, post-2007, did not scrap communal bloc designations, whereby Assembly members have to designate as 'unionist', 'nationalist' or, controversially, merely 'other', a device which can reduce the voting importance of 'others'. The First and Deputy First Minister are denied choice in the selection of Ministers, preventing their removal of incompetent (or sectarian) office holders. The removal of a nationalist Minister by a unionist First Minister, or vice versa, would be likely to result in severe sectarian squabbling. The First Minister's attempt to prevent Sinn Féin Ministers participating in the North–South Ministerial Council in 2001, as animosities within the Executive increased, offered an example of how the enforced removal of government Ministers could entrench hostility.

The committee system of the Northern Ireland Assembly, as it operated between 1999 and 2002, offered a more encouraging version of how cross-community, consensual politics might be built without ethnic 'grandstanding'. These committees were quietly effective in scrutinising and, on many occasions, introducing legislation. A majority of committee meetings were not open to the public, which, whilst raising questions of input and accountability, facilitated cross-party co-operation not always visible when the parties sought to pander to their rival constituencies. Consensus was not always apparent; *ad hoc* committees on such issues as the display of flags witnessed sectarian division, whilst the largest committee, the Committee of the Centre, was presided over by a DUP chair who declined initially to acknowledge Sinn Féin's presence. Departmental committees were, however, mildly effective in producing non-partisan legislation and introducing some form of accountability of Ministers, however limited.

The Assembly committees represented the closest the institution came in its early years, beyond the breadth of its representational content, to becoming the 'pluralist parliament for a pluralist people' envisioned by the original First Minister, David Trimble, in his opening address to the Assembly. The work of the committees was, however, largely unpublicised. On the floor of the Assembly ethnic partisanship tended to prevail. Despite the Executive's indifferent performance, public opinion among Protestants and Catholics remained in favour of the Assembly and devolution, even though Protestant disaffection with the GFA markedly increased.[13]

Within the sectarian divide: the ethnic appeal of parties

For evidence that the parties are serious concerning the need for collective government, one needs to look for signs of appeal beyond their ethnic core vote. While electoral imperatives determine that such appeals will necessarily be limited, the willingness to share power with traditional foes is indicative of how politics in Northern Ireland have undergone revision. The DUP, previously the most implacably hostile party in respect of power sharing with Sinn Féin, abandoned its opposition to the concept in favour of a stance that demanded the fulfilment of its prior conditions for entering government with Gerry Adams's party. Sinn Féin dropped its policy of abstention to enter the Northern Ireland Assembly post-GFA and campaigned fervently for the restoration of the institution after its suspension. The more participatory form of politics promised in Northern Ireland has not, however, reduced their communal basis, as voters have backed those perceived as the stoutest defenders of the interests of specific ethnic blocs.

The honeymoon period enjoyed by the GFA and its institutions – in their first phase – was brief. Support for the DUP rose in the 1998 Assembly elections, a process which accelerated dramatically as unionists, having narrowly backed the Agreement initially, began to display wariness of its possible implications. The DUP's pitch was to accentuate the negative. Changes in policing, prisoner releases (two-thirds of those released were republicans), the lack of compulsion upon paramilitary groups to decommission their weapons and the presence of Sinn Féin in government were all highlighted as detrimental to unionist interests, claims which clearly resonated within that community.

Although the constitutional architecture of the GFA was criticised by the DUP as encouraging the transition to a united Ireland, the party's principal concerns were with those measures within the GFA which it regarded as eroding the 'British ethos' of Northern Ireland in favour of neutral symbols and the ambiguities within the deal which allowed Sinn Féin to enter government with the IRA and its weaponry still intact. The DUP's appeal was twofold: first as the party which would negotiate much more vigorously on behalf of unionism and secondly as a party strongly committed to the maintenance of a particular form of Protestant unionist Britishness. Given that the GFA affirmed the status of Northern Ireland within the United Kingdom, it was unsurprising that the DUP's main concern lay in opposition to the non-constitutional issues associated with the deal. Successive opinion polls and survey data showed that, although many Protestants expressed fears over the constitutional direction of the GFA, these concerns were less extensive than opposition on more immediate issues such as policing.[14] Although the DUP could do little to reverse the changes wrought by the GFA, an oppositional stance was useful as a means of communal mobilisation.

In contrast, the UUP could offer only the '*status quo* minus some changes' to the unionist electorate. An appeal based upon the argument that the GFA was 'as good as it gets' in terms of forcing concessions from republicans was scarcely likely to enthuse a community which had long perceived itself as being in retreat, no matter how often the principle of consent to constitutional change in Northern Ireland has been reasserted by the British (and Irish) government(s). As UUP leader from 1995 until

2005, and as First Minister of Northern Ireland in the Executive established in 1999, David Trimble saw the GFA as the means of securing
Northern Ireland's place within the United Kingdom and as the potential
instigator of a civic unionism that respected the equal integrity of Ulster
Unionism and Irish nationalism.

Trimble's pluralist vision was undermined by internal party dissidents
and growing disaffection with the GFA and the UUP among the unionist
electorate.[15] Under these constraints, Trimble oscillated between genuine
commitment to political pluralism, exemplified by entrance into government with Sinn Féin with the IRA still intact, and ritualistic playing of an
ethnic unionist card, rhetoric that was never likely to be sufficiently radical
to offset a swing to the DUP. Perhaps the most notorious example of the
retreat towards cruder expressions of cultural and political unionist
supremacy was Trimble's invitation to compare Northern Ireland with the
'pathetic, monocultural, sectarian state to our South'.[16] Although the UUP
leader used the same speech at the Ulster Unionist Council (UUC) annual
general meeting in 2002 to caution against unionist retreat into a 'sectarian laager', the denunciation of the Irish Republic – with which Trimble
had of course agreed to do business in strand two of the GFA, which established all-island cross-border bodies – emphasised that any revision of the
unionist outlook was vulnerable to recurrent appeals to exclusive ethnic
sentiment. Trimble's failure to sell the GFA to a sufficient swathe of the
unionist electorate led to his political demise in the 2005 Westminster
election. Ousted from his Upper Bann Westminster seat, Trimble resigned
the party leadership, to be replaced by Sir Reg Empey. Yet 'Empeyism', in
so far as it constituted a vision, had hitherto amounted to proclaiming
'how the institutions of the Agreement had delivered for the common
good'.[17] Given unionist scepticism over the initial terms and implementation of the Agreement, it remained unclear how the UUP might be restored
to former electoral glories and the party was eclipsed by the DUP.

Within nationalism, although the GFA was heavily influenced by the
political thinking of the SDLP, it was Sinn Féin that would be primarily
entrusted with the defence of the Agreement's gains. The communal
divide was scarcely breached by the 1998 GFA referendum campaign.
The UUP's appeal for a 'yes' vote was based upon how the deal allegedly
secured the Union; Sinn Féin's pitch for a similar outcome was partly
(and unconvincingly) based upon the potential of the GFA as marking a
transition to a united Ireland. Sinn Féin has subsequently emphasised the
equality agenda of the GFA as a key benefit for nationalists, a none too
subtle redefinition of the original primary goal of the party. 'Dissident'
republicans have been critical of the reordering of Sinn Féin priorities by
which contests for civil rights and equality within the British state have

Table 3.1 Responses to the possibility of Northern Ireland never voting to
become part of a united Ireland, by religion (%)

Question	Prot.	RC	Total
If the majority of people in Northern Ireland never voted to become part of a united Ireland, do you think you would:			
Find this almost impossible to accept?	1	4	3
Not like it, but could live with it, if had to?	13	31	25
Happily accept the wishes of the majority?	74	55	67
Don't know	11	10	6

Source: Northern Ireland Life and Times Survey, Political Attitudes, 2006,
www.ark.ac.uk. For a discussion of earlier, similar, figures see M. Bric, and
J. Coakley, 'The roots of militant politics in Ireland', in M. Bric and J. Coakley
(eds), *From Political Violence to Negotiated Settlement: The Winding Path to
Peace in Twentieth Century Ireland* (Dublin: UCD, 2004), pp. 1–12.

partially displaced issues of national sovereignty and Irish unity. This critique was most clearly expressed by Bernadette Sands-McKevitt, sister of
the republican hunger striker Bobby Sands, who declared that her
brother had not died for 'nationalists to be equal British citizens within
the Northern Ireland state'.[18]
    While Sinn Féin continues to press to 'make partition history', the
more immediate and tangible gains of the 'equality agenda' make the
party's revisionist republicanism attractive to a nationalist electorate for
which armed struggle and militant paths to unity were always a minority taste. This is perhaps most clearly illustrated in responses to the survey
question of what would happen if a majority of people in Northern
Ireland never voted to become part of a united Ireland (Table 3.1).
    Some caution needs to be exercised in analysis of such surveys. Aside
from the curious figure of 13 per cent of Protestants who declare they
'would not like it' if the people of Northern Ireland did *not* vote for a
united Ireland, it should be noted that there is a marked tendency for
respondents in opinion polls conducted in the region to offer what they
consider to be socially or politically 'acceptable' answers. Underestimation
of the electoral appeal of Sinn Féin and the DUP appears to be a permanent feature of data gathering in Northern Ireland. For example, the 2004
edition of the (generally admirable) Northern Ireland Life and Times
(NILT) survey identified the UUP as the largest unionist party, polling at
21 per cent to the DUP's 16 per cent, a finding starkly contrary to the
evidence from all four types of elections in Northern Ireland which took
place from 2003 to 2005. Nonetheless, the message from Table 3.1

appears unambiguous. One-third of Catholics do not like the idea of the goal of a united Ireland never being attained, but few find the non-realisation of the dream absolutely unacceptable. More than half could 'happily accept' the prospect of no united Ireland if there was insufficient desire among the population. Few Protestants (only 14 per cent in the 2006 NILT survey) declare that they would find the prospect of a united Ireland 'almost impossible to accept' if a majority in Northern Ireland voted in favour. Against this, however, only 31 per cent indicate that they 'would happily accept the wishes of the majority'.[19]

Sinn Féin has adapted to the traditional strength (the extent of desire for a united Ireland) and weakness (the intensity of that desire) of nationalism, by promoting a united Ireland but not at the expense of 'other', non-constitutional politics, which are important to nationalists, given that Irish unity is far from imminent. The *extensiveness* of the desire for a united Ireland across Ireland remains undiminished.[20] The proportion of the Northern Ireland population believing the best long-term policy for Northern Ireland is to remain part of the United Kingdom is lowest among eighteen to twenty-four-year olds, at only 45 per cent.[21] The *intensity* of desire for a united Ireland, however, remains significantly less than that of unionists to resist incorporation into such a state.

In moving into constitutional politics Sinn Féin began to control a space that was previously the preserve of the SDLP. This shift presented the SDLP with various choices, none of which was particularly promising. The first was the consolidation of a robust cross-community coalition of political moderates with the UUP within the Assembly and Executive. Given the internal and electoral disintegration of the UUP, this prospect quickly disappeared. The alternative position for the SDLP was to portray itself as the more trustworthy custodian of the GFA than Sinn Féin for the nationalist community. Having largely written the deal, this was a logical position for the SDLP to adopt, but after the GFA nationalists looked for a party to advance the agreement.

Sinn Féin positioned itself as the stouter defender of a nationalist 'equality agenda' within Northern Ireland, on which changes in policing, the work of an Equality Commission and recognition of the legitimacy of the nationalist tradition provided compensation for the shelving of long-term constitutional ambitions. Republicans were rewarded for the shift from violence by a nationalist electorate, a majority of which have usually eschewed such a tactic. Nonetheless, the nationalist electorate also wished for robustness from its representatives, given the challenges of DUP hostility to the original terms of the deal.

An alternative for the SDLP was merger with a major party in the Irish Republic to counter Sinn Féin's all-Ireland organisational advantages.

However, this was a move likely to be opposed by members of both parties hostile to any prospective merger and would undermine the SDLP's evenhandedness in dealing with the Irish government. The idea has elicited little enthusiasm among SDLP members.

Gauging polarisation: voting patterns

The rise of the DUP and Sinn Féin has undoubtedly been the most important feature of the political process since the signing of the GFA. Table 3.2 records the parties' progress in eclipsing their rivals, the UUP and SDLP. Given that Sinn Féin has come to advance a rather less radical political agenda and that the DUP has a commitment to devolved power sharing, the frequent interpretation of the electoral advance of the parties as the growth of 'extremism' was perplexing. Crucially, however, electoral 'moderation' has been *asymmetrical*. Sinn Féin has been rewarded for its willingness to abandon support for the IRA's armed campaign, which had only ever been supported by a minority of nationalists, notwithstanding the considerable sympathy that key moments in the history of republicanism such as the 1980–81 hunger strikes were able to generate within the broader nationalist fold. Sinn Féin's new agenda has led to perceived gains for nationalists within the northern state and has thus drawn considerable support from the Catholic community. Any early DUP appeal to moderation would not have brought similar reward among its electorate, given the initial perception of the GFA among unionists as, at best, a 'necessary evil' in terms of the concessions in relation to prisoner releases and policing changes and, at worst, part of an ongoing process of 'greening' Northern Ireland.

Nonetheless, the ousting of the traditional moderates within each bloc probably amounts to permanent realignment, the end game of which could potentially result in the competition between two parties within each ethno-religious bloc being replaced with single-party dominance. Such a development may ease the implementation of power sharing, as intra-bloc rivalry is eliminated.

Elections in Northern Ireland remain contests marked by almost total correlation between religious affiliation and political preference. Use of the 2001 census data and the 2005 Westminster election results in each constituency reveals an extremely strong link between the percentage of Protestants and the combined unionist vote in a given constituency and an almost identically strong link between the percentage of Catholics and the combined nationalist vote.[22] Admittedly, the single plurality ('first past the post') voting system employed alone for Westminster elections encourages voting within ethno-religious blocs, given the absence of lower

Table 3.2 Party vote shares in Northern Ireland elections, 1997–2007

Election	First preference party vote share (%)			
	DUP	*UUP*	*SF*	*SDLP*
Pre-GFA				
1997 Westminster	13.6	32.7	16.1	24.1
1997 Council	15.6	27.9	16.9	20.7
Post-GFA				
1998 Assembly	18.1	21.3	17.6	22.0
1999 European	28.4	17.6	17.4	28.1
2001 Westminster	22.5	26.8	21.7	21.0
2001 Council	21.4	22.9	20.7	19.4
2003 Assembly	25.7	22.7	23.5	17.0
2004 European	31.9	16.5	26.3	15.9
2005 Westminster	33.7	17.7	24.3	17.5
2005 Council	29.6	18.0	23.2	17.4
2007 Assembly	30.1	14.9	26.2	15.2

Source: Ark, Northern Ireland Social and Political Archive, www.ark.ac.uk/
elections/.

preference votes. Regardless of the specific voting system employed, however, elections in Northern Ireland remain sectarian head counts. The outbreak of optimism that marked the elections to the Assembly held immediately after the signing of the GFA, in which a sizable minority of SDLP supporters transferred final vote preferences across the divide to the UUP where an Alliance Party candidate was not standing, was destined to be brief. Over 90 per cent of surplus vote transfers from parties at the 2007 Assembly elections remained within the same ethnic bloc.

The lack of voting across the communal divide is further illustrated by survey evidence. Table 3.3 indicates how the four main parties draw only miniscule support from outside their ethno-religious bloc. Whilst the Life and Times survey hugely overstates UUP and SDLP support at the expense of the DUP and SDLP (even allowing for a high rate of abstention from voting among UUP sympathisers) there is little reason to doubt that the association between religious affiliation and political preference is as stark as suggested in Table 3.3.

The absence of significant breaches of the sectarian fault line is unsurprising when the extent of hostility to the 'hard line' parties in the 'other' ethnic bloc is considered. An almost total absence of lower preference vote transfers across the divide between DUP and Sinn Féin voters is a recurrent feature of elections. For example, in the 2004 European elections, of the DUP's 38,441 surplus votes, 87 per cent were transferred to the UUP and only 1 per cent crossed the divide, going exclusively to the

Table 3.3 Party support, by religion (%)

Party	Prot.	RC
UUP	27	1
DUP	34	1
SDLP	1	29
Sinn Féin	0	25
None/other	38	44

Source: Northern Ireland Life and Times Survey, 2006, Political Attitudes, www.ark.ac.uk.

SDLP. In the 2007 Assembly elections less than 0.1 per cent of DUP surpluses transferred to Sinn Féin, a figure reciprocated in terms of Sinn Féin's surplus transfers to the DUP.

The 2001 Northern Ireland General Election Survey asked electors to grade their feelings towards each political party.[23] By far the largest single category of feeling towards the DUP and Sinn Féin was the maximum 'strongly dislike' permitted on the scale. These maximum dislikes amounted to 27 per cent of electors in respect of the DUP and 41 per cent in respect of Sinn Féin. As respective party leaders, Ian Paisley and Gerry Adams attracted similar maximum dislike ratings. Given that the bulk of these strong dislikes may reasonably be assumed to emanate from the 'rival' community, the extent of polarisation becomes readily evident. The leading two parties in Northern Ireland are thus strongly disliked by a large swathe of the electorate. In contrast to this, the UUP and SDLP attract rather less hostility. Only 10 per cent of respondents felt maximum dislike for the UUP, even fewer being so antipathetic to the SDLP, at 6 per cent. This lack of enmity suggests that the *possibility* of lower preference vote transfers between the SDLP and UUP remains intact, but in reality the bulk of voters have moved towards more 'green' or 'orange' representatives.

Moreover, there is little incentive for parties in Northern Ireland to appeal beyond their ethno-religious community. For either unionist party such a choice would hardly be rational, given the risk to core support within the ethnic bloc which is antipathetic to the 'other' side. For nationalist parties an appeal to Protestants has often been part of their rhetoric, traditionally expressed in the form of the need for an agreed Ireland (SDLP) or through the guarantee of civil liberties and rights in a united Ireland (Sinn Féin). Election campaigns, however, are based primarily upon the mobilisation of nationalist voters. The appeal by Gerry Adams in the 2003 Assembly elections for Sinn Féin voters to support UUP candidates who backed GFA after registering higher preferences for Sinn

Féin and SDLP candidates was widely ignored. The new moderation of Sinn Féin has in fact accentuated communal voting by keeping the votes of SDLP first-preference supporters within the ethnic bloc. When support for Sinn Féin could readily be construed as a vote for the IRA campaign of political violence a majority of SDLP terminal lower-preference votes went to the non-confessional Alliance Party where an SDLP candidate was unavailable, not to Sinn Féin.[24] By the 2003 Assembly election almost three-quarters of the final votes of SDLP first preference voters transferred to Sinn Féin. The size of the confessional and non-confessional blocs is shown in Table 3.4.[25]

The table illustrates the gradual rise of the nationalist bloc and the slight decline in the unionist bloc vote. However, the prospect that the nationalist vote may overtake the unionist one remains distant. In elections from 1998 until 2007 the mean share of the vote was 50.0 per cent unionist and 41.7 per cent nationalist. While this gap is likely to close, it will probably do so only gradually, given the slowing of the rise in the Catholic population.

The Alliance Party of Northern Ireland (APNI) has long been the only significant centrist party in the region. Unsurprisingly, Alliance does not attract the opprobrium associated with the likes of the DUP or Sinn Féin.[26] Although its centrist position retains some advantage in attracting votes from those unwilling to cross the communal divide, there is little to disguise the longer-term decline of the only sizable party capable of attracting support from Protestants and Catholics alike.

The APNI's status as a non-confessional party is secured on the basis of its appeal for votes across the sectarian divide. Whilst all parties ritually claim to appeal across the chasm and welcome support from both communities, the membership, appeal and campaigning techniques of the larger parties often suggest that this is mere tokenism. In arguing for a one-community approach to politics, as distinct from the bipolar and ethnically exclusive politics evident since the formation of the state, APNI has assumed a distinctive niche in Northern Irish political life. Alliance has sought to dismantle the structures of communalism. Whilst supportive of devolved power sharing, the party has been very critical of the reductionism of the 'unionist, nationalist or other' designations required of Assembly members and opposed the Catholic and non-Catholic quota recruitment system for the Police Service of Northern Ireland (PSNI). Alliance argues that binary recruitment or designation procedures reinforce rather than challenge sectarian division. What is needed, according to the party, is the fostering of a sense of Northern Irishness rather than the strengthening of existing Protestant-Unionist-British and Catholic-Irish-Nationalist communalisms.[27]

Table 3.4 Bloc voting, 1992–2007

	Bloc										
	Unionist				Nationalist				Non-confessional		
Election	UUP	DUP	Other	Total	SDLP	SF	Other	Total	APNI	Other	Total
1992 general	34.5	13.1	2.7	50.3	23.5	10.0	–	33.5	8.7	7.5	16.2
1993 local	29.4	17.3	2.7	49.4	22.0	12.4	0.3	36.7	7.6	7.8	15.4
1994 European	23.8	29.2	–	53.0	28.9	9.9	–	38.8	4.1	4.0	8.1
1996 Forum	24.2	18.8	9.3	52.3	21.4	15.5	–	36.9	6.5	4.3	10.8
1997 general	32.7	13.6	4.2	50.5	24.1	16.1	–	40.2	8.0	1.3	9.3
1997 local	27.9	15.6	4.1	47.6	20.7	16.9	–	37.6	6.5	8.4	14.9
Post-GFA											
1998 Assembly	21.3	18.1	11.1	50.5	22.0	17.6	–	39.6	6.5	3.4	9.9
1999 European	17.6	28.4	6.3	52.3	28.1	17.4	–	45.5	2.1	0.1	2.2
2001 Westminster	26.8	22.5	3.4	52.7	21.0	21.7	–	42.7	3.6	1.0	4.6
2001 local	22.9	21.4	3.0	47.3	19.4	20.7	–	40.1	5.1	7.5	12.6
2003 Assembly	25.7	22.7	2.6	51.0	17.0	23.5	–	40.5	3.7	4.8	8.5
2004 European	16.5	31.9	–	48.4	15.9	26.3	–	42.2	–	9.4	9.4
2005 Westminster	17.7	33.7	–	51.4	17.5	24.3	–	41.8	3.9	2.9	7.8
2005 Council	18.0	29.6	1.0	48.6	17.4	23.2	–	40.6	5.0	6.4	11.4
2007 Assembly	14.9	30.1	2.6	47.6	15.2	26.2	0.5	41.9	5.2	3.0	8.2

Sources: Adapted and updated from P. Mitchell, 'The party system and party competition', in P. Mitchell and R. Wilford, (eds), *Politics in Northern Ireland* (Oxford: Westview Press, 1998), pp. 40–63; S. Elliott and W. Flackes, *Northern Ireland: A Political Directory* (Belfast: Blackstaff Press, 1999), and the Conflict Archive in Northern Ireland at www.cain.ulster.ac.uk For a pre-1990s version of the data see B. O'Leary, 'Party support in Northern Ireland, 1969–1989', in J. McGarry and B. O'Leary (eds), *The Future of Northern Ireland* (Oxford: Oxford University Press, 1991) pp. 342–57.

Table 3.5 Political identification

Question	Prot.	RC	Total
Generally speaking, do you think of yourself as a unionist, a nationalist, or neither?			
Unionist	69	3	36
Nationalist	0	54	23
Neither	30	42	40

Source: Northern Ireland Life and Times Survey, 2006.

Given its largely middle-class origins, membership and support base, Alliance has never been in a strong position to challenge communalism where is has been most visible, between rival working-class communities at sectarian interfaces.[28] The party could also be charged with underplaying the legitimacy of Irish nationalism, given the *de facto* unionism of its essentially uncritical acceptance of the legitimacy of the constitutional *status quo* and its initial belief in the superior liberalism of the British state as the guarantor of the rights of all the people of Northern Ireland. Over 60 per cent of the support attracted by Alliance comes from Protestants, yet there is evidence that Alliance ought to do better electorally *per se* and particularly among Catholics, a larger percentage of whom identify as neither unionist nor nationalist than do Protestants (Table 3.5).

Those identifying as unionist or nationalist may have a greater propensity to vote than non-identifiers, but the discrepancy between the proportion of the Northern Irish population that seemingly eschews the unionist–nationalist dichotomy – perhaps as many as two in five – and that which has been willing to support the Alliance Party in recent elections – stuck around 5 per cent – is stark. The 2001 General Election Survey, the most recent exhaustive study of a Northern Ireland Westminster election, also suggested the existence of a substantial centrist constituency to which a party such as Alliance might perhaps be expected to appeal. Asked to grade themselves on a scale of 0 (republican) to 10 (loyalist) by far the largest category of respondents, some 34 per cent, placed themselves in the middle at 5.[29]

There are rather more 'non-identifiers' than nationalists within Northern Ireland if – and it is admittedly a big if – the survey evidence is to be believed. In principle, the electoral performance of Alliance really *ought* to have been altogether more impressive. The age categories that have the largest percentage of non-identifiers with unionism and nationalism are those between eighteen and twenty-four and between twenty-five and thirty-four. While in principle the Alliance Party might be expected to perform best among these age cohorts, it is in fact among these younger voters that it performs most poorly, attracting a mere 2 per cent of first preferences.[30]

However, the survey evidence suggesting the existence of a large group of non-identifiers with the unionist–nationalist contest should be treated with considerable caution. Firstly, there is a tendency in surveys for respondents to portray themselves as liberal-minded, non-sectarian pluralists, whatever their private prejudices. Secondly, as noted, the survey findings are not replicated by electoral evidence in terms of party support. Thirdly, there is a sizable, if unquantifiable, body of opinion which eschews the labels unionist or nationalist but whose sympathies nonetheless lie in one direction or the other. Fourthly, some of those professed non-unionists or non-nationalists have disengaged from the electoral process, allowing elections to become increasingly contests of 'true believers'.

Two concurrent trends may be identified. There appears to be considerable indifference to the traditional unionist–nationalist zero-sum-game politics among the younger members of Northern Irish society. Equally, however, there has been a hardening of attitudes among other younger members of both ethno-religious blocs. Support for the UUP among eighteen to twenty-four-year olds was recorded at a mere 4 per cent by the 2006 Northern Ireland Life and Times survey, a figure only a quarter of that found for the DUP and only just over one-fifth of that shown for the UUP among over-sixty-fives. Sinn Féin's support among eighteen to twenty-four-year-olds year olds was substantially greater than among any other age category and the party's electoral strength would seem to be premised largely upon the mobilisation of young voters and former non-voters.[31]

Table 3.5 also indicates how few Protestants and Catholics are willing to adopt the political label associated with their 'rival' community. Whilst successive public opinion surveys (e.g. the annual Northern Ireland Life and Times surveys) show that a minority of Catholics accept Northern Ireland's place in the United Kingdom, Table 3.5 indicates that only a tiny percentage of such Catholics are prepared to describe themselves as unionists. This may be due to communal pressure, or the perceived sectarian nature of unionist parties. Almost no Protestants are willing to define themselves as 'nationalists'.

As conflict has subsided amid a polity where a sizable section of the electorate professes to eschew the traditional unionist–nationalist binary, the question that springs to mind is whether political parties will mobilise voters around the old constitutional issues or develop a new politics centred upon social issues and resource allocation. Given the impermanence of devolution thus far, and the resultant impotence of the local parties, it has been difficult to enthuse electors as to the possibilities of local control or radical change.

In recent years there would appear to have been a trend towards voter disengagement in Northern Ireland, although this pattern can be found in most Western democracies. As examples, turnout has fallen in Westminster, European and local elections. There is a negative relationship between votes for unionist parties and turnout. The general rule is that the higher the unionists' share of the vote the lower the turnout. Despite the bitterness of the intra-unionist rivalry of the immediate post-GFA years, a substantial section of the unionist community disengaged from the political process. Although communal polarisation emerged as a trend if one examines the (crude) measurement of increased DUP support, the negative relationship between DUP vote and turnout indicated that apathy had also become an important feature of the political disposition of the unionist community.

Party membership and polarisation

It is clear from the earlier data that an electoral thaw among DUP and Sinn Féin supporters is unlikely, given the extent of their mutual antipathy. Yet the perceptions of moderation seen in relation to the UUP, SDLP and APNI still offer some prospect, however slight, of an erosion of the sectarian voting barrier among those with less distance to travel. It should be acknowledged, though, that parties are reluctant to attempt to become 'catch-all' organisations, given the associated risk of alienating their core ethnic support. As an intermediate tier between elites and voters, party members can be important in rebranding parties or resisting such change.

Academic analyses of political parties elsewhere in the United Kingdom have suggested that members tend to be more hard-line than ordinary voters.[32] While there would appear to be some common ground between the relatively moderate memberships of the UUP and SDLP, this is probably insufficient for the parties to develop a coherent strategy that transcends their established ethnic bases. The UUP and SDLP draw their membership almost exclusively from discrete and different ethno-political communities. Only 1 per cent of UUP members are Catholics; the same figure is recorded for the percentage of Protestants among the membership of the SDLP.[33] The APNI is much less exclusive than either in its membership base, comprising 20 per cent Catholics, 63 per cent Protestants and 17 per cent those of no religion or other affiliation.[34]

For those seeking common ground the good news lies perhaps in the belief in the potential for devolution. A majority of UUP, SDLP and APNI members have consistently believed that a Northern Ireland Assembly would improve local services, and they appear to have been joined by Sinn Féin and DUP backers. Only 14 per cent of UUP members disagreed, and the figure was even lower within Alliance and the SDLP.[35] Moreover, a majority of the members of all three parties support power sharing within the Assembly and Executive. However, there are aspects of the GFA which still appear divisive. Even among UUP members, more associated with moderation, there is an almost equal division over whether cross-border bodies should be attached to institutions in Northern Ireland, and there is also a substantial body of the party, some 45 per cent, that favours the full integration of Northern Ireland into the United Kingdom.[36] Polarisation of party positions becomes evident when non-constitutional aspects of the GFA are examined. Whilst 94 per cent of SDLP members endorse the changes in policing introduced since the GFA, only 19 per cent of the UUP membership are similarly inclined. Paramilitary prisoner releases produce a similar asymmetry. While the assertion of the unqualified marching rights of the Orange Order divides the UUP, members of the SDLP are strongly opposed to loyalist parades passing though nationalist districts. Even in the case of the APNI opinion is divided along religious lines, with Protestant members showing much greater hostility to prisoner releases and policing changes than their Catholic counterparts.[37] The divisions within republicanism were apparent in the presence of 'dissident' candidates at the 2007 Assembly elections, although they fared badly, whilst the DUP's entry into government with Sinn Féin provoked disquiet and several resignations within the party but little serious dissent.

In relation to 'normal' issues there is considerable division both between and within the political parties. Members of the UUP tend, for instance, to be opposed to the abolition of the eleven-plus test that has for the last half-century determined the type of secondary level school that Northern Irish children attend. The membership of the SDLP, in contrast, strongly support the transfer procedure being changed. In addition, abortion splits the UUP, half its members being in favour of its legalisation whereas SDLP members are strongly opposed.[38]

Would party members take the lead in being willing to diminish polarisation by voting for a party from the rival ethnic bloc? The general pattern that emerges is of solidarity within competing ethnic blocs, albeit tempered by attitudes to the GFA within the UUP. On a scale of 1 (very likely to transfer lower-preference votes to the DUP) to 4 (no possibility of such a transfer) supporters of the GFA within the UUP offered a mean figure of 2.6, compared with 1.5 for anti-Agreement UUP members. Almost half (47 per cent) of SDLP members desired an electoral pact with Sinn Féin in which the parties might not fight each other, but such pacts are most unlikely.[39] The SDLP is a potential repository of lower-preference votes from UUP members, only 31 per cent of whom declared that 'under no circumstances' would they vote for the nationalist party.[40] Despite the Protestant background of the majority of APNI members, the SDLP is slightly favoured over the UUP as a lower-preference voting choice and Alliance is positioned closer to the nationalist bloc on a number of ideological and policy perspectives.[41]

Conclusion

The communalism that pervades Northern Irish society assumes many different forms. Residential segregation and cultural separation are two readily apparent expressions of the distinctions between people living in the region. Equally stark, however, is the political divide. The politics of peace and (eventually) devolved power sharing in post-conflict Northern Ireland have not seen an end of occasional zero-sum contests between unionists and nationalists, despite their combining in an elite level consociation to govern the region. The polity remains one in which the past, present and future are contested, even by those whose contributions are generally regarded as essentially moderate and constructive. Argument over whether a united Ireland is attainable or desirable in the future persists.

Even optimists have conceded that 'the end of sectarianism is at least two generations away'.[42] A historically determinist reading could be yet more pessimistic, given the propensity of Northern Ireland politics to oscillate between constitutionalism and more militant activity. Given the disappearance of meaningful armed conflict, however, the question that arises is whether the stark unionist–nationalist political division can ever be breached. The demise of the Provisional IRA, the modest growth of secularism and the possible turn in the region's economic fortunes have not erased the traditional fault lines within the region.

The focus is now upon the impact of political arrangements in post-conflict Northern Ireland. Advocates of consociation continue to offer its management of ethnic tensions as the most realistic and ultimately productive means of harnessing political divisions. The willingness of Sinn Féin and the DUP to enter a power sharing arrangement provided vindication that institutional accommodation can reshape politics. The assumption is that a combination of a technocratic reordering of power sharing procedures within the Assembly and Executive and the shift towards a bloc system in which one party dominates each ethnic group will both facilitate a more durable form of cross-community government which does not merely divide up political power. Considerable goodwill towards the concept of devolution has always been apparent and was eventually accompanied by the willingness of all the main forces within unionism and nationalism to share power. However, continuing inter-communal mistrust and the fear that power shared is actually power divided has meant that doubts over the durability of devolved power sharing have remained.

Given the absence of decisive movement towards joint authority, inte-gration or a united Ireland, the ambitious alternative to consociation, of building consensus at the grass roots, relies upon an incremental process of diminishing mistrust and lessening communal antagonism. Such move-ment is entirely possible, given the relatively peaceful backdrop in which paramilitary activity has become comparatively rare. Reintegration is already under way and is likely to accelerate when the physical symbols of division, notably 'peace walls', are removed. Consensus building from below will nonetheless be obliged to contend with a legacy of communal hostility, divergent identities, split allegiances and the potentially desta-bilising ritual expressions of cultural and political identity in the form of parades. Benign apartheid and a two-community suspicious coexistence, rather than the emergence of consensual one-community politics, remain the more likely short-term scenarios.

Notes

1 R. Taylor, 'Northern Ireland: consociation or social transformation?' in J. McGarry (ed.), *Northern Ireland and the Divided World* (Oxford: Oxford University Press, 2001), pp. 37–53.
2 A. Oberschall and L. Kendall Palmer, 'The failure of moderate politics: the case of Northern Ireland', in I. O'Flynn and D. Russell (eds), *Power Sharing: New Challenges for Divided Societies* (London: Pluto Press, 2005), pp. 77–91.
3 A. Lijphart, *Democracy in Plural Societies: A Comparative Exploration* (New Haven CT: Yale University Press, 1975); J. McGarry and B. O'Leary, *Explaining Northern Ireland: Broken Images* (Oxford: Blackwell, 1995), pp. 320–6.
4 G. Gillespie, 'The Sunningdale Agreement: lost opportunity or an agreement too far?' *Irish Political Studies* 13 (1998), pp. 100–14.
5 B. Hayes and I. McAllister, 'Who voted for peace? Public support for the 1998 Good Friday Agreement', *Irish Political Studies* 16 (2001), pp. 61–82.
6 A. Lijphart, 'Democracy in plural societies', in J. McGarry and B. O'Leary (eds), *The Northern Ireland Conflict: Consociational Engagements* (Oxford: Oxford University Press, 2004).
7 T. Hadden, 'Reviewing the Agreement', *Fortnight*, January 2004, p. 7.

8 A. Aughey, *The Politics of Northern Ireland: Beyond the Belfast Agreement* (London: Routledge, 2005), p. 88.

9 M. Laver, 'Coalitions in Northern Ireland: Preliminary Thoughts', programme for government conference, Belfast, June 2000. For a slightly more sanguine view of the post-GFA polity see S. Wolff, 'The peace process in Northern Ireland since 1998: success or failure of post-Agreement reconstruction?', *Civil Wars* 5:1 (2002), pp. 87–116.

10 In the 1999–2002 Executive, party Ministerial entitlements under the D'Hondt system were as follows: UUP three, SDLP three, DUP two and SF two.

11 See Taylor, 'Northern Ireland: consociation or social transformation?'; R. Wilson, 'The apartheid thinking of the Agreement', *Fortnight*, December 2002, p. 6. R. Wilford, 'The Assembly and Executive', in R. Wilford (ed.), *Aspects of the Belfast Agreement* (Oxford: Oxford University Press, 2001), pp. 107–28, offers a mildly sceptical view.

12 B. O'Leary, 'The British–Irish Agreement: consociation-plus', *Scottish Affairs* 26 (1999), pp. 1–22; McGarry and O'Leary, *The Northern Ireland Conflict*.

13 C. Irwin, *The People's Peace Process in Northern Ireland* (Basingstoke: Palgrave, 2002); Northern Ireland Life and Times Survey, 2003, Political Attitudes, www.ark.ac.uk.

14 Irwin, *The People's Peace Process*; J. Tonge and J. Evans, 'Party members and the Good Friday Agreement', *Irish Political Studies* 17:2 (2002), pp. 59–73.

15 For a discussion of the concept of civic unionism see N. Porter, *Rethinking Unionism: An Alternative Vision for Northern Ireland* (Belfast: Blackstaff Press, 1996).

16 D. Trimble, speech to Ulster Unionist Council annual general meeting, Belfast, October 2002.

17 Aughey, *The Politics of Northern Ireland*, p. 127.

18 T. Hennessey, *The Northern Ireland Peace Process: Ending the Troubles?* (Dublin: Gill & Macmillan, 2000), p. 112.

19 For a discussion of earlier, similar figures see M. Bric and J. Coakley, 'The roots of militant politics in Ireland', in M. Bric and J. Coakley (eds), *From Political Violence to Negotiated Settlement: The Winding Path to Peace in Twentieth Century Ireland* (Dublin: UCD, 2004), pp. 1–12.

20 W. H. Cox, 'Who wants a united Ireland?' *Government and Opposition* 20 (1985), pp. 29–47; B. Hayes and I. McAllister, 'British and Irish public opinion towards the Northern Ireland problem', *Irish Political Studies* 16 (2001), pp. 61–82; B. Hayes and T. Fahey, 'National identity in the Republic of Ireland: does religion matter?' Paper presented to the Irish Protestant Identities conference, University of Salford, 17–19 September 2005.

21 Northern Ireland Life and Times Survey, 2006.

22 At the 2005 election the r^2 for the Protestant population and the unionist bloc vote was 0.974; the r^2 for the Catholic population and the nationalist bloc vote was 0.975.

23 For details see www.bes.ac.uk.
24 Terminal votes are the final transfers of votes from candidates who have already been elected or eliminated. Their votes are redistributed until the requisite number of representatives for a constituency has been elected. Most such transfers in Northern Ireland are to parties within the same ethnic bloc.
25 The term 'confessional' refers to those parties which draw support from an almost exclusively religious support base and whose electoral appeal is pitched overwhelmingly to that base. It does not infer a formal connection between the party and any religious organisation. The term 'non-confessional' refers to those parties which draw significant (above 10 per cent) support from both the main religious traditions in Northern Ireland. Of the parties with elected representatives above council level, only the Alliance Party achieves this.
26 In the 2001 Northern Ireland election survey Alliance scored a central 5 on the 0 (strongly dislike) to 10 (strongly like) scale.
27 See for example, Alliance Party of Northern Ireland, *Agenda for Democracy: Alliance Party Proposals for the Review of the Agreement* (Belfast: Alliance Party, 2004).
28 For details of this manifestation see P. Shirlow, 'Who fears to speak? Fear, Mobility and Ethno-sectarianism in north Belfast', paper presented to the ESRC Northern Ireland Research Group seminar, Belfast, May 2003.
29 www.bes.ac.uk.
30 Northern Ireland Life and Times Survey, 2006.
31 I. McAllister, 'The Armalite and the ballot box: Sinn Féin's electoral strategy in Northern Ireland', *Electoral Studies* 21:1 (2004), pp. 123–42.
32 See as examples P. Seyd and P. Whiteley, *Labour's Grass Roots* (Oxford: Clarendon Press, 1992); P. Seyd, P. Whiteley and J. Richardson, *True Blues* (Oxford: Clarendon Press, 1994).
33 These and subsequent figures for the UUP are drawn from the author's membership survey, conducted in 2002. For more details of attitudes within the UUP and UUC see J. Tonge and J. Evans, 'Fault lines in unionism: division and dissent within the Ulster Unionist Council', *Irish Political Studies* 16 (2001), pp. 111–31. These and subsequent figures for the SDLP are drawn from the author's membership survey as part of the ESRC New Nationalism in Northern Ireland project, 2000, R000222668. See also G. Murray and J. Tonge, *Sinn Féin and the SDLP* (London: Hurst, 2005).
34 Figures based upon the author's membership survey, ESRC project, R000223414, Third Traditions in Northern Ireland. See J. Evans and J. Tonge, 'The future of the "radical centre" in Northern Ireland after the Good Friday Agreement', *Political Studies* 51:1 (2003), pp. 26–50.
35 Tonge and Evans, 'Party members and the Good Friday Agreement'.
36 Tonge and Evans, 'Fault lines in unionism'.
37 Evans and Tonge, 'The future of the "radical centre" in Northern Ireland'.
38 See note 28.

39 J. Evans, J. Tonge and G. Murray, 'Constitutional nationalism and socialism in Northern Ireland: the greening of the Social Democratic and Labour Party', in P. Cowley, D. Denver, A. Russell and L. Harrison (eds), *British Elections and Parties Review* 10 (London: Frank Cass, 2000).
40 Tonge and Evans, 'Fault lines in unionism'.
41 Evans and Tonge, 'The future of the "radical centre" in Northern Ireland'.
42 Speech by the Irish ambassador to the United Kingdom, Daithi O'Ceallaigh, Institute of Irish Studies, University of Liverpool, 19 October 2005.

4

Belfast: a segregated city

Peter Shirlow

'Belfast is ready for the party to begin'

The headline above, provided by the *New York Times* journalist Stuart Emmrich,[1] airs the view that all is well in Belfast and that it is high time, after the traumas of three decades of conflict, that everyone in the city let their hair down. This optimism echoes a common internal and external view of the positive changes that have occurred in Northern Ireland since the advent of the paramilitary cease-fires of 1994. Belfast, the city in which it was often difficult to find a centrally located restaurant open at night, is now portrayed as a small metropolitan site that has shaken itself free from the dire old world of the bomber and a far from sophisticated past that lacked deeply commodified 'lifestyles'.[2] This was once the very city in which the City Fathers (and the very occasional City Mother) chained up public playgrounds on Sundays, dare anyone enjoy the Sabbath beyond the confines of religious indignation.

The manifestation of social well-being and the rise of the 'chic' bar and bistro are presented as a sign of normality and security. State expenditure, in particular on the riverfront, and the use of funds to create a modern cityscape clearly benefit a middle-income group who suffered less than their working-class counterparts who bore and bear the brunt of violence and who cannot easily afford the benefits of opulent living. But the veneer of sophistication and more observable signs of a metropolitan lifestyle cannot undermine other realities of social truncation and sectarian asperity.

The key ideological message driven by both the Irish and the British states is that peace dividends are to be achieved through economic upgrading and the related 'benefits' of global living. No space within such representations is permitted for the growth in relative poverty, the rise in racism and the mounting exploitation of sex workers, mostly women, who have provided an alternative mode within the service economy. Even less time is to be dedicated to appreciating how Belfast's future remains tied to enduring ethno-sectarian separation. This is a city within which some 1,500 people were killed and tens of thousands victimised and traumatised in a conflict that rumbles on, although thankfully in a less dramatic fashion.

Policy makers aim to construct Belfast via non-controversial representations. Illusionary and buoyant renditions of Belfast are linked with somewhat surreal distortions. It is not that those who frame policy have an inability to see beyond immediate events but that they aim to transcend what they view as the complex, bizarre and illogical through reasserting ethno-centric separation while at the same time denying that ethno-sectarianism exists. Belfast's policy makers and tourist officials aim to corral Belfast's more unsightly problems into the inner and outer-city housing estates and consequently have failed to show the commitment required to genuinely address the injustices associated with segregation and socio-spatial exclusion.

The fate of the city lies somewhere between the uneven developments that arise out of globalisation and the balkanisation that defines ethno-sectarian life. In recent times we have also witnessed some of the most inexcusable scenes of violence since the paramilitary cease-fires of 1994. The Holy Cross dispute, in 2001, presented loyalists hurling abuse at Catholic[3] schoolgirls aged four to eleven as they walked to school through 'loyalist' territory. The murder of Robert McCartney by members of the Irish Republican Army and the attempted cover-up undertaken by republicans, including the harassment of the victim's sisters, who 'dared' to demand justice, testify to old habits surviving in new times.

For those who promote Belfast as a tourist site it is hoped that the sightseers, of whom there are now many, will be directed to those parts of the city which will ensure that visitors are physically and cognitively distant from the more 'unsavoury' parts of the city. Ironically, it would appear that most tourists aim to seek out the 'dangerous' and 'perverse' as they head into the inner city in search of opportunities to photograph paramilitary wall murals and Orange bands. In spite of official attempts to promote the city in an 'apolitical' manner, visitors have failed to be entirely convinced by recent attempts to represent and repackage what Belfast 'really' means. This chapter explains the nature and extent of ethno-sectarian problems that remain and the reasons why it is not time to party – or, at least, not just yet.

Space matters

Developing processes of conflict transformation must be linked with the development of space sharing and a challenge to those localised discourses which view segregation, in whatever form, as protecting identity. Segregation provides the capacity to subvert civic responsibility through encouraging territorial disputes that draw sustenance from the need for inter-community separation. Negative inter-community relations are tied to the promotion of exclusivist renditions of belonging within which spatial bordering[4] is centred upon the practice and definition of an ethno-sectarian 'other' that is viewed as repressive and deviant. In antithesis to this, the community-based definition of the 'in-group' positions those deemed to be kin as both pure and legitimate.[5]

The need remains, despite noteworthy political changes and a decrease in violence, to establish the structural relations of power, displacement and conflict which pinpoint how spaces are both (re)constructed and contested.[6] This means analysing the media through which Belfast's residents transform daily occurrences and sentiments into a symbolic system of territorial belonging.[7] These constantly negotiated and contested social and spatial practices matter in that they are interpreted and given significance by their participants. Within Belfast, obvious forms of social, cultural and political belief are linked across spatial scales including residential segregation, schooling, leisure, sport, consumption, socialising and work. As noted by Shirlow and Murtagh:[8]

> The desire to champion political discourses and violence as 'veritable', 'virtuous' and legitimate has led to a conspicuous failure to recognise how ethno-sectarianism conflict has reproduced spatial enclosure and behavioural practices that are partly dictated by widespread fears and prejudices.

A central problem is the connection between territoriality and the political organisation of space. Space is continuously divided through a combination of physical and symbolic forces and the expression of social power. Not only is such power aggressive, especially within the context of inter-community violence, it also encourages identity performance. Thus Orange marching and discouraging such parading in republican areas are based upon a mutually inclusive relationship between alternative territories, their control and ultimate meaning.

Wall murals, for example, are a distinguishable form of territorial marking. The utilisation of selective events and images in such murals is tied to the managing of senses of territorial belonging and of struggle, suffering and resistance. The marking of space pinpoints political selection by reminding the viewer of 'oppression' and the perpetual need to celebrate examples of armed and civil resistance.

Muralists use defined spaces within which to operationalise a propaganda-conditioning perspective that encompasses signals of territorial demarcation. The key issues in terms of interpreting the meaning

Table 4.1 **Relationship between politically motivated deaths and interfaces**

Distance from interface(m)	Share of all deaths within Belfast urban area (%)
Less than 100	13.47
Less than 200	28.89
Less than 300	44.25
Less than 400	57.28
Less than 500	66.53
Less than 600	71.88
Less than 700	75.91
Less than 800	79.39
Less than 900	81.53
Less than 1,000	84.25
Over 1,000	15.74

Source: P. Shirlow and B. Murtagh, *Belfast: Violence, Segregation and the City* (London: Pluto Press, 2006), p. 73.

and nature of interfaces[9] are those of memory. Victimhood within the post-conflict period has been employed as a key tool in the promotion of oppositional histories. Presentations of anguish rarely consider the impact of loss between communities, and as a result we are left with a sterile repetition of suffering within rather than between communities.

Violence and segregation

The rise of ethno-sectarian violence in the late 1960s led to greater segregation and new interfaces across the city.[10] The creation of rigid boundaries between communities aided the capacity to target the 'other' community. In particular the presence of the British army and police within such boundary zones also led to a concentration of violence in such places. Indeed, the escalating relationship, in the 1970s, between residential segregation and violent enactment intensified hostility. Ironically, the 'protective' walls that were assembled in order to protect communities were the very places within which the most numerous, insistent and unremitting violence was located.

A third of the victims of politically motivated violence died within 250 m of an interface (Table 4.1). The data further indicate that around 70 per cent of deaths occurred within 500 m of all interfaces. In addition, over 80 per cent of deaths occurred within places that were at least 90 per cent Catholic or Protestant.

The high rates of violence within these areas highlight the relationship between factors such as residential segregation, interfacing and social class. It is not surprising that violence buoyed up political and

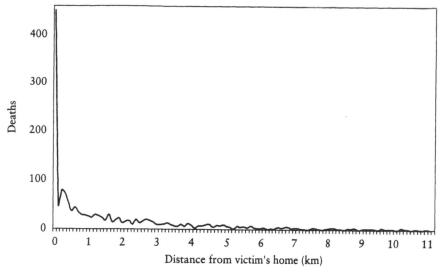

Figure 4.1 Distance between the location of conflict-related fatalities and the
victim's home, Belfast, 1966–2004.
Source: P. Shirlow and B. Murtagh, *Belfast: Violence, Segregation
and the City* (London: Pluto Press, 2006), p. 74

cultural retrenchment. Violence not only increased separation but it also
re-emphasised the rudimentary nature of ethno-sectarian 'difference'.

The proportion of Belfast citizens who died close to their home address
is worthy of note (Figure 4.1). Nearly one-third of all victims were murdered at home or only a matter of metres from their place of residence,
a reality that promoted the notion that violence was based upon an
assault upon community. Given the proximity of death to residence it is
understandable why conflict related deaths are understood as a form of
group suffering. Such an interpretation reduced the capacity and/or
desire to link deaths within one's own community with those happening
within the 'other' community. Such limited readings regarding which
community was 'harmed more' furthered processes of territorial entrap-
ment. Although the number of violent deaths has declined significantly
since the 1990s the legacy of inter-community violence maintains the
polarised relationship between and towards communities.

Segregated places

The population of Belfast is comprised more or less equally of the
two main ethno-sectarian groups. However, as shown in Tables 4.2–3, the
majority of persons from a Catholic or Protestant community background

Table 4.2 **Segregation in Belfast, by Catholic community background**

Percentage of district that is comprised of Catholics	*Percentage of Catholics living in such Districts*
0–20	4.7
21–40	3.6
41–60	10.7
61–80	13.8
81–90	9.3
91–100	58.0

Source: Census of population, 2001.

Table 4.3 **Segregation in Belfast, by Protestant community background**

Percentage of district that is comprised of Protestants	*Percentage of Protestants living in such districts*
0–20	3.4
21–40	7.3
41–60	7.0
61–80	9.3
81–90	28.4
91–100	44.6

Source: Census of population, 2001.

live in places in which at least 81 per cent of people are from the same ethno-religious background. Just over two-thirds of Catholics (67.3 per cent) and almost three-quarters of Protestants (73 per cent) live in such places. A mere 10.7 per cent of Catholics and 7.0 per cent of Protestants live in places that are between 41 per cent and 60 per cent Catholic or Protestant, the very places that could be described as mixed. The Northern Ireland Housing Executive (NIHE) argues that housing areas are 'segregated' if over 90 per cent of residents within each area are from one particular community background. Its research constantly confirms that around 98 per cent of NIHE[11] estates in Belfast are segregated, compared with a rate of 71 per cent for Northern Ireland as a whole. Their general conclusion is that segregation within social housing estates is rising.[12]

The mosaic of segregation within the city is complex, given the combined issues of scale and interpretation. There are evidently large areas, such as west Belfast, the Shankill and extensive parts of east Belfast that are dominated by one of the two main communities. Such large single identity zones are places within which the interface between communities derives from an historical lineage that dates back to the mid part of the nineteenth century but which has been reinforced by the violence of more recent times.

The intricate territorial divisions of north Belfast create some of the most complex spatial demarcations within the city, a reality that has been reflected in the performance of violence in recent years. Within North Belfast the borders between nationalist/republican and unionist/loyalist communities are constantly being altered by a series of demographic shifts. Unlike most parts of the city, north Belfast has a complex series of ever-changing interfaces and spatial juxtapositions. Boundaries within north Belfast have tended to increase as relatively mixed areas, such as the Antrim Road and Cliftonville Road, have become more national-ist/republican. New interfaces have also been created between private housing areas and public-sector housing estates. The interface, for example, between White City and Whitewell – a loyalist public housing estate and a predominantly Catholic private residential area respec-tively – has become a relatively new arena within which ethno-sectarian violence has been played out. Such contemporary interfacing reflects the fluidity of demographic shifts within the private housing sector, whereas the social housing stock, and the commitment to identity within such places, present a rigid and enduring set of boundaries.

The most evident interfaces are those marked by high walls that both sunder and demarcate the boundaries between communities, and a list of the current physical divisions in the city, as acknowledged by the NIHE, is provided in Table 4.4. Somewhat ominously, there were sixteen inter-face walls in 1994, the year in which almost all the principal paramili-taries in the region announced a cease-fire. Since then most of these constructions have been either extended or heightened. Nine additional walls have been constructed owing to interface-related violence since 1998. The first meeting of the Northern Ireland Assembly in 1998 was held on the same day as an interface wall was built though Alexander Park, a public park located in north Belfast.

Linked with the particular spatial dynamics of ethno-sectarian rela-tions is the issue of population mass and the institutions, facilities and services that a population can support. There is a close connection between population decline and a community feeling uncertain about its ability to safely occupy a particular locality. The Torrens estate in north Belfast was depopulated by the gradual and then rapid out-migration of the unionist/loyalist community that had lived there. This area had become cut off from other unionist/loyalist communities via a process of long and slow exodus.

There is a close relationship between the twenty-five physical inter-faces in Belfast and social inequality. These places cover twenty-two

Table 4.4 Physical interfaces in Belfast, 2005

Interface
Cluan Place
Bryson Street
Lower Newtownards Road
Mountpotinger Road–Woodstock Link
Duncairn Gardens
Henry Street–West Link
Manor Street–Roe Street
Crumlin Road
Alliance–Glenbryn
Elmgrove Street
Alexander Park
Hallidays Road–Newington
Mountcollyer
White City
Longlands
Mountainview
Squires Hill–Hazelbrook
Northumberland–Ardmoulin
Cupar Way
Ainsworth
Springmartin
Springhill
Suffolk
Roden Street
Carrick Hill–Peters Hill

Source: P. Shirlow and B. Murtagh, *Belfast: Violence, Segregation and the City* (London: Pluto Press, 2006), p. 72.

wards and, of these, seventeen are in the top 10 per cent deprived wards as measured by the Noble index.[13] Added to this are the daily experiences of people living in an area affected by often low-level but constant violence, pervasive fear and the threat of attack. For example, Shirlow and Murtagh[14] found that the residents of interface areas typically experienced higher rates of long-standing illness, attendance at doctors' surgeries and stress than the rest of the Northern Ireland population.[15] The demographic characteristics of Protestants and Catholics also differ significantly in interface areas. Catholic communities are characterised by higher than average family sizes, higher fertility rates and a more youthful demographic structure. The Protestant population is older, with smaller household sizes and lower than average fertility rates. When these demographics are acted out in highly segregated space, very different housing need profiles are reflected in terms of the number, size, type and location of accommodation required. The negative image that brutal lines of division, physical dereliction and poverty project to a wider audience can also be a major obstacle to investment and tourism. Problems caused by interfacing range from the monetary to the symbolic.

Interfaces vary with regard to form, style, meaning and both visibility and invisibility. However, they will most certainly be known and understood as such by those who live in such places. A local knowledge of spatial demarcation is centred upon territorial marking. Such a process is a common feature for many who have grown up in the city. The marking of space, via murals and flags, can be reinforced by a sectarianised and location-driven knowledge. The telling of division and the 'need' for separation are also founded upon a system of signs that are attached to deciphering territory via an ethno-sectarian lens.

Owing to such extensive segregation there are whole sections of the city that are virtually unknown to citizens living within Belfast. Older persons (those aged over sixty) tend to posses a more comprehensive and informed geography of the city. Such knowledge tends to pre-date the extensive sundering of place that followed in the wake of the contemporary conflict. Boundaries between communities did exist prior to the conflict, but such boundaries were easily and often readily crossed. Older residents tend to remember more evident forms of inter-community engagement, especially with regard to sharing space. As noted by a respondent, aged seventy, from the predominantly republican Ardoyne area:

> Before all them troubles and the like we used to live here with Protestants. Good and very decent people. My best friends were from among them. They left, forced out, as it were, and now they're a memory. Lost times – that's all we ended up with was lost times.

Younger people tend to have a more limited knowledge of places within the city. Growing up within a more intensively segregated city, within which boundaries have become more rigidified by violence, has a momentous impact upon the understanding of place. As shown in the next section, age and the experience of segregation influence the form, meaning and reading that shape various geographies of separation.

Fear, prejudice and separation

A survey looking into the relationship between segregation and mobility was conducted in 2004 and included 1,750 individuals living within interface communities in Belfast. As indicated, the level of socio-economic interaction between communities remains low. A mere one in twelve people worked in areas dominated by the 'other' religion. Seventy-eight per cent of respondents could provide examples of at least three publicly funded facilities that they would not use simply because it was on the 'wrong' side of an interface. The disturbance of everyday living in such places is even more distressing when it is recognised that interfaces are areas which contain the most excessive forms of social dislocation.

The evidence collected[16] showed that around one in eight people forgo health care for themselves and younger members of their families rather than use the nearest health facilities because these are located in areas dominated by the other community. Other data gathered by the survey indicated that 82 per cent of respondents would not enter at night an area dominated by the other community. Almost half those surveyed (48 per cent) would not travel even during daytime through an area dominated by the other community.

In overall terms, a mere 18 per cent of respondents undertook, on a weekly basis, consumption activities in areas dominated by the 'other' community. Such low levels of interaction were explained by the finding that 58.9 per cent of respondents would not undertake journeys into areas dominated by the 'other' community owing to fear of either verbal or physical violence. Around 9 per cent stated that they would not undertake such journeys owing to a desire to remain 'loyal' to their own community by not spending money in areas dominated by the 'other' side.

The findings located in Table 4.5 would seem to suggest that fear of being attacked by the 'other' community is central in determining low levels of cross-community contact. Fear, as shown in Table 4.5, is a much stronger determinant in the choice of facilities than 'loyalty' to the home community. However, 13.5 per cent of respondents would not undertake journeys into areas dominated by the other community through fear of being ostracised by their own community for so doing. A similar proportion stated that fear of both the 'other' and the 'home' communities was instrumental in their refusal to enter areas dominated by the other ethno-religious bloc. Fear of 'my own community' was directly linked with the belief that entering areas dominated by the 'other' sectarian group would lead to individuals being 'punished' by members of their own sectarian group. As such, fear operates as both an inter- and intra-community-based understanding.

The interviews conducted after the survey was completed revealed a series of complex cultural and demographic positions. Pensioners were those least likely to perceive the 'other' community as a menacing spatial formation. As shown in Table 4.5, pensioners are less likely to fear the 'other' community than is the case among younger age groups. For pensioners, fear of 'my own community' or both communities was more palpable than it was among those aged sixteen to forty-four.

Table 4.5 Percentage of those who do not use facilities in areas located in the
other community, by age and reason

Age	Fear of the other community	Fear of my own community	Fear of both communities	Loyalty[a]	Other
65+	45.6	20.2	20.2	8.5	5.5
45–64	49.6	16.2	14.2	13.5	6.5
25–44	64.6	9.4	9.2	8.8	8.0
16–24	75.8	8.4	6.2	5.6	4.0
Average	58.9	13.5	12.4	9.1	6.0

Notes: 'Loyalty' refers to the notion that to spend money in areas dominated
by the 'other' community rather than in one's own community is
dishonourable and undermines community solidarity.
Source: P. Shirlow and B. Murtagh, *Belfast: Segregation, Violence and the City*
(London: Pluto Press, 2006), p. 86.

Virtually all the respondents of pensionable age who are able-bodied
used facilities in areas dominated by the 'other' community. Interviews
among the pensioner group disclosed that the majority are not afraid to
enter 'alien' territory for three main reasons. Firstly, social relations that
existed prior to the contemporary conflict have tended to endure, and
older people visit the other community in order to maintain such friendships. Secondly, pensioners were three times more likely than the other
age groups to have either Catholic or Protestant relatives within each
respective community. This would suggest that inter-faith marriages were
more numerous, according to respondents, prior to the present conflict.
Thirdly, older people tended to be more likely to be repulsed by violence,
which they contended had destroyed a previous society within which
community relations were relatively 'normal'.

Although pensioners conceded that their communities had been victimised by sectarian violence, it was also conceded that their community
had been involved in transgressive sectarian behaviour as well. A belief
that it is immoral to judge whole communities as abnormal and abhorrent was also evident within this group. It is apparent that lived social histories, within which there has been an extensive form of inter-community
linkage, are capable of diluting the rationale of ethno-sectarian sentiment
and, as a result, fear of the 'other' community is tempered by more experienced forms of cultural understanding.

More vehement and sectarian attitudes were located among those aged
between sixteen and fifty-five, who comprised 86 per cent of all respondents. Few within this group undertook, by choice, any form of inter-
community linkage or visits to areas dominated by the 'other' religious

group. For this group the experience of residential segregation was articulated through a framework of exclusive and sectarian representations and ideological 'tradition'. Sectarianism and fear of the 'other' community are not viewed as either repressive or irrational but rather as driven by a reasonable need to encourage separation.

Space, for those who articulate sectarian discourses, is seen to function in such a manner that it hosts historical 'truths' and collectivised communications. Community and history, for this group, serve as territorial constructions that strengthen the way in which spatial division presents sectarian hostility as a valid understanding of loyalty. Among those who advanced ethno-sectarian opinions, the need to perpetuate residential segregation is imperative in order to operate and promote inter-community difference. During conversations with those who assumed ethno-sectarian positions it was asserted that all social space should be coded through a hostile and belligerent lens. It was also understood that space is produced by a need for ideological and physical separation. However, one of the most pronounced factors that distanced the vociferously sectarian from others was that they eulogised the communities within which they lived. Each member of the 'sectarian'[17] group discussed their community via utopian discourses of integrity, loyalty, kinship and symbolic purity. In comparison, those who considered themselves to be non-sectarian denoted that 'their' communities contained multiple forms of impurity, transgression and deviance. The interviews conducted among the 'sectarian' group produced passionate and partial narratives and the most pronounced sense that the 'other' community was abnormal, antagonistic and obdurate. The share of those who had experienced physical harm at the hands of the sectarian 'other' was similar to that amongst pensioners (40 per cent and 38 per cent respectively). Unlike 'non-sectarians', this sectarian group tended to maintain that they could not understand why their community had been victims of sectarian violence. Members of this group tended to argue that their community was victimised and that the perpetrators of such attacks were abhorrent representatives of a homogeneous community. The failure by the majority of these respondents to identify that analogous threats are an encumbrance upon the 'other' community meant that communal separation was comprehended through a unidimensional ethno-sectarian logic.[18]

Within this group, fear was explained via the framework of reproaching the rival community. As a result, sectarianised readings are constantly linked with acknowledgement of spaces of fear and the location of unsafe places. Within such a climate of ethno-sectarian cognition and telling, cross-community contact was discussed through tales of violence and aggression. Violence from within the 'home' community which had been directed at the 'other' community was nearly always articulated as a strategy of defence or as rational patterns of reprisal.

Without doubt, paradigms of ethno-sectarian purity and impurity predicate social relations to such an extent, and with such power, that the capacity exists to silence the dialogue capable of challenging ethnosectarian discourses. This implies that, tellingly, violence and the reproduction of fear are based upon sectarianised relations which aim not only to reproduce residential segregation but also to restrain any belief system which identifies ethno-sectarian purity as a socially constructed and imagined set of relations. It is clear that preserving the capacity to control sectarian belonging is facilitated through spreading the notion that the 'other' community is to be feared. Sectarianised relations will continue to be achieved through endorsing the morality of cultural and political sectarianism.

Moving on

Belfast's slow transition from 'troubled' city to a less violent city is under way. Yet the impact of decades of conflict endures and encourages the 'logic' of spatial separation between a constitutionally divided people. Memory and the reproduction of low-level violence are intertwined in the promotion of ethno-sectarian attitudes. The fear held by unionists that they will be subsumed within a united Ireland and the related desire of Irish nationalists for constitutional reunification mean that the conflict cannot be resolved. Conflict resolution will not pertain in a discord driven by the existence of the Irish border, as even the removal of that construct will produce instability.

The prospect of conflict transformation and the reduction and near removal of violence is achievable but only through politics that confront mythic reiteration of community belief. The peace accords and the return of political devolution did not undermine political antagonisms which remain ingrained within the continuation of various forms of partition and the territorialisation of wider cultural, social and economic allegiances. Northern Ireland is a more agreeable and less threatening place but its future remains disagreed. In spite of the supposedly homogenising effects of globalisation and the alleged post-nationalist turn, there has in fact been no drift towards consensus in the region. Any failure to recognise that political power brokers seek a settlement for their own community as opposed to meaningful compromise between communities leads to a delusional belief that identities are being sourced beyond an ethno-sectarian frame.

For there to be genuine progress we require governance structures that shift from being highly centralised and locally unaccountable. A recognition that the development of civil society is retarded by persistent ethno-sectarian relationships is also required. In addition, the formation of the built environment, where state and private enterprise dominate land use, where security consciousness produced fragmented spatial arrangements, and where clientelist politics promote resource competition, is also of concern. Civil enterprise in any post-conflict situation must claim a pivotal role in shaping a less contested city. Neutral spaces and their protection are a crucial formation in the presentation of de-segregated space. At present the desire to de-segregate such a divided city remains a minority pursuit and is articulated only by those who challenge ethno-sectarian belonging. The essential problem that afflicts Belfast is that geography matters in a way that is explicit and unconcealed. The cantonisation of life is a forceful impediment to the creation of a new city. The debate on developing a less contested city will remain subsumed by the ability of political entrepreneurs to mobilise space as a variable within identity construction. However, it is a debate that must continue and move forward.

Fear and residential segregation impede the search for work, the uptake of training and education and the use of public services. In addition, fear creates socio-spatial burdens which are mostly endured by socially deprived communities. The potential to reconstruct Northern Ireland's production and consumer arenas in order that they respond to equality of opportunity and parity of esteem is a major factor in the creation of long-term political stability. Few if any of the policies which aim to challenge socio-economic dislocation link the realities of spatialised fear to the reproduction of social deprivation and communal polarisation.

The analysis of fear and prejudice underpins the need to translate policy and political rhetoric around segregation into practice and to connect practice with the reality of sectarianised habituation. Given the sectarian nature of political practice and control in Northern Ireland, much of the commentary dedicated to challenging segregation and ultimately the reproduction of fear is ambiguous and difficult to distinguish in the detail of policy-making instruments. Belfast, despite change, remains a sectarianised place.

Notes

1 The article appears in the 21 August 2005 edition. It is accessible at http://travel2.nytimes.com/2005/08/21/travel/21belfast.html?ex=11625300 00&en=4ae6936e0cda1898&ei=5070.

2 P. Shirlow, ' "Who fears to speak": fear, mobility and ethnosectarianism in the two Ardoynes", *Global Review of Ethnopolitics* 3:1 (2003), pp. 76–92; P. Shirlow and B. Murtagh, 'Capacity building, representation and intra-community conflict', *Urban Studies* 41:1 (2004), pp. 57–70; S. Maguire and P. Shirlow, 'Shaping childhood risk in post-conflict rural Northern Ireland', *Children's Geographies* 2:1 (2004), pp. 69–82.

3 The terms 'Catholics' and 'Protestants' are used although the conflict is not based upon religious belief. Religious is merely one of many boundary markers. These terms are the most common identifiers.

4 The process that creates territorial divisions.

5 E. Soja, *Postmetropolis: Critical Studies of Cities and Regions* (London: Blackwell, 2000).

6 E. Heikkila, 'Identity and inequality: race and space in planning', *Planning Theory and Practice* 2:3 (2001), p. 266.

7 For more on this see P. Shirlow and B. Murtagh, *Belfast: Segregation, Violence and the City* (London: Pluto Press, 2006).

8 *Ibid.*, p. 28.

9 An interface is a boundary between Catholic and Protestant communities. Many of these interfaces are marked by walls, some by roads and others by derelict housing.

10 Due to technical reasons it is difficult to show if segregation within the city has increased or decreased since 1991. The argument is not being made that it has.

11 Northern Ireland Housing Executive, *Building Good Relations: Community Cohesion* (Belfast: NIHE, 2005).

12 For further discussion see Shirlow and Murtagh, *Belfast*.

13 The Noble index (2001) is a multivariate measurement of deprivation in Northern Ireland.

14 Shirlow and Murtagh, *Belfast*.

15 *Ibid.*

16 *Ibid.*

17 The categories of 'sectarian' and 'non-sectarian' are not absolute. However, 'sectarians' are those who articulate a desire for segregation and non-sectarians are those who view segregation as a problem that needs to be resolved through challenging the nature of separation.

18 Sectarianism is relative. Unidimensional sectarians view sectarianism as a positive and justified part of their identity/actions.

5

Spatial planning in contested territory: the search for a place vision after the 'troubles'

William J. V. Neill and Geraint Ellis

The purpose of this chapter is to review the history of strategic spatial policy in post-partition Northern Ireland. The principal focus of the chapter falls on developments since the Good Friday Agreement in 1998, especially in relation to the vision of regional planning as a whole and physical image enhancement of the 'post-conflict' city of Belfast in particular. The starting point here is the realisation that the establishment of Northern Ireland by the Government of Ireland Act in 1920 was a process of re/deterritorialisation of the UK state which satisfied neither unionists nor nationalists. Unionists saw the creation of a Northern Ireland parliament as a partially successful challenge to an ascendant cultural Irish nationalism from which they felt alienated.[1] For nationalists, the very existence of Northern Ireland was seen as an artificial remnant of an incomplete process of decolonisation, marking the tail end of centuries of British domination of Ireland. Indeed, from a nationalist perspective, the Northern Ireland state has traditionally been characterised as being embedded in, and a symptom of, social relations of subordination.[2] The understanding of spatial governance and planning amid such contestation thus cannot be divorced from a deeper appreciation of two cultural identities in conflict where the meaning of place is constitutive of identity itself. This remains the case in a 'post-troubles' environment.

The symbolic language of territory and identity

The meanings that people attach to place are now recognised as a key concern of any sensitised approach to spatial governance.[3] Both the principal cultural traditions in Northern Ireland draw emotional sustenance from contrasting place visions of territory which, while becoming gradually outdated in an increasingly multicultural Britain and Ireland, remain powerful nonetheless. On the one hand, there is a nationalist cultural tradition that focuses, *inter alia*, upon a Gaelic vision of Ireland based on pre-Christian folk lore, the Great Famine and the 1916 Easter Uprising. Although northern nationalists have forged their own distinct post-partition identity, this broader cultural persona retains considerable resonance.[4] On the other hand, unionists, post-partition, have expressed a sense of exclusion and alienation from Irish nationalism and culture, seeing the south as Gaelic, dominated by the Catholic Church and harbouring territorial claims over the north. This view was summed up in 2002 by David Trimble, then leader of the Ulster Unionist Party, when he referred to the Republic of Ireland as 'a sectarian, mono-ethnic, mono-cultural state'.[5]

Unionism, however, has itself never convincingly established its own cultural image as having a legitimate territorial claim. While the unionist tale is a complex one with roots in centuries of contact and mixing on an archipelago of islands on the edge of Europe, to most of the world, particularly following the coverage of the annual stand-off at Drumcree or the harrowing pictures from the school blockade in Ardoyne, unionists appear as intransigent, even bigoted, settlers who have refused to integrate. Although republicans have accused Ulster Scots of being a 'rediscovered identity' as a reaction to the greater cultural fluency of nationalism, it is one that is gradually being presented with increasing self-confidence, as evidenced in the musical *On Eagle's Wing*.[6] However, one can argue that as the cultural tradition that has had dominant political control of Northern Ireland for most of the twentieth century, the 'corrosive siege mentality'[7] of the unionist psyche can be linked with the weak production of a territorial imagination for the region. This has been overly influenced by notions of the greatness of a British past[8] now forced into re-evaluation by a multicultural Britain[9] and a propensity to appropriate territory with intensity through the spatial practice of marching. The cultural identity of unionism, dominant until the 1970s at least, forms one of the ethno-tectonic plates with which spatial management of Northern Ireland has been confronted.

Spatial planning: the early years

Northern Ireland's settlements have long faced intractable problems arising from ethnic segregation – even today 68 per cent of all wards in Northern Ireland have a population of more than 70 per cent of one ethno-religious community or the other.[10] At a regional level, there is a danger of oversimplifying the complex ethnic geography, which features many enclave communities living in the territory of the 'other'.[11] One bold demographic generalisation stands out, however. Crude statistical analyses show that, since its creation, the east of Northern Ireland has remained predominantly Protestant and the west predominantly Catholic. The river Bann dividing east and west also runs through the mind. Population data demonstrate that roughly two-thirds of the population west of the Bann are Catholic and over 70 per cent east of the Bann are Protestant. The latter figure rises to 75 per cent if Catholic west Belfast is excluded from the calculation.[12] In general demographic terms there are, therefore, two Northern Irelands, which has occasionally even prompted commentators to make the case for repartition.[13] While such drastic re/deterritorialisation is not a likely prospect, ethnic demographic asymmetry does cast a shadow over many spatial planning concerns in the north.

In the early years of Northern Ireland's existence it could be argued that the economic viability of the region depended upon the considerable concentration of unionist industrial capital in the Belfast area, integrated as it was with the economies of Liverpool and Glasgow, part of the workshop of the world, which made the British Empire possible.[14] This in turn relied on the western counties for agricultural produce. The *laissez-faire* approach that defined regional policy prior to World War II inevitably ensured that the economic geography of Northern Ireland was somewhat skewed. In 1935 over 60 per cent of all jobs in manufacturing employment were in the Belfast county borough alone,[15] while the rural west was characterised by intense poverty.

Spatial modernisation in the 1960s

In the late 1940s, with almost 80 per cent of the insured work force concentrated within a thirty-mile radius of Belfast, the Northern Irish economy still remained heavily specialised around its nineteenth-century industrial base of linen, shipbuilding and engineering.[16] The devolved government's post-war policy to modernise the region's economic base was strongly supported by reformist unionism, faced with the pressure of growing international competition in Northern Ireland's traditional markets. Yet it is against the perceived shortcomings of the economic and spatial modernisation plans of this era that all subsequent spatial policy in Northern Ireland has been judged. The new spatial vision that emerged in the 1960s reflected the Anglo-modernist planning paradigm of the time and drew heavily on the work of 'mainland' planning consultants, especially the views of Sir Robert Matthew.[17] The strategy can be summarised around a few key points, including the establishment of a development 'stop line' around Belfast to contain the outward sprawl of the city,[18] a major programme of transport investment, following the principles of the Buchanan Report in Britain, for a car-based urban future,[19] which involved a motorway building programme focused on Belfast,[20] and, most controversially, the dispersing of development away from Belfast by designating other growth centres aimed at spreading international investment more widely, although these largely remained east of the Bann.

Although it was presented as a result of the cold economic calculus of the technical reports, nationalist opinion was critical of this policy approach for neglecting spatial equity, a view that was only reinforced by other aspects of unionist spatial governance of the time. For example, the major new growth centre, the new city of Craigavon, was named after the first Prime Minister of Northern Ireland, who famously referred to Stormont building in Belfast as 'a Protestant parliament for a Protestant people'. Furthermore, the region's new university was controversially located near the predominantly Protestant town of Coleraine rather than in the second city of Derry/Londonderry, which has a Catholic majority, while the motorway network snaked towards the major unionist towns of Ballymena, Portadown and Enniskillen but left most of the Derry–Belfast link as single-carriageway. All these decisions compounded nationalist feeling that reformist unionism, whatever battles it had to fight with defenders of the *status quo*, was 'fine sentiment but little substance'[21] and contributed to priming the conflict that was to dominate the region for the next three decades.

Spatial planning under Direct Rule

The re-emergence of the 'troubles' in the late 1960s and the subsequent suspension of the devolved government in Northern Ireland in 1972 were to be accompanied over the next twenty-five years by Westminster-determined planning policy that struggled to cope with the socio-spatial expression of ethnic identity. Abstract regulations and statistical classifications of space in the 1960s planning documents were to quickly pale before the brute reality of the hastily prepared Orange and Green maps of sectarian space familiar at every 'security force' base in the region. The hard edge of ethnic spatial management was evident in the all too visible presence of CC-TV surveillance, watch towers, listening antennae, fortified police stations and 'peace' walls. The suspicion that in the military management of ethnic conflict urban planning decisions involving roads and housing layouts, not to mention ethnic interfaces or 'peace walls', involved direct, if subtle, military and security considerations still lingers.[22] Indeed, the foremost ethnographic mapper of Northern Ireland's divisions has argued that 'such considerations must have impinged'.[23]

Strategic spatial management during these years of Westminster rule did, however, have a softer side. Foremost in tackling some of the background causes of conflict was the vigorous approach to social housing provision started in the 1970s and pursued with increased zeal in the 1980s by the Northern Ireland Housing Executive (NIHE) even when such programmes were being decimated by the Thatcher government in every other region of the United Kingdom.[24] The marshalling of development as a feel-good factor and the promotion of spaces of consumption as 'oases of normality'[25] were to achieve prominence in the 1980s.[26] In terms of strategic planning, the basic foundations of policy, without explicit acknowledgement, were subject to radical change during the 1970s, as the Regional Physical Development Strategy for Northern Ireland[27] put forward for public discussion no fewer than six spatial options with relative degrees of *laissez-faire*, intervention, agglomeration and dispersal. A 'district towns' strategy of relative dispersal was eventually adopted as official policy. Acknowledging 'the peculiar circumstances of Northern Ireland',[28] the principal aim of the planning strategy would be 'to distribute population, development and activities of all kinds in such a way that, irrespective of place of residence, everyone will enjoy at least reasonable access to a high level of employment opportunities and to services and facilities of all kinds'.[29] In 1978 a relaxation of policy with regard to development in the open countryside added a greater leaning towards settlement diffusion and away from the growth centre thinking of the 1960s. Although this policy draws on a range of issues related to rural development, in the political context of the 1970s it cannot be disengaged from issues of often uncritical 'territorial equity' which was to become, in fact, the spatial orthodoxy or 'planning doctrine' for Northern Ireland.

Regional spatial strategy since the Good Friday Agreement

The Good Friday Agreement of 10 April 1998 has formed the basis of future governance in Northern Ireland and represents a significant re/deterritorialisation of relations between the United Kingdom and Republic of Ireland. The Irish government, following a referendum, has removed the strong territorial claim on the north from its constitution and the British government has revised the Government of Ireland Act 1920, which instituted partition. The Agreement also proposed and initially instigated more plural forms of Irish–British political association, which included a north–south Ministerial Council on the island of Ireland and a British–Irish Council (the Council of the Isles) bringing together no fewer than eight governmental entities from the British

Isles.[30] One commentator optimistically sums up the new constitutional arrangements thus:

> With the ratification of the 1998 Belfast Agreement, both sovereign governments signed away their exclusivist sovereignty claims over Northern Ireland – and came of age. This signalled, I believe, the cessation of the long constitutional battle over the territory of Ulster: that contentious piece of land conjoining and separating the islands of Britain and Ireland for so long. The Siamese twins can now, one hopes, learn to live in real peace, accepting that their adversarial offspring in Northern Ireland may at last be British or Irish or both.[31]

More pessimistically, the relatively novel consociational[32] basis of government set out in the Good Friday Agreement[33] explicitly recognises and entrenches cultural difference on a constitutional basis. This carries the possibility that, despite far-reaching equality legislation in Northern Ireland,[34] cultural differences will remain sharp and more integrationist and assimilationist outcomes impeded.[35] The reinstitution of the Assembly in May 2007, bringing Ian Paisley and Martin McGuiness together to lead the Executive, opens a new chapter in how the spatial geography of the region will evolve. The Assembly immediately faces a number of acute challenges to environmental and spatial governance inherited from the outgoing Direct Rule administration, all of which are primarily framed in terms of the principles embedded in the Good Friday Agreement. Indeed, the north's statutory regional spatial plan (Regional Development Strategy for Northern Ireland 2025, or RDS) carries the distinction of quasi-constitutional status being explicitly mentioned in the Good Friday Agreement itself, with the British government pledging to make rapid progress with:

> a new regional development strategy for Northern Ireland, for consideration in due course by the Assembly, tackling the problems of a divided society and social cohesion in urban, rural and border areas, protecting and enhancing the environment, producing new approaches to transport issues, strengthening the physical infrastructure of the region, developing the advantages and resources of rural areas and rejuvenating major urban centres.[36]

The process leading up to the production of the RDS has been documented elsewhere.[37] In essence, the final plan was published in late 2001[38] and endorsed by the Assembly before its suspension in 2002. The main aim of the strategy is to:

> Together create an outward-looking, dynamic and livable region with a strong sense of its place in the wider world; a region of opportunity where people enjoy living and working in a healthy environment which enhances

the quality of their lives and where diversity is a source of strength rather than division.[39]

To achieve this, the strategy and policies cover a wide range of issues, including natural resources, urban and rural development, economic development, tourism, community integration, transport and infrastructure. The RDS relies on a number of 'daughter' documents for its implementation, including the Regional Transportation Strategy[40] and Planning Policy Statements.[41]

In essence, the RDS does not stray far from the doctrinal principles endorsing relative economic and population dispersal embodied in Northern Ireland's previous 1975–95 Regional Physical Development Strategy. This time, in order to achieve 'balanced development', alignment is sought with the vanguard of European spatial planning thinking by adopting abstract spatial generalities of 'hubs, gateways and corridors',[42] all servicing a happy 'family of settlements'.

While it is a notable achievement to produce a spatial plan in the context of ongoing ethnic strife, the success of the strategy has been unduly exaggerated,[43] particularly given the lack of evidence of how successful its implementation will be. A full judgement of the RDS can reasonably be made only in the fullness of time. There has, however, already been some critical evaluation of how the plan was developed.[44] A critique of the final strategy raises four principal concerns, each of which is considered in turn below.

The aspirational rhetoric of the plan

The preparation of the RDS rode a wave of post-Agreement optimism that appeared rather naive in the context of faltering devolution, continuing incidents of acute sectarian violence and ongoing lack of agreement on the nature of power sharing that dominated the first six years of the strategy's life. Indeed, the RDS was drafted at a time of innocence when it appeared that a lasting peace had been struck with the Good Friday Agreement and before this was sullied by protracted debates over decommissioning and the future of policing. This led commentators to describe the strategy as a 'society-wide hug'[45] or a 'cotton-wool approach to spatial ethnic management'.[46] Others, in contrast, have defended the metaphors and vocabulary of the RDS as helping mobilise an alternative spatial imaginary that could help displace the geography of old sectarian politics.[47] Here Graham correctly points out that 'one of the primary cultural factors demarcating Northern Ireland from its southern neighbour is that it has never evolved that sense of an invented landscape which might help unify its population in a shared communal sense of identity'.[48]

The jury remains out on whether the conceptualisation of Northern Ireland's settlements as 'European gateways and corridors', as noted in the RDS, will provide the final solution to the region's contested spatial governance.

The rhetoric of the RDS may also be critically evaluated from more functional perspectives. In attempting to 'go beyond land use planning'[49] the strategy attempted not just to shape physical development but also to influence the spatial expressions of other forms of environmental policy and socio-economic development. However, this aspiration already appears to be having difficulty dealing with its initial challenges. In the wake of the RDS the Department of the Environment has embarked on an ambitious programme of Area Plans, through which the RDS objectives should have be given statutory status. However, even before the first of these plans reached its public inquiry stage, those interests raising issues marginally beyond the scope of traditional land use planning (but covered by the RDS), such as promoting higher proportions of affordable housing or the integration of environmental objectives, were met by blanket rebuttals from the Planning Service on the grounds that they were outside the organisation's statutory remit. Hence it would appear that the RDS's loftier aims will simply not be reflected in this lower tier of policy. On economic issues, also, the RDS's vision of 'balanced development' across the region remains disconnected from the prioritisation of public expenditure commitments, leading one local think tank to criticise it for steering clear of controversy rather than tackling key economic questions,[50] such as asymmetric urban growth, leaving Belfast as the only realistic monocentric driver of a reinvigorated regional economy. Apart from the anathema of raising the ghost of the Matthew Report, a recent research study points to a reason for this:

> the public finance culture of Northern Ireland has to change. There has been a financially irresponsible culture, in the sense that the UK Exchequer would insulate the residents of Northern Ireland from the cost of internal conflict and the resulting inefficiency in both microeconomic and macroeconomic terms. Even when – perhaps especially when – there are generous fiscal equalisation arrangements, there has to be a credible budget constraint[51]

The truncation of discussion of possible spatial futures
As already indicated, the previous regional strategy for Northern Ireland did at least try to articulate some alternative spatial scenarios. No such thinking informed the public consultation process associated with the RDS – despite the intervening technological revolution, paradigm shifts in terms of debates over sustainable development and the relationship

between development and transport infrastructure. Thus the strategy sought to apply a neutral concept of territorial equity, with little or no debate on the relative merits of settlement concentration and dispersal,[52] the potential for public transport-led development patterns[53] or how the development of telecommunications infrastructure could inform spatial trade-offs and choices.[54]

Uncritical acceptance of the nature of rural development

The RDS sets out a specific spatial framework for rural Northern Ireland, identifies key driving forces for rural change,[55] sets out rural development objectives and specifies five main policies.[56] Despite this attention, the Strategy still highlights how the failure to have an informed debate over the fundamental nature of social needs and the distribution of economic development in the region partly stems from unwillingness to address a number of contentious issues related to the economic, environmental and cultural dimensions of rural development. When the RDS was being drawn up, the agricultural sector dominated by small, family run farms was beginning to face major uncertainties, with collapsing farm incomes, major readjustment in the face of Common Agricultural Policy (CAP) reform and, specifically in Northern Ireland, potential major environmental restrictions on agricultural practices arising from enforcement of the European Union's Water Framework Directive and the end of structural funds in 2006. The failure of the RDS to grapple seriously with these issues has been subject to an extensive critique, particularly on the links between its land use planning objectives and the needs of rural development.[57]

Significantly, the RDS did not challenge the prevailing policy that there would be 'a presumption in favour of planning permission for single new dwellings in the countryside, outside of Greenbelts and Countryside Policy Areas'.[58] Although this was abruptly and controversially reversed in March 2006 with the publication of a new Planning Policy Statement,[59] it has not come soon enough to avoid the rural landscape being subjected to an extraordinary level of dispersed housing, making satellite pictures of rural Northern Ireland appear as if it has caught a nasty rash, reflecting the smattering of housing development across the rural region. This dispersed pattern of housing has severe consequences for water quality,[60] car dependence and the viability of public services,[61] and is storing up substantial difficulties in relation to social support as the dispersed population enters old age. Figures released by the Department of Regional Development show that over 12,608 planning consents for single dwellings in the Northern Irish countryside were awarded in 2005/06 alone, compared with nearly 20,000 in the entire period of 1984–2006. Indeed, it has been suggested that this rate of development is treble that of England, Scotland and Wales combined and that the government's policy response, including that of the RDS, has been described as 'an objective lesson in obfuscation'.[62] This criticism goes on to note that:

> The cumulative effect of the discussion of the single dwellings issue in planning documents is a wringing of hands about the unfortunate adverse effects accompanied [by] no real action to address the issue. Policy is aimed at ducking and weaving around the personal interests of the beneficiaries of current policies. The manner of the wording and implementation of policy is to guarantee that constraint on development is minimal now and, by placing in its own way a quagmire of impediments to change, is clearly intended to remain so. Indeed it is remarkable that so much policy text should be devoted to doing so little. This is bureaucracy with hardly any benefit and rules without any regulation. This is simply not tolerable in 2004.[63]

Despite the environmental, social and economic unsustainability of one-off houses in the country, the discussion of alternative paths to development remains taboo in Northern Ireland. This is reflected in the incredulity on the part of agricultural and development interests that the most fertile and profitable crop in recent years – housing sites – now faces lean years.[64] The apparent strength and mobilisation around what is an accepted policy position in the rest of the United Kingdom highlights how Northern Irish rural society continues to be a repository of political power and cultural imagination for both sides of the sectarian divide.

For unionists, particularly those supporting the Democratic Unionist Party, agricultural policies are seen as being 'very important',[65] and, with dwindling farm incomes, the territorial holdings of the (Protestant) farming class have looked increasingly vulnerable. Because of this, unionists have taken the chair of the agricultural policy committee under both phases of devolution. Indeed, so important are rural issues to maintaining the broad-based support of the DUP that one of its key policy papers specifically addresses 'rural reform and rejuvenation', which describes Ian Paisley as 'the farmers' friend'[66] and, incredibly, advocates even further relaxation of planning controls in the countryside.

This is not however, just a unionist issue, as nationalism is also imbued with strong rural narratives,[67] but for very different reasons. As Greer and Murray point out, 'the public discourse on rural disadvantage as conveyed by its spatial representation has become a powerful metaphor of key socio-economic differentials which have built up over time between the competing traditions in Northern Ireland'.[68] Gerry Adams, the leader of Sinn Féin, which is now the North's largest nationalist party, argues that the skewing of resources, infrastructure and job investment to the more deprived areas 'west of the Bann and along the border' are issues that should be dealt with on a statutory basis,[69] which echoes the call for 'rural-proofing' contained in the RDS. A Sinn Féin spokesman has associated attempts to restrict single dwellings in the countryside under the rationale of sustainable development as an 'attempt to kill off a rural way of life that has existed for 800 years'.[70] Furthermore, those concerned with rural deprivation also contribute to the 'obfuscation' identified by the Northern Ireland Planning Commission by suggesting that concerted planning efforts aimed towards the Belfast Metropolitan Area Plan are 'relegating the rural to a state of limbo'[71] while accusing the RDS of offering 'almost primeval antipathy to new single homes in the countryside'.[72]

Indeed, all the main political parties had manifestoes for the 2007 Assembly elections in which the key planning issue was opposition to the restrictions on housing in the countryside introduced under Direct Rule in the form of PPS 14. The discourse of the opposition is, however, subtly different according to the political audience being addressed – nationalists tend to stress the eroding effect it has on a rural community forged out of ties with the land, while unionists emphasise the impact on the valiant farmer seeking to scratch a living on his homestead. Indeed, discourse on this controversial issue appears to purposely avoid the key fact of spatial equity in the context of ethnic division,[73] and for fear of exposing sensitive questions of ethnic geography the fundamental issues of sustainability, service efficiency and economic development performance are suppressed – illustrating perhaps how some issues remain too hot to handle in the still fragile post-conflict society of Northern Ireland.

Lack of consideration of cross-border governance issues

A further dimension where the RDS has failed to live up to its expectations is in facing up to the realities of cross-border governance. Indeed, unique as it is within the United Kingdom in having an international land border and sharing a broad ecological niche with a neighbouring sovereign state, the regional strategy makes only the feeblest attempt to place Northern Ireland in its island context. There are of course, intense unionist sensitivities about the territorial relationship with the Republic of Ireland but, as with other aspects of the Strategy, any engagement with such issues is therefore shunned to achieve the vague consensus needed for cross-party support. This has been done even in a context where not only is there some history of cross-border co-operation on a range of environmental matters[74] but also all the major parties have signed up to the need for increased co-operation on 'strategies and activities which would contribute to a coherent all-island approach to the achievement of sustainable development'.[75] Indeed, in the last UK region to produce its own sustainable development strategy[76] the RDS was seen by some as the next best thing. The new strategy, produced as a result of 'constipated deliberation',[77] also fails to grapple with a more progressive all-island approach to sustainable development, the possibilities of which have been highlighted by Ellis *et al.*[78] These include not only resource management issues, where the RDS claims some competence (e.g. habitat conservation, waste management, transport, coastal management and tourism), but also issues that are unique within the United Kingdom, including cross-border distortions of economic and environmental regulation and a duty to recognise trans-boundary participation rights in environmental decision making.[79]

Belfast spatial strategy since the Good Friday Agreement

Such matters, however, have been of little more than background interest to the main thrust of post-conflict urban planning in Belfast, Northern Ireland's main shop window. Here, despite the production of a draft Belfast Metropolitan Area Plan[80] concerned with narrow land use planning issues and virtually ignoring the sectarian nature of Belfast's spatial geography, the emphasis has been on fashioning a physical image for the 'city in transition' and riding the benefits and challenges caused by the dramatic surge in house prices.

Since a great deal of the established cultural life of the city remains too sensitive and controversial to facilitate a common vision of place, the image makers have preferred instead to turn to the shock of the new. Here the major parting shot from the soon to be wound up Laganside Corporation, which has led Belfast's riverfront reimaging over the last fifteen years, will be a new glass skyscraper for the city, at twenty-six storeys the tallest building in Northern Ireland. The complex, which is intended to transform the Belfast skyline, will incorporate hotel, entertainment, apartment and office uses and, according to the developer, by being 'breathtaking in its stature . . . will become an icon for the city'. The building comes with its own ready-made nickname: the Obel, apparently the short form of Obelisk.[81] Glass is now the representational form of choice for development in the post-conflict city, offering as it does an obvious contrast to the brutalist terror-proofed buildings of the 'troubles'. The massive new Victoria Square retail complex in the city, which sadly saw the demolition and relocation of the old Kitchen Bar, a time capsule of the now unfashionable Belfast of yesteryear, will be topped with a glass dome. A newly planned 'Hope and History Centre' in Belfast will be dominated by a glass enclosure, as will a new extension of the Grand Opera House. That the design of the 'post-conflict' city is insufficiently reflective of the character of Belfast has not gone without comment. In 2005 a £200,000 15 m high statue appeared on the banks of the river Lagan courtesy of the Laganside Corporation, intended to be yet another icon of post-troubles Belfast. Entitled 'The Ring of Thanksgiving', and looking like what appears to be a girl holding aloft a hoop while standing on a ball, one wag has named it 'Nuala and her hoola', while a frank local journalist remarked:

> If Belfast is to have a huge statue that is in some way meant to speak for the city, shouldn't the people of the city have had a say in it? That way we might have had something that looks better than a sketch lifted from a child's storybook.[82]

This was to bring a swift, imperious retort from the president of the government-appointed committee responsible for commissioning the 'symbol of hope'. This suggests that the critic was ignorant in not understanding that the statue 'contains all the symbolism of the feminine principle in mythology, including the Classical Greek and the Celtic traditions'.[83]

However, it is to the mythology of the Belfast-built *Titanic* and not classical Greece that the post-conflict city primarily looks to reimage itself in the twenty-first century. The centre of attention here is a 185 acre site formerly part of the Harland & Wolff shipyard, now a pale shadow of its former self. In the biggest property development scheme ever undertaken in Northern Ireland the developer on the official web site entices entry with the words 'Welcome to Titanic Quarter . . . a new brand emerging on the horizon.'

The idea of creating a new precinct for Belfast described as a 'city within a city' dates to the aftermath of the Belfast Agreement and originated with the privately owned shipyard itself, faced with rapidly disappearing orders for ships but the prospect of large profits from land development. The project concept and brand launched in 1999 and based on the salvage of *Titanic* heritage has been embraced with gusto by all official place promotion agencies in Belfast, including Laganside, Northern Ireland Tourist Board and Belfast City Council. That a city should promote its heritage for profit is of course unremarkable, given the current imperatives that drive the representation and promotion of place. What is remarkable in 'post-conflict Belfast' is that in less than a decade the city has gone from leaving the memory of *Titanic* 'on a sunken plain of the psyche', not wishing to draw much attention to its 'ambiguous pride and embarrassment',[84] to active celebration in representing the post-conflict city through association with one of the twentieth century's most dramatic symbols of hubris and lost confidence in modernity. The advent of the Oscar-winning 1997 film starring Leonardo Di Caprio and Kate Winslet, which popularised 'the brand' and made tragedy good for business, undoubtedly contributed to this apparent change of heart. The massive east Belfast landmark shipyard cranes Samson and Goliath, now in their impotence symbolising the decommissioning of the yard as Protestant space, better leave the way open for the joint appropriation of the project of bringing the legacy of the *Titanic* home.

While this in principle could be a worthy and overdue endeavour, the crassness of commercial exploitation of a memory lodged deep in the troubled consciousness of Western culture still rankles. The leasehold of the Harland & Wolff land was sold for a reported price of £48 million by its Norwegian owner, Fred Olsen, in 2004, with Belfast Harbour Commissioners, who administer the Port of Belfast, holding the freehold and the right to a share of future increases in development value. The purchaser, now with lead responsibility for the *Titanic* 'brand', is the Dublin-based development company Harcourt Developments. The latter, through a wholly owned subsidiary, Ivy Wood Properties, has the development rights to the Titanic Quarter. In the wake of the Northern Bank robbery,[85] the political establishment in Ireland, north and south, was to shudder when a prominent board member of Harcourt resigned following Gardai investigations into IRA money laundering.[86] Reverberations were felt in the north when the head of the Northern Ireland Policing Board, also a non-executive director of Ivy Wood Properties, with no suggestion of wrongdoing, felt obliged to step down from both positions. Two weeks later Harcourt Developments launched plans for the new city which will arise over the next fifteen to twenty years not in Belfast itself but at an international property exhibition in Cannes.[87] The project, which amounts to a vast extension of Belfast city centre eastwards, involves mixed use of 3,300 new homes and waterfront apartments (which from artist drawings look as if they belong in Cannes itself), around 3.3 million ft² of new business/office/R&D and other commercial space, a cruise liner berth and a large-scale leisure development featuring restaurants and hotels.

The application of the *Titanic* stamp to this new post-conflict city is still subject to some debate, although the headquarters of the ship's makers will definitely be converted into a four-star hotel. Already, at the *Titanic* Bar and Grill in the nearby Odyssey complex, diners can enjoy their *Titanic* burger while on a multi-screen surround the famous 1958 film *A Night to Remember*[88] plays in a silent continuous loop. No doubt the audible distress of passengers being led to lifeboats by Kenneth

Moore as the brave Second Officer Herbert Lightoller would bring reality rather too close for comfort. As a contribution to raising the quality of the *Titanic* brand the developers in 2005 were in discussion with heritage experts Universal Studios, with Belfast City Council and the Northern Ireland Tourist Board also commissioning a consultants' study to recommend an iconic *Titanic* exhibit for the Quarter to open in time for the centenary of the ship's sinking, and the UK Olympic Games, in 2012. The proposal finding favour is a ghost ship in the form of a light sculpture of the stricken vessel, which from artist's impressions looks like bent coat hangers draped with fairy lights.[89] First prize, however, in the ideas competition to use the *Titanic* motif to brand post-conflict Belfast must go to one offered by the artist Rita Duffy and supported by Belfast's mayor at the time. Described by one commentator as 'plumbing the deaths',[90] this would involve towing an iceberg into the quay from which the ship first sailed, the iceberg then becoming yet another symbol of hope as it melts.[91] In the words of the poet Thomas Hardy – who addressed the disaster of the *Titanic* in 1912 with, as Foster rightly says, 'the authority of mature expression'[92] – icebergs deserve rather more respect.

A key factor in the optimism of the regeneration plans for Belfast lies in the surge of house prices that has gathered momentum from the mid-1990s to the point that prices are increasing faster than anywhere in the United Kingdom – up 37 per cent in 2006 and 22 per cent in 2005.[93] While this has led to optimistic chatter in bars and cafés as property owners return home every evening to assets of ever increasing value, it has led to significant affordability issues, further fuelled debates over housing in the countryside and glossed over the effect of the different housing markets that exist in places still dominated by ethnic segregation. This has further polarised both local ethic tensions and the wealth distribution across society. As a review has noted,[94] the planning system has simply failed to respond to the pressing issue, fuelling demands for a more drastic reflection of how Northern Ireland regulates land use and formulates a regional spatial vision.

Conclusion

The Good Friday Agreement of 1998 marked a critical milestone in Irish history, seemingly breaking an impasse that had plunged Northern Ireland into three decades of bitter ethnic conflict. In reality, the signing of the Belfast Agreement would, as most would now acknowledge, mark only the beginning of another chapter in the endeavour to resolve an enduring dispute. In contrast to previous conflict resolution schemes applied to the region, however, this one has taken place in a context defined largely by the absence of political violence. The Agreement may also be considered novel in that for the first time spatial planning was acknowledged as having a crucial and constitutionally recognised role in preparing the region for what it is hoped will be an enduring peace. In the optimistic culmination of the 1998 peace talks the Agreement pledged to deliver a regional development strategy that would, *inter alia*, tackle 'the problems of a divided society and social cohesion'. While we should acknowledge the fact that a regional strategy did actually emerge out of difficult circumstances, we should not deceive ourselves that it has the competence to really address these issues. A critical cause of this is not only the historical and contemporary context of a sectarian society but also the unwillingness of planners to raise sensitive issues of territory and the expression of cultural identity. Unfortunately, in the re-imaging of 'post-troubles' Belfast, this results in a city which too often settles for third-rate copies of originals that exist elsewhere, leaving a swath of historic challenges that the recently revived Assembly will now have to address.

Notes

1 A. T. Q. Stewart, *The Narrow Ground: Aspects of Ulster, 1609–1969* (Belfast: Blackstaff Press, 1989).
2 L. O'Dowd, B. Rolston and M. Tomlinson, *Northern Ireland: Between Civil Rights and Civil War* (London: CSE Books, 1980).
3 P. Healey, 'Towards a more place-focused planning system in Britain', in A. Mandanipour, P. Healey and A. Hull (eds), *The Governance of Place: Space and Planning Processes* (Aldershot: Ashgate, 2001), p. 278; J. Hillier, 'Imagined value: the poetics and politics of place', in A. Mandanipour, P. Healey and A. Hull (eds), *The Governance of Place: Space and Planning Processes* (Aldershot: Ashgate, 2001), p. 71; W. J. V. Neill, *Urban Planning and Cultural Identity* (London: Routledge, 2004).
4 F. O'Connor, *In Search of a State: Catholics in Northern Ireland* (Belfast: Blackstaff Press, 1993).
5 *Belfast Telegraph*, 'Trimble in new swipe at republic', 14 March 2002, p. 11.
6 *On Eagle's Wing* is a full-scale musical that traces and celebrates the history of the Scots Irish over 500 years, in particular their influence on American culture and music. 'As a people, like many displaced peoples, they face poverty, hardship, religious persecution and loss of their loved ones, but in a new world they find freedom, friendship and inclusion contributing to a new world called America' (see www.oneagleswing.co.uk).
7 M. Elliott, *The Catholics of Ulster* (London: Penguin Press, 2004).
8 B. J. Graham, 'Heritage conservation and revisionist nationalism in Ireland', in G. J. Ashworth and P. J. Larkham (eds), *Building a New Heritage: Tourism, Culture and Identity in the new Europe* (London: Routledge, 1994).

 9 B. Parekh, *The Future of Multi-ethnic Britain* (London: Profile Books, 2000).
10 B. Murtagh and P. Carmichael, *Sharing Place: A Study of mixed Housing in Ballynafeigh, South Belfast* (Belfast: NIHE, 2006).
11 B.Murtagh, 'Dealing with the consequences of a divided society in troubled communities', in J. Greer and M. Murray (eds), *Rural Planning and Development in Northern Ireland* (Dublin: Institute of Public Administration, 2003).
12 P. A. Compton, *Demographic Review: Northern Ireland* (Belfast: Northern Ireland Economic Development Office, 1995).
13 L. Kennedy, *Two Ulsters: A Case for Repartition?* (Belfast: Queen's University Belfast Press, 1986).
14 O'Dowd *et al.*, *Northern Ireland*, p. 30.
15 R. Wiener, The *Rape and Plunder of the Shankill: Community Action, the Belfast Experience* (Belfast: Farset Press, 1980), p. 29.
16 O'Dowd *et al.*, *Northern Ireland*, pp. 30–1.
17 R. H. Matthew, *Belfast: Regional Survey and Plan* (Belfast: HMSO, 1964); T. Wilson, *Economic Development in Northern Ireland*, Cmd 479 (Belfast: HMSO, 1965); Travers Morgan & Partners, *Belfast Transportation Plan* (Belfast: Travers Morgan, 1969); Building Design Partnership, *Belfast Urban Area Plan* (Belfast: DoENI, 1969).
18 This 'stop line' has been successfully upheld until the present day in delineating the outer edge of the Belfast urban area, although, as noted below, one-off housing development has continued unabated in the countryside beyond.
19 C. Buchanan, *Traffic in Towns* (London: HMSO, 1963).
20 This could also be regarded as being successful in terms of the policy's objectives, with Northern Ireland having 2.2 times more road length *per capita* than Great Britain (source: Department of the Environment (Northern Ireland) (DoENI), *Transport Statistics, 1998–1999*, Belfast: DoENI, 1999) and created the conditions for Belfast to become the most car-dependent city in Europe. See J. Cooper, E. Granzow, T. Ryley and A. Smyth, 'Contemporary lifestyles and the implications for sustainable development policy: lessons from the UK's most car-dependent city, Belfast', *Cities* 18:2 (2001), pp. 103–13).
21 R. Osborne and D. Singleton, 'Political processes and behaviour', in F. W. Boal and N. J. Douglas (eds), *Integration and Division: Geographical Perspectives on the Northern Ireland Problem* (London: Academic Press, 1982), p. 177.
22 C. Cowan, 'Belfast's hidden planners', *Town and Country Planning* 51:6 (1982), pp. 163–7; G. Dawson, 'Defensive planning in Belfast', *Irish Geography* 17 (1984), pp. 22–41; P. Hillyard, 'Law and order', in J. Darby (ed.), *Northern Ireland: The Background to the Conflict* (Belfast: Appletree Press, 1983).
23 F. W. Boal, 'Belfast: hindsight or foresight? Planning in an unstable environment', in P. Doherty (ed.), 'Geographical perspectives on the Belfast region', *Geographical Society of Ireland*, Special Publications 5 (1990), pp. 4–14.

24 C. Brett, *Housing a Divided Community* (Dublin: Institute of Public Administration, 1986).

25 Northern Ireland Information Service, *Nine-point Package to spell the Rebirth of Belfast* (Belfast: NIIS, 1978).

26 W. J. V. Neill, 'Physical planning and image enhancement: recent developments in Belfast', *International Journal of Urban and Regional Research* 17:4 (1993), pp. 595–609.

27 Department of the Environment (Northern Ireland), *Regional Physical Development Strategy for Northern Ireland* (Belfast: DoENI, 1975).

28 *Ibid.*, p. 32.

29 *Ibid.*, pp. 25–6.

30 This includes the administrations covering the United Kingdom, the Republic of Ireland, Scotland, Wales, Northern Ireland, Jersey, Guernsey and the Isle of Man.

31 R. Kearney, 'Ireland and Britain: towards a Council of the Isles', in R. Savage (ed.), *Ireland in the New Century* (Dublin: Four Courts Press, 2003), pp. 28–42.

32 Consociational government is where major internal differences are acknowledged in the context of a stable form of administration based on consultation with the elites of its major groups and is contrasted with those based on majority rule.

33 A. Lijphart, *Democracy in Plural Societies* (New Haven CT: Yale University Press, 1977).

34 G. Ellis, 'Addressing inequality: planning in Northern Ireland', *International Planning Studies* 5:3 (2000), pp. 345–64.

35 R. Wilson, *Northern Ireland: What's going Wrong?* Institute of Governance, Queen's University Belfast, Working Paper 1 (Belfast: Queen's University of Belfast, 2003).

36 This is included under Section 6 (Rights, safeguards and equality of opportunity – Economic, social and cultural issues, Section 2 (i). See www.nio.gov.uk/the-agreement.

37 M. Murray and J. Greer, *The Northern Ireland Regional Strategic Framework and its Public Examination Process: Towards a New Model of Participatory Planning?* (Belfast: Rural Innovation and Research Partnership, 2000); J. M. McEldowney and K. Sterrett, 'Shaping a regional vision: the case of Northern Ireland', *Local Economy* 16:1 (2001), pp. 38–49; W. J. V. Neill and M. Gordon, 'Shaping our future? The regional strategic framework for Northern Ireland', *Planning Theory and Practice* 2:1 (2001), pp. 31–52.

38 Department of Regional Development, *Shaping our Future: Regional Development Strategy for Northern Ireland* (Belfast: DRD, 2001).

39 *Ibid.*, p. 20.

40 Department of Regional Development, *Regional Transportation Strategy, 2002–2012* (Belfast: DRD, 2002).

41 These cover land use issues that apply to the whole of Northern Ireland and are issued by either the Department of the Environment or the Department

of Regional Development. Examples include PPS 5, *Retailing and Town Centres*, and PPS 10, *Telecommunications*.

42 'Hubs', 'gateways' and 'corridors' are key concepts in the *European Spatial Development Perspective*, a strategic spatial framework for the EU, pub-lished in 1999. 'Hubs' represent nodes or places of key infrastructural inter-connections (e.g. Schipol airport in the Netherlands), 'gateways' are those places that offer entry into major hinterlands (e.g. major ports, such as Rotterdam) and 'corridors' are infrastructure chains that open up possibili-ties of development, such as the M4 in England. (See European Commission, *ESDP – European Spatial Development Perspective: Towards a balanced and sustainable Development of the Territory of the European Union*, Luxembourg: Office of Official Publications of the European Communities, 1999.)

43 For example, B. Morrison, 'Staying ahead of the game on the quality front', special Irish supplement, *Planning Magazine*, 8–9 June 2000; M. McEldowney, K. Sterrett, F. Gaffikin and M. Morrissey, 'Shaping our future: public voices – a new approach to public participation – the Regional Strategic Framework for Northern Ireland', paper presented at Planning Research conference, London School of Economics, March 2000; Royal Commission for Environmental Pollution, *Twenty-third Report: Environmental Planning*, Cm 5459 (London: Stationery Office, 2002).

44 Neill and Gordon, 'Shaping our future?'

45 J. Greer and M. Murray, 'Rethinking rural planning and development in Northern Ireland', in J. Greer and M. Murray (eds), *Rural Planning and Development in Northern Ireland* (Dublin: Institute of Public Administration, 2003), p. 293.

46 Neill, *Urban Planning and Cultural Identity*, p. 202.

47 P. Healey, 'The treatment of space and place in the new strategic spatial plan-ning in Europe', *International Journal of Urban and Regional Research* 28:1 (2004), pp. 45–67.

48 B. J. Graham, 'Interpreting the rural in Northern Ireland: place, heritage and history', in J. Greer and M. Murray (eds), *Rural Planning and Development in Northern Ireland* (Dublin: Institute of Public Administration, 2003), pp. 265–6.

49 Neill, *Urban Planning and Cultural Identity*, pp. 198–9.

50 Northern Ireland Economic Council, *A Response by the Northern Ireland Economic Council to 'Shaping our Future'*, NIEC advice and comment series (Belfast: NIEC, 1999), p. 7.

51 D. Heald, *Funding the Northern Ireland Assembly: Assessing the Options*, Northern Ireland Economic Council, Research Monograph 10 (Belfast: NEIC, 2003), p. 59.

52 For example, K. Williams, *Achieving Sustainable Urban Form* (London: E. & F.N. Spon, 2000).

53 Transport 2000 (Northern Ireland), *Response to 'Shaping our Future'* (Belfast: Transport 2000 NI, 1999).

54 N. Blair, 'Telecommunications Infrastructure in Northern Ireland', unpublished Ph.D. thesis (Belfast: School of Environmental Planning, Queen's University Belfast, 2004).

55 For example, rising public concern for the protection of high-quality rural landscapes and increased agricultural diversification.

56 RNI 1, To maintain a working countryside with a strong mixed use rural economy. RNI 2, To create and sustain a living countryside with a high quality of life for all its residents; RNI 3, To support the network of service centres based on main towns, small towns and villages in rural Northern Ireland; RNI 4, To create an accessible countryside with a responsive transport network that meets the needs of the rural community; RNI 5, To continue to create and sustain an attractive and unique rural environment in the interests of the rural community and the region as a whole.

57 J. Greer and M. Murray (eds), *Rural Planning and Development in Northern Ireland* (Dublin: Institute of Public Administration, 2003).

58 DoENI, *A Planning Strategy for Rural Northern Ireland* (Belfast: DoENI, 1993), p. 43.

59 Department of Regional Development (DRD), *Planning Policy Statement 14: Sustainable Development in the Countryside* (Belfast: DRD, 2006).

60 For example, most of these dwellings are reliant on septic tanks for sewerage disposal, which with poor maintenance can become a significant health hazard, causing seepage of pathogens into the water table.

61 For example, the cost of postal delivery, education, waste collection and water connections all fall dramatically with population density, while other services, such as public transport, are simply unviable in rural areas.

62 Northern Ireland Planning Commission, *A Sense of Place: Planning for the Future in Northern Ireland* (Belfast: National Trust, 2004), para. 3.5.7.

63 *Ibid.*, para. 3.5.9.

64 An example of the discourse of opposition to this recent policy announcement can be viewed at www.pps14.com.

65 C. Irwin, *The People's Peace Process in Northern Ireland* (London: Palgrave, 2002).

66 Democratic Unionist Party (2003), *Rural Reform and Rejuvenation: Policy Paper* (Belfast: DUP, 2003), p. 10.

67 Graham, 'Interpreting the rural in Northern Ireland', p. 269.

68 Greer and Murray, *Rural Planning and Development in Northern Ireland*, p. 17.

69 G. Adams, 'The equality agenda', *Belfast Telegraph*, 17 January 2001.

70 *Belfast Telegraph*, 'Plan to kill off countryside', 27 September 2004, p. 7.

71 Greer and Murray, *Rural Planning and Development in Northern Ireland*, p. 297.

72 *Ibid.*, p. 298.

73 W. J. V. Neill and H. U. Schwedler, 'Planning with an ethic of cultural inclusion', in W. J. V. Neill and H. U. Schwedler (eds), *Urban Planning and*

Cultural Inclusion: Lessons from Belfast and Berlin (London: Palgrave, 2001), p. 209.

74 J. Buick, *Crossing the Border: A Regional Approach to Environmental Management*, Report 2002.2 (Lund: International Institute of Industrial Environmental Economics, 2002).

75 North–South Ministerial Council, *Joint Communiqué, Environment Sector*, Interpoint (Belfast, 28 June 2000), see www.northsouthministerialcouncil.org.

76 Department of Environment, *First Steps towards Sustainability: A Sustainable Development Strategy for Northern Ireland* (Belfast: DoENI, 2006).

77 As noted by Jonathan Porritt, Chair of the UK Sustainable Development Commission, at the launch of the Northern Ireland Sustainable Development Commission in May 2006, in a speech that did little to hide disappointment with a protracted policy process and its ultimate outcome.

78 G. Ellis, B. Motherway, W. J. V. Neill and U. Hand, *Towards a Green Isle? Local Sustainable Development on the Island of Ireland* (Armagh: Centre for Cross-border Studies, 2004).

79 R. Macrory and S. Turner, 'Participatory rights, trans-boundary environmental governance and EC law', *Common Market Law Review* 39 (2002), pp. 489–522.

80 DoENI, 2004.

81 G. Blackbourne, spokesperson for Karl Properties Ltd, quoted in 'Obel: new landmark for Belfast', *Ulster Architect* 21:3 (2005), pp. 22–5.

82 M. O'Doherty, '"Symbol of hope" a pathetic icon of the spirit of Belfast', *Belfast Telegraph*, 20 December 2004, p. 14.

83 R. Appleton, 'Sculpture will be stunning addition to Belfast skyline', *Belfast Telegraph*, 27 December 2004, p. 12.

84 J. W. Foster, *The Titanic Complex: A Cultural Manifest* (Vancouver BC: Belcouver Press, 1997), p. 15.

85 On 19 December 2004 £26.5 million was stolen from the Northern Bank in Belfast city centre. There have been many claims that the raid was carried out by the IRA, but as yet no successful prosecutions have taken place.

86 M. Sheehan, 'Unravelling the threads of Phil Flynn's tangled life', *Belfast Telegraph*, 1 March 2005, p. 13.

87 N. Tilson, '£1 billion Titanic Quarter blueprint is unveiled', *Belfast Telegraph*, 11 March 2005, p. 2.

88 *A Night to Remember* is the best known pre-1997 *Titanic* film, starring Kenneth Moore and directed by Roy Baker. It is a less romantic and melodramatic portrayal of the sinking of the vessel that relies on historical accounts of the tragedy.

89 A. Clements, '*Titanic*'s lights fantastic!' *Belfast Telegraph*, 12 August 2005, p. 3.

90 S. Denham, 'Belfast's civic dignity melts away as *Titanic* iceberg sails into town', *Sunday Times*, 27 February 2005, p. 21.

91 *Ibid.*

92 Foster, *The Titanic Complex*, p. 27.
93 P. Davy 'Northern Ireland: housing hotspot', *Guardian*, 16 May 2007, www.guardian.co.uk/print/0,,329855047-103588,00.html.
94 J. Semple, *Affordability Review* (Belfast: DSD, 2007), www.dsdni.gov.uk/hsdiv-housing-affordability.htm.

6

Policing change: to reform or not to transform?

Mary O'Rawe

When the Good Friday Agreement[1] was signed following multi-party negotiations in 1998, policing[2] loomed large on the peacemaking agenda. This should come as little surprise, given that, from the inception of Northern Ireland, policing had been one of the most controversial features[3] of the political and legal fiction that democracy prevailed in the region. The Royal Ulster Constabulary (RUC) was overtly political,[4] in many respects espousing a British, unionist culture, and was used by successive governments to shore up a repressive and discriminatory regime.[5] Well over 90 per cent of police officers were drawn exclusively from Protestant/unionist/loyalist communities.[6] Many within these sections of Northern Irish society[7] understandably, therefore, felt a strong identification with the police, bordering at times on a sense of ownership. The deaths of over 300 police officers during the conflict and the fact of thousands more injured and maimed impacted very keenly upon these communities, and strengthened allegiance and commitment to the force.

Meanwhile, perceptions in the minority community were that policing was neither fair nor impartial and that the structures ostensibly set up to hold the police to account were partisan, grossly incompetent or both. The RUC operated with a wide range of 'emergency' powers, which were often used in an arbitrary, discriminatory and insufficiently accountable manner. Many human rights abuses, ranging from the misuse of stop and search powers and ill treatment in detention up to and including controversial killings by the security forces themselves as well as collusion with loyalist and republican paramilitaries in a number of further murders were denied and covered up by government and the forces of law and order. Hence policing Northern Ireland was, from the outset, mired in the same complex contestation of identities, ownership, power and legitimacy that led to, exacerbated and perpetuated violent conflict in the region over a period of many decades.[8]

In these attributes and features, policing in Northern Ireland merely mirrored much of what is wrong with policing in violently conflicted societies around the world. This chapter reflects on whether changes made to policing in the wake of the Patten Commission on policing, although in many respects dramatic, visible and far-reaching, have been sufficient to effect the transformation in policing required for Northern Ireland to leave its troubled past behind. Following the decision of Sinn Féin in January 2007 to finally come on board with the new policing arrangements and the reinstatement of the power sharing Assembly at Stormont in May 2007, the chapter further aims to revisit the police change process with a view to articulating some remaining governance challenges for accountable and legitimate policing post-conflict.

The road to the Patten Report

In 1998 an independent commission was established to consider what should be done about policing in Northern Ireland – partly because acceptable and legitimate policing was deemed vital to securing the peace. In this, Northern Irish society faced issues similar to those confronting other transitional societies. The main stumbling block was essentially how to effect that change in such a way as to create policing arrangements acceptable to all sections of a divided community, at a time when peace itself was very fragile. Following the IRA cease-fire in 1994 and the subsequent Loyalist cessations, Northern Irish society appeared to group around two diametrically opposed demands. One of these insisted that the RUC should not be 'poked', 'prodded'[9] and tinkered with. The police required no reform and had done the best job possible in difficult circumstances. The other end of the spectrum articulated, in an equally trenchant and vocal manner, that the RUC should be disbanded, as it was incapable of engendering loyalty from the section of the population it had repressed and misused over several decades.

In the mid-1990s popular opinion began not just to group around these positions but to explore what they might mean in practice. Several conferences and events were held at grass-roots level to begin the difficult societal conversation involved in making acceptable policing change a reality. By and large, police and government did not engage in these events. This lack of openness and candour at a key stage in the peace process retrenched defensive positions and contributed to the pressure on unionists and loyalists to stay loyal and not be seen to criticise the organs of the state that had traditionally held their allegiance. This had the effect of masking the degree of working-class loyalist dissent against the RUC at a stage when more openness and honesty might have smoothed the path of the peace process. That said, for the first time, during this period, loyalists began to articulate cautiously, but publicly, that their own experience of policing was far from entirely positive. This commonality of experience led to a dialogue with republicans which, hitherto unthinkable, was hugely important in terms of building bridges to other realities.

The ambition of government and the police to 'hold the line' following the cease-fires also neutralised the impact of the scaling down of some of the more visible aspects of security policing. Any attempts made by the RUC to engage with ordinary citizens thereafter were viewed by many as part of a cosmetic and surface-level charm offensive. This was further cemented by the unpublished RUC internal 'Fundamental Review of Policing', which attempted to paint the principal issues requiring consideration purely in terms of modernisation, professionalism and managerialism rather than vital transformation.

The failure to capitalise on the opportunity presented by the cease-fires to 'go deep' on the issue of policing meant important ground was lost at a key transitional moment. This failure to push out the boundaries and create a safe space for 'policing' as opposed to 'police' issues to be played out, in all likelihood contributed to the breakdown of the IRA ceasefire in 1996.[10] Meanwhile the important exchanges that had begun to happen in small, but important, ways between republicans and loyalists had at least allowed initial exploration of how the police apparatus affected the poorer communities in Northern Ireland. Grass-roots loyalism, and in particular the Progressive Unionist Party, thus played an important role in beginning to articulate the need for 'open admission' of the reality of the legacy of bitterness fostered by 'the long history of RUC actions and attitudes towards Catholics'.[11]

The months that followed the breakdown of the first IRA cease-fire were categorised by massive failures in public order policing[12] as the police moved back to a conflict-based militaristic approach to problems. Meanwhile the political debates as to whether the RUC was inherently good or intrinsically bad continued apace. What the Good Friday Agreement attempted – successfully or otherwise – to do in 1998 was to sow the seeds of a consensus in principles of fairness, impartiality and accountability. Policing was acknowledged as a key source of hurt and tension which would continue to frustrate the fledgling peace process if left unaddressed. All parties to the agreement acknowledged the need for the police service to be 'professional, effective, efficient, fair and impartial, free from partisan political control; accountable both under the law for its actions and to the community it polices; and [to] operate within a coherent and co-operative criminal justice system which conforms with human rights norms'.[13] The parties to the Agreement created some societal distance from the ultimate outworkings of this in the establishment of an independent international commission to consider future arrangements for policing that would be acceptable to all sections of Northern Irish society in the transition from violent conflict to durable peace.

The establishment of such a commission had been suggested in a number of different quarters, not least by the Committee on the Administration of Justice (CAJ), Northern Ireland's foremost civil liberties organisation, which had commissioned a major piece of research drawing on international experience of transition and exploring the benefits of using human rights as both a tool and an indicative measure for the success of the change process.[14] The level of civil society activity around this issue from the earliest moments of the peace process indicates the degree to which policing mattered to people at a symbolic as much as a practical level, and demonstrated the difficulties in cutting through the feelings, emotions and experiences to the heart of what needed to happen to move society and policing forward.

The Patten Commission and its journey

The task of the Patten Commission was to walk a tightrope between the past and the future. The commission, established by the British government in 1998, was charged with ensuring that future policing arrangements in Northern Ireland conformed to the norms expressed in the Agreement.[15]

What the Patten Commission had in its favour which made it different from previous government-sponsored police reform initiatives[16] was that it was not boycotted by any section of the community. The commission was, therefore, introduced to the multiple experiences and agendas of different sections of a divided community. At a very basic level, the commission acted as a precursor to a *bona fide* Truth Commission, hearing many stories of pain and loss, from both the families of murdered and injured police officers, and also from those who had experienced death and brutality at the hands of the police. The commissioners were conscious of the difficulties arising if they were seen to ground their recommendations in one or other of two bitterly divided camps[17] and, therefore, tried not to apportion blame or get drawn into making pronouncements on the past, in the hope that this would allow for a focus on the future.

The commission was hamstrung to a certain extent by various pronouncements by government that disbandment was not an option and that it had complete confidence in the RUC. The government also used the period of Patten's deliberations to bring in a new Police (Northern Ireland) Act[18] which, among other things, established a much diluted and more toothless version of the Police Ombudsoffice originally proposed by Maurice Hayes in 1997.[19] This unseemly rush to pre-empt Patten's judgement on a number of issues allowed the government to lay claim to basic legislative principles that would have to be overturned if Patten were to come up with anything too radical.

In part this speaks to a dichotomy and a fundamental flaw within the whole tenor of the rights agenda in both the Good Friday Agreement and the official discourse surrounding it. Human rights had been offered a little space in the rhetoric – but in ways that served to mask the fact that, on the ground, government still clung tenaciously to the notion that the RUC was principally a victim of circumstances, its main problem being its lack of representativeness. This, in turn, was portrayed solely to have been caused by paramilitaries intimidating young Catholics to the point where they felt unable to join what was assumed to be a good and heroic force. Although certainly a consideration, the emphasis on paramilitary intimidation as the sole explanation for the dearth of police officers from a nationalist background allowed the government to distract attention from its own role and that of its agents in rendering the police force unacceptable. While extolling the virtues of equality and dignity for all, policing reforms were styled as potential concessions to nationalists, with human rights viewed as bargaining chips, rather than as a framework to make Northern Ireland a more inclusive and vibrant democracy. The language of pluralism and equity was being spoken, but not necessarily understood. This double-speak and double-think is a feature of any transitional process where sands are shifting yet all parties are keen not to concede too much ground. It is, however, important that this phenomenon is recognised for what it is to try to guard against the persistence of established and iniquitous political practices.

At a moment when much could have been done to create a new and more fluid space for working through common agendas, government actions served to preserve old realities and perceptions, simultaneously ignoring the possibility that widening the conversation might actually create the means of circumventing old debates. Eventually the Commission premised its recommendations on the notion that the 'fundamental purpose of policing should be . . . the protection and vindication of the human rights of all . . .There should be no conflict between human rights and policing. Policing means protecting human rights.'[20]

The Patten Report: new beginnings and new directions?

The Patten Report talked of the need for professional police officers to 'adapt to a world where their own efforts are only part of the policing of a modern society' and the need to 'reorient their approach' to allow policing to become 'a genuine partnership for peace on the streets with those who live, work and walk on those streets'.[21] Very clearly, the report concluded, 'holistic change of a fundamental nature' was necessary. It argued further that reform could not be seen as 'a cluster of unconnected adjustments in policy that can be bolted or soldered on to the organisation that already exists'.[22] This analysis was an important one in terms of a post-conflict society. The Patten Commission attempted to shift the focus from an organisation that drew a range of very different responses and emotions to a much broader conception of policing and how it might be done. In so doing the body's report opened up some new spaces for thinking and acting.

The findings of the Patten Commission further exhorted that politics should be taken out of policing in Northern Ireland. This may be deemed naive in that there will always be some political dimension to state policing. However, it did send a strong – and much needed – message to government not to fall into the trap of tying police reform too closely to political agendas. The changes that needed to be made were valid and vital in and of themselves, irrespective of the constitutional question or whether the fledgling institutions of devolved government in Northern Ireland survived or fell.[23] Patten's proposals were rooted firmly in principles of human rights aimed at improving the policing service for the whole of society – whatever ultimate shape that society might take.

The Patten approach, therefore, definitively articulated the need to place human rights at the centre of policing and integrate this logic into every aspect of police service delivery. Unfortunately it then failed to follow through the logic of its own arguments in a number of important respects. It permitted the personnel of the RUC to remain largely intact, albeit with a change of name,[24] uniform and badge. However, it made no provision for how those guilty of human rights abuses in the past should be either purged from the force or successfully rehabilitated within it. It did not deal with how a human rights culture could be inculcated while policing continued to be premised on the use of wide-ranging 'emergency' powers. The commissioners were also particularly weak in the area of diversity. Ethnic and other minorities were insufficiently accommodated within the proposals. Further, in recommending a period of 50:50 recruitment for Catholics and Protestants, and making no creative provision to increase the representation of women, the commission effectively missed the gender challenge. Women have historically been unrepresented and poorly accommodated in police forces around the world. A well thought through focus on gender and other aspects of enhanced diversity might have taken some of the sting out of the proposals that were made in terms of increasing the quota of Catholics in the organisation. In failing to see and work with this reality the Patten commissioners effectively denied themselves an important key to unlock the diversity debate more comprehensively and less controversially than they did. Instead, a too singular focus on Catholics and Protestants inadvertently perpetuated the pre-eminence of sectarian politics as a defining feature of their post-conflict policing solutions.

That said, a policing blueprint had been established on many levels which could work to the benefit of Northern Irish society. However, scarcely before the ink was dry on the Patten Report there were forces at work to claw back the parameters of the debate and hurl policing once more into the party political disputes which had necessitated an independent commission in the first place. As has been stated, the signs that this would happen were already there in the run-up to the establishment of the Patten Commission and in government action during its period of deliberation. Unfortunately the replaying of old mistakes was assisted by a process failure of the Patten Commission itself. The commission either underestimated or ignored the need to build political and social consensus around the 'transformation' it proposed. It failed to recognise the level of resistance there would be to its recommendations, and that it was ideally placed to pre-empt and counter that resistance in key areas. Rather than validate its conclusions or ground its recommendations firmly in areas where consensus existed or could be created, the Patten Commission 'disbanded' itself only hours after its report was laid before the public, leaving the old guard to resume command of the process.

Paradoxically, but not unexpectedly, it was precisely the old guard – those who had maintained and managed old-style policing – who viewed themselves as the rightful and most effective authors of change. When no change is not an option, experience attests to a creeping tendency for police organisations to take ownership of a process which then tends to be managerial, technocratic and reformist, rather than radical and transformative. In this, police organisations tend to be supported by politicians and civil servants, who share a narrow security analysis of the problems and see change in terms more of modernisation, professionalisation and cost-effectiveness than anything more fundamentally challenging to the *status quo*. The parameters of the debate are thereby narrowed and the gap between commitment and delivery allowed to widen. In large measure, although there have clearly also been dedicated and committed reformers among those involved in change management within the police, this is what has happened in Northern Ireland.

The post-Patten period, despite ushering in obvious and apparently extensive changes, still attests to the past being allowed to reassert itself in a new guise. Despite the surface rhetoric of human rights and representative policing, all is not as well as it might be. For all that has happened and all that is different, it would appear that change is continuing to build on a false premise – that 50:50 recruitment of Catholics and Protestants, and a number of other less dramatic changes, deal effectively with the diversity challenge and that the legacy of the conflict in terms of past police wrongdoing does not need to be explicitly addressed for the change process to be truly transformative.

The role of the International Oversight Commissioner proposed by the Patten Commission to monitor and copper-fasten the change process has had its share of limitations in ushering in a transformation of policing in Northern Ireland, as have the new domestic accountability structures such as the Policing Board, the Police Ombudswoman and the District Policing Partnerships. These will be addressed shortly.

First, it is only in setting out what Patten actually proposed that we can ascertain whether it is what is being delivered. Space precludes a full examination of the 175 recommendations in the report, but the main ones may be considered as follows:

1 Human rights to be accepted as the core function and guiding principle, with a comprehensive programme of action to focus policing in Northern Ireland on a human rights approach

2 Changes in the name, badge and uniform and the assessed maintenance of a neutral working environment.

3 A 'flattening' of police structures and a reduction in the number of officers.

4 Fifty-fifty recruitment for a time-limited period to address the imbalance of Catholics in the organisation.

5 Establishment of a nineteen-member Policing Board to hold the Chief Constable publicly to account and to monitor police performance in respect of human rights as in other respects. This board would also oversee and support the development of District Policing Partnership boards. These were designed to reflect and engage with concerns and priorities around policing at a more local level. Patten, in particular, recommended that these bodies should have access to their own separate funding stream to spend on local policing initiatives.

6 A strong Ombudsoffice to investigate complaints against the police, make research-based recommendations on policy and practice and undertake its own investigations ('own motion' investigations in the absence of a complaint) in the public interest (with more powers than accorded by the Police (Northern Ireland) Act 1998).

7 Changes in training, education and development with a view to assessing what was being delivered, establishing a much more problem-solving, scenario-based approach and integrating human rights into every module. As much as possible, it was felt by the commission, training should be outsourced and done in partnership with the community and local universities. A new purpose-built police college was also recommended
8 Changes in organisational structures, including decentralisation, demilitarisation, civilianisation, the disbandment of Special Branch, and the amalgamation of criminal investigation and intelligence functions under a sole command
9 Legislative and other human rights compliant changes to covert policing to try to put an end to Special Branch acting unaccountably as a force within a force.
10 Severance packages for those wishing to leave the force
11 Provision concerning funds and memorials to honour RUC victims and their families

The government welcomed the Patten Report and then instigated a further period of consultation after which it claimed that it would implement the report's recommendations. During the period of consultation the debate returned pretty much to the level it had been at before the Patten Commission process intervened. There were emotive arguments around the symbols of policing. The media concentrated on the same divisive points of the debate. The government awarded the RUC the George Cross for gallantry yet said nothing about those who had been victims of members of the same force.

Driving Patten forward

In January 2002 a new Secretary of State, Peter Mandelson, announced the government's plans for implementation of the Patten Report. Mandelson's statement to Parliament was explicitly predicated on full support for the job the RUC had done over the previous thirty years. That Patten had not done this was a deliberate and very important strategy. The commission chose not to comment on the merit or the weight of allegations against the RUC, nor to heap fulsome praise upon the organisation for a very specific reason. It did not feel the need to do so, as it deemed its recommendations valid irrespective of whether the RUC were the 'best police force in the world', institutionally sectarian and rotten through and through, or somewhere in between. Politically this was probably quite astute but for one thing – the fact that, where narratives compete, government has always been very clear which truth should be prioritised. In this instance, too, the government simply moved back into its traditional space as if the Patten Commission process had never happened.

The failure to move to a speedy implementation of the Patten package thereby consolidated ownership of the change process in the very bodies that had been responsible for policing prior to the Patten Report.[25] The Northern Ireland Office set up a Patten Action team. The RUC also established a high-level team to manage change within the organisation. The two bodies spoke to each other (and the Police Authority) but to precious few others. The draft legislation and implementation plans when they surfaced looked like the work of the same people who had resisted much real change prior to the Patten Report. And indeed they were.

Legislative changes were brought in by means of another 'Police' Act. The attempts of Patten to broaden the sites of community safety were thereby nullified from the outset. The 'Policing Board' legislated for was in fact essentially a 'Police Board'.[26] The District Policing Partnerships, by which Patten had attempted to inject a further level of democratic accountability and encourage a further sense of focus on policing as opposed to the police, bore little resemblance to what the commission had envisaged. Most significantly, they were deliberately not given financial power to buy in improved policing services at district level, whether from the police or elsewhere.[27] The Police Ombudsoffice, initially proposed by Maurice Hayes in 1997, and legislated for prior to Patten in the Police (Northern Ireland) Act 1998, continued to be tied very tightly into individual complaints by individual members of the public about individual officers. This was despite Patten's clear exhortation that this office would be a key lynchpin of policing governance and a very visible symbol of what had changed for the better. As such, it should have had powers to instigate investigations of its own accord (own motion powers) and to make recommendations on what it deemed to be problematic policies and practices above and beyond individual complaints.

Despite this, the government was keen to emphasise how the Police (Northern Ireland) Act 2000 would implement both the letter and the spirit of Patten,[28] clinging to this fantasy despite irrefutable evidence that the legislation fell far short of Patten in very many respects. Even after extensive discussion and over 100 amendments, most of them substantive, the legislation still failed to convince either the SDLP or Sinn Féin to commit to taking their seats on the new Policing Board.[29] The majority of Patten's 175 recommendations did not make it into legislation. They were dealt with by way of an implementation plan drawn up by the NIO, which, unsurprisingly, gave lead responsibility for implementing many of the proposals to the Chief Constable and the NIO.[30] Even when this plan was reissued in 2001, lead responsibility for the Patten recommendations on community policing, normalisation, and policing structures, for example, continued to be vested in the Chief Constable. It appeared from this that the government did not foresee the board having any major responsibility in a number of areas, from creating an unarmed police force, to establishing a police appraisal system, to integrating the work of Special Branch more fully into the organisation.

With this afoot, a great deal required to be salvaged by the one legacy the Patten commissioners had left in terms of seeing their recommendations through. An Oversight Commissioner was to be appointed to copper-fasten the changes proposed and ensure a real and visible high-level scrutiny of the process. Patten had recommended that this person should be appointed 'as soon as possible' with responsibility for 'supervising the implementation of our recommendations'.[31] The failure to appoint Tom Constantine[32] until June 2000, months after the consultation process on Patten, may be considered one of the most regrettable aspects of the post-Patten process.

By the time the appointment was made, government had already repackaged Patten in its own likeness. Yet it was the legislation and implementation plan, rather than the Patten Report itself, that the commissioner took as his brief. When it was pointed out to him[33] how valuable and, indeed, necessary it might be for him to consider how far the draft legislation and implementation plan fell short of truly implementing the Patten Report he refused to contemplate this as coming within his remit. Essentially, his argument was that he had no democratic mandate to substitute his views for those of an elected legislature. On one level, his logic is quite proper and understandable. However, most of the manoeuvring that was going on was at the level of the Executive and its advisers. The majority of MPs in the Westminster Parliament were not familiar enough with the problems, or sufficiently concerned with the detail, to either realise or to care what was happening. Given the circumstances pertaining in Northern Ireland at the time, and the need to avoid previous mistakes, this attitude of the Oversight Commissioner actually impacted quite significantly on whether he would genuinely be able to supervise the Patten implementation process as a transformative one.

The Oversight Commissioner was strategically well placed to raise these issues and to have them taken on board. He could also have alerted the legislature to the need for greater vigilance. In practice, however, he did neither. Rather than look at the vehicle for change in terms of its roadworthiness, Constantine preferred to leave both the design and the mechanics of the process in the same hands that had driven policing prior to the Patten Report. He saw his role as ensuring that these people did what they said they were going to do, rather than look behind this to see if more needed to be done.

In keeping with this same narrow reading of the situation, the commissioner chose not to bring a partnership approach to the oversight process. This could have drawn on local strengths and knowledge to complement international expertise and could have helped test the feasibility of Patten's proposed partnership approach to policing generally. The commissioner seemed to believe that outreach to the policed was important, but did not see it as impacting on his role. Instead the commissioner gathered around him a cohort of white North American males, mostly from police backgrounds, with a combined 221 years' policing experience behind them. This is certainly one part of an effective dynamic – but the process is poorer for assuming it can be an effective dynamic in and of itself. An expert 'police' mind-set was once again applied to a 'problem' of policing, with this team largely considering it unnecessary to meet on a regular basis with anyone other than the policing establishment. A partnership approach to oversight could have had real and symbolic value during this period of transition. The opportunity to capitalise on either aspect was missed.

Instead the Oversight Commissioner set out 772 performance indicators[34] developed by his team and 'those individuals who will be subject to the monitoring process' and based on the 175 recommendations of the Patten Report. The oversight process then set itself to verify administrative compliance with each of the performance indicators, placing the process firmly within the professional, managerialist, policing model, where transformation ultimately gave way to the ticking of boxes.

The stance of the Oversight Commissioner made it even more important that domestic accountability structures were 'of the community' and indeed were seen to be so. Particularly in a society in transition, there is a need to distance the police from identification with any particular section of the community or any specific political agenda. Effective oversight, in the words of the current Chief Constable Hugh Orde, is 'not about cosy relationships'.[35] It is not about defending the police in the face of criticism, a misguided strategy much beloved of the erstwhile Police Authority of Northern Ireland. Not only are critics unconvinced by such an approach, but in the long run it serves to erode the legitimacy of the very structures established to ensure transparency, openness and accountability. Effective oversight needs to be about ensuring a broad societal stake in a democratic policing process. It is about the development and maintenance of systems which hold police organisations effectively to account, whether on the use of resources, the manner in which services are delivered or the attitudes and actions of staff. The Policing Board set up initially lacked the degree of diversity one might have hoped for, with only two women and many of the ten 'independent' members having some party political affiliation.[36] Part of the board's remit was to act as a conduit for other voices not represented round the table. It is questionable to what extent it has succeeded in this remit.[37] Probably the board's most notable achievement to date has been the appointment of external advisers to draw up a framework for monitoring human rights compliance in police performance.[38] This finally concretised in human rights terms how measures and indicators needed to be looked at, and has provided a very useful model not just for the PSNI but for other services to learn from.

The Police Ombudswoman for Northern Ireland (PONI) has been another important strand in the change process. In many ways it has been the most visible in terms of tackling the legacy of conflict, albeit in an *ad hoc* and piecemeal way. The Ombudsoffice[39] opened its doors on 6 November 2000. As with Patten, much goodwill surrounded its establishment, though doubts continued to persist on all sides as to the extent to which it might signal a break with the past.[40] Although on a surface level entirely accepting of the new organisation, a rather more negative police view of the Ombudsoffice occasionally comes to the fore. This was evidenced most strongly following the PONI investigation into the RUC handling of events around the Omagh bombing of 15 August 1998, in which thirty one people, including two unborn children, were killed. The resulting report[41] raised serious concerns as to how RUC Special Branch[42] had handled information given to them prior to the bombing, and how the investigation following the bombing had been hampered by the failure of Special Branch to hand over relevant information to the criminal investigation team. The report concluded, among other things, that the leadership of Sir Ronnie Flanagan, then Chief Constable, was 'fatally flawed'.

Predictably, an enormous backlash against Nuala O'Loan and her integrity ensued. The very existence of such a report created enormous controversy, with the Chief Constable denouncing its findings as unfair and the Ombudswoman's investigation as less than rigorous. He claimed not to have been interviewed in relation to the Omagh investigation, or given a chance to respond prior to the report being published. Rather than accepting that mistakes were made and that systems were less than perfect, the Chief Constable's response was to state he would publicly commit suicide if the report's claims were true. Thus, in time-honoured tradition, the most senior police officer of the day attempted to deflect attention from the shortcomings of his force, pointing the finger at the

Ombudswoman for her failure to understand how the police have to operate in the face of a terrorist threat. Amid this intense personal and professional vilification, the Police Federation launched judicial review proceedings aimed at declaring the Omagh report null and void. These were eventually dropped only in January 2003, and the findings of the Omagh report vindicated. By that time the media had lost interest in the story and the damage visited on the credibility of the Office by months of constant haranguing had taken its toll.

The lessons of this whole sorry affair are salutary. They point to a degree of discomfort and simmering anger about a process of change, which on a surface level is accepted. The backlash against reform partly contests what the Good Friday Agreement stands for, and continues the fight as to what the conflict was about. It is very much in keeping with a society in transition that those who have previously held power feel the need to flex their muscles as the old, the new and the not-so-new stakeholders vie to amass control of a fluid situation post-conflict. In such transitional spaces a lot of power seems 'up for grabs'. The extent to which this is truly the case lies in the extent to which government proactively supports its new improved systems in the face of traditional loyalties and allegiances. The Policing Board and the Secretary of State are certainly not beyond criticism for how they responded to the very public controversy created by the report. There should have been mechanisms put in place to verify the accuracy or otherwise of the Ombudswoman's findings at the earliest juncture. The government and the Policing Board would then have been in a position to stand over her recommendations where they related to preventing similar occurrences in the future. Although a number of recommendations were eventually acted upon, in many ways the Ombudswoman was allowed to become isolated and had very much to fight her own corner. It is unlikely to contribute to public faith in the process when the very government which set up the Office appears less than willing to ensure its effectiveness. Despite the rhetoric of managerialism, professionalism and openness to the new dispensation, the Omagh controversy symbolises how difficult it has been for the PSNI to transform rather than merely reform itself.

The 'Operation Ballast' report published by Nuala O'Loan's office in 2007 pointed very starkly to how, despite all the rhetoric, changes implemented up until 2003 had been insufficient to curb the power of Special Branch acting as the supreme force within the police. The British state – despite having handed out around £80,000 to a serial killer for his services as a police agent between 1997 and 2003 – refused to allocate resources requested to speed up the O'Loan investigation, which ultimately took over three years to come to its conclusions. The investigation was also hampered by missing, destroyed or concealed documentation and other evidence and the ongoing unwillingness of a number of retired and serving officers to co-operate with the Ombudsoffice's most serious investigation to date. Shockingly, but not surprisingly, this investigation ultimately found security force collusion to have been established in at least ten murders in north Belfast between 1997 and 2003. The report also linked one particular special branch informer and his associates with a range of other criminal activities into which there was no effective investigation, but rather evidence of Special Branch officers thwarting any such investigation by their colleagues. The Operation Ballast report produced a more nuanced response to that concerning the Omagh bomb investigation in that government and police officially accepted the findings and based their defence on the fact that action had now been taken to remedy the deficiencies set out in the report in terms of the handling of informers (Covert Human Intelligence Sources), etc. The Police Federation found cause to doubt the rigour of the O'Loan investigation and government saw no need to castigate Sir Ronnie Flanagan, who was permitted to remain as head of Her Majesty's Inspectorate of Constabulary (HMIC) despite having presided over this collusion during his time as head of Special Branch and, later, Chief Constable of the RUC/PSNI.

A third strand to the Patten Report's accountability framework was the creation of District Policing Partnership Boards (now DPPs).[43] These were intended to take democratic participation in policing to the most local of levels. However, alongside these fora, which were denied spending powers, the government separately established Community Safety Committees, as a result, not of Patten, but of a parallel Criminal Justice Review. The existence of these two sets of bodies attests to the continuing desire of the state to keep issues compartmentalised. The Northern Ireland Office (NIO) retains much more control of the latter process – and it is here that funds seem to be available to spend on community safety initiatives approved by the powers that be. The acronyms may change, but the same bodies retain control of both the process and the purse strings. An assessment of attendance of the public at DPP meetings has shown no more than a handful turning up at meetings, while the cost of DPPs has exceeded £12 million since they were established in 2003.[44] However, it must be noted that £12 million still represents only a very small part (0.5 per cent) of the overall policing budget allocation, and it is certainly possible that DPPs would be much more effective public accountability fora had they been set up and resourced as recommended by Patten.

Following a Review of Public Administration, plans were introduced to decrease the number of district councils from twenty-nine to seven.

This has resulted in a corresponding decrease in police District Command Units to eight, with a corollary of fewer DPPs. Local accountability and local policing issues are bound to suffer as a result of these moves. In the words of the Oversight Commissioner, 'While this decision can be supported on the grounds of efficiency, it may have unintended consequences with respect to the dilution of accountability, community involvement and representation.'[45] Thus, the little that was given by Patten is already being taken away. The narrative of policing change is still being dictated at very many levels by a state that does not sufficiently value what local communities can bring to the process.

As regards the PSNI itself, massive change has happened, and this author does not wish to detract from much difficult work that has been done and that is still being undertaken. For example, Catholics now make up 23.74 per cent of the force's regular officers, with females accounting for 22 per cent.[46] Strides have been taken to incorporate human rights into training and other aspects of service delivery. An in-house human rights lawyer is in post, and more recently a human rights lawyer advising specifically on training, was recruited although that post is not filled at the time of writing.

However, despite the achievements, because concepts like consultation and partnership have been defined to suit the interests of the police, and because the role of past policing has not been fully engaged with,[47] the opportunities created by this transitional moment have not been fully realised. The final report issued by the Oversight Commissioner in May 2007 concluded that:

> While there has been substantial overall progress, and the institutions of policing are performing their respective roles of delivery, governance and accountability, there are Independent Commission recommendations that remain unfulfilled and there are significant future challenges that place recommendations at risk.[48]

On a number of levels the PSNI has left itself open to the assertion that the ostensible process of change has in fact been merely one of rebranding rather than substantive change. This is particularly apparent in the training arena[49] and in continuing concerns about the extent of collusion with paramilitary groups. In both these areas, further steps have eventually had to be taken to meet the human rights challenge and conflict legacy more fully – but there is still some way to go. The difficulties in taking those steps cast doubt on how firmly the human rights agenda is embedded in the organisation as a whole, and on the government's commitment to deliver transformed policing.

Conclusion

Transitional societies need to recognise the tendency of government and police agencies to keep a tight hold of the policing agenda, for good reasons and bad. The Northern Ireland experience indicates the folly of compartmentalising interdependent issues, and trying to deal with policing change in a vacuum or in the context of a security-led agenda. The principles of human rights can provide a valuable tool to mobilise consensus around changes for the good of police and policed alike, but only where they go to the heart of state governance and are not viewed as pawns to be used for short-term political gain. Where the state clings to a desire to maintain central control of policing and the broader change process the process will not be as holistic as is required to effect a transformation in policing. Mistrust and fear of the community, and a sense that the vagaries and demands of operationalising policing are capable of being understood by the select few, will continue to ensure that, for all the rhetoric, the 'policed' are not viewed as equal partners in the policing project.

Traditional police reform methods shot through with a degree of professionalisation/managerialism will never suffice to legitimise policing in transitional societies. Where the rule of law has been badly damaged, the conditions for its very existence, in any transitional society, need to be carefully crafted[50] and cannot be assumed. However, in Northern Ireland, as elsewhere, there remains a lingering denial of the extent of change necessary to bridge the police/policing gap. Change to the extent demanded by 'others' would require deconstruction of dearly held truths and assumptions and contribute to further fluidity and uncertainty in power relations.

To avoid this, government has deliberately chosen to 'compartmentalise' issues,[51] narrowing the focus to deal in micro-management rather than look at the big picture. All this has contributed to a climate of 'false change'[52] – a range of scenarios which appear on a surface level to be dynamic and vibrant yet which miss the point that what is needed is not merely to reform a state police institution but to transform the experience of policing for police and policed alike. The entire focus is on 'building for the future' without realising that a past not properly laid to rest will provide a very unsteady foundation for the new project.

While these issues are not satisfactorily addressed the conflict will continue to be fought out on another plane. Difficulties in the policing change process symbolise and reflect what has inhibited change for many years at a broader political level. Engaging courageously with the full gamut of challenges in the policing arena may help unblock some of the resistance still being experienced in the broader peace process. At base, this means dealing with the legacy of conflict rather than trying to avoid what inevitably will demand attention. This is hard, but not impossible, and requires a fuller degree of co-operation and candour from all the concerned parties than we have witnessed to date. Only in beginning to speak frankly about 'the war' can we really hope to achieve societal consensus on what the conflict has been about and finally put the appropriate mechanisms and processes in place to ultimately end it.

Notes

1　Agreement Reached in the Multi-party Negotiations, 10 April 1998, available at www.nio.gov.uk/issues/agreelinks/agreement.htm (hereafter, the Good Friday Agreement).
2　Throughout this chapter reference will be made to 'police' and 'policing'. The two terms are used deliberately and are not interchangeable. 'Police' refers specifically to the police organisation – in this case the RUC/PSNI. 'Policing' refers to a much broader construction of the tasks and roles involved in creating and keeping individuals and communities safe, some of which may be carried out by police, others of which will not, and should not, be.
3　A steady catalogue of wrongdoing by state actors has formed the basis of concerns from a range of bodies and individuals, internationally and domestically. For instance, the use of lethal force by the security forces in disputed circumstances has received much attention over the years. See, for example, Fionnuala Ní Aoláin, *The Politics of Force: Conflict Management and State Violence in Northern Ireland* (Belfast: Blackstaff Press, 2000), which provides evidence of multiple failures to adequately investigate or prosecute in such cases. The extent of collusion by members of the security forces with loyalist and republican paramilitaries has not yet been fully acknowledged or acted upon. See statement of Stevens 3, 19 April 2003 (full report not published); also Operation Ballast Report of Police Ombudswoman for Northern Ireland, 22 January 2007, available at www.policeombudsman. org/publicationsuploads/BALLAST%20PUBLIC%20STATEMENT%2022-01-07%20FINAL%20VERSION.pdf). Statistics on the differential deployment of plastic bullets against the Catholic/nationalist/republican population and on the thousands of people arrested over the years under successive 'Emergency Provisions' and 'Prevention of Terrorism' Acts, held without access to a lawyer or their family for up to forty-eight hours and, in the vast majority of cases, released without charge after up to seven days in detention, attest to oppressive and partisan policing over many years. Criticisms by international bodies such as the United Nations Human Rights Committee and the European Committee for the Prevention of Torture on conditions in 'holding centres' such as Castlereagh in east Belfast again raise issues around

policing in an 'emergency' when that emergency is the norm. Reports by non-governmental organisations such as Amnesty International, Human Rights Watch, British Irish Rights Watch, the Pat Finucane Centre and the Committee on the Administration of Justice (CAJ) all highlight how accountable and impartial policing has suffered in the government's 'fight against terrorism' and how, rather than solve the problem, this exacerbated the situation, fed a culture of repression and created more volunteers for republican paramilitarism. Various judgements of the European Court of Human Rights – for instance, Murray *v*. UK (1996) 22 EHRR 29, McCann *v*. UK (1995) 21 EHRR, Jordan *v*. UK (2001) 37 EHRR 2 and Finucane *v*. UK (2003) 37 EHRR 656 – are further testament to the breach of key aspects of the right to life, abuses in detention and the denial of the right to a fair trial, among other things.

4 The RUC's role as the 'armed wing of unionism' became particularly apparent in the policing of the civil rights movement in the 1960s and throughout the subsequent years of violent conflict. On one hand, the RUC may legitimately be viewed as merely operating under legislation and government policy that the force itself did not design, leaving it very much a tool in the hands of its political masters. There is also evidence that this legislation and these policies were wholeheartedly embraced and lobbied for at senior levels within the organisation throughout this period to the extent that police recommendations as to the need for further powers were generally given precedence over any calls for the tempering or dismantling of the 'emergency' regime. See K. Boyle and T. Hadden, *Northern Ireland: The Choice* (London: Penguin, 1994).

5 The Stormont government over many decades operated a policy of discrimination against Catholics with a view to maintaining Protestant ascendancy. See, for example, the report of the Cameron Commission in this regard. Under Direct Rule from Westminster the RUC's state security function, coupled with extensive powers accorded by successive Emergency Provisions Acts (EPAs) and Prevention of Terrorism Acts (PTAs), together with a lack of proper accountability mechanisms, ensured that policing continued to be highly politicised.

6 Although increasingly, and particularly from 1985 onward, working-class loyalist communities became more and more alienated from the police and experienced much of what had been problematic for Catholics, nationalists and republicans over the years. The extent of the breakdown of trust between police and loyalists has been evidenced very starkly by public disorder, e.g. in September 2005.

7 By the late 1990s, when the Independent Commission on Policing (the Patten Commission) published its report on future policing arrangements for Northern Ireland, 92 per cent of the force was drawn solely from the Protestant tradition, the majority community (57 per cent) which has historically favoured Northern Ireland's status as part of the United Kingdom. Census figures for Northern Ireland (2001) report that while 14 per cent of

the population do not declare a religion, the remainder of the population reflect a 53:47 ratio of Protestant to Catholic.

8 Rather than hold agents of the state effectively to account, successive governments have denied or ignored much wrongdoing and instead allowed division to fester and grow. This failure in the proper administration of justice allowed police officers to be set up as 'legitimate targets' for those with a grievance against the state or the organisation. The stress and danger of being in such a position, coupled with the broad powers permitted under emergency law, at the same time fuelled the mistrust that led to human rights abuses occurring and recurring. Meanwhile, those who criticised state or police action in this regard were dismissed and vilified as dangerous subversives. See Kieran McEvoy and John Morison, 'Beyond the "constitutional moment": law, transition, and peacemaking in Northern Ireland', *Fordham International Law Journal* 26 (2003), pp. 961–95, on the dangers of providing secureaucratic responses to conflict management.

9 Sir John Wheeler, Minister of Security at the NIO, in his speech to the annual conference of the Police Federation in the Europa Hotel, Belfast, on 4 June 1996, asserted that 'one of the most distasteful consequences of the ceasefires was the poking and prodding at the police service.'

10 This and the loyalist ceasefires were later reinstated, and remained in place at the time the Patten Commission reported in 1999.

11 Progressive Unionist Party Submission to the Northern Ireland Office on Policing and Related Matters (1995).

12 The initial police decision to ban an Orange Order parade through the nationalist Garvaghy Road district of the mainly unionist town of Portadown in July 1996 was met with loyalist protests that proved so alarming that the decision was reversed and the march pushed through. This sparked violent confrontations between nationalists and the security forces (see Misrule of Law, CAJ and documentation put together by the Pat Finucane Centre, 1996). The Parades Commission, established in 1998, has responsibility for deciding on the legality and route of marches, which at least now means that police are not left to make their own decisions.

13 Good Friday Agreement, Cmnd 3883 (Belfast: HMSO, 1998), p. 22.

14 See M. O'Rawe and L. Moore, *Human Rights on Duty: Principles for Better Policing – International Lessons for Northern Ireland* (Belfast: CAJ, 1997).

15 For the full terms of reference see appendix 1 to the Patten Report, *supra*, note 1.

16 For instance, the review conducted by the Police Authority for Northern Ireland in 1994.

17 In part this stemmed from their mandate to find means of ensuring widespread community support for policing arrangements (Good Friday Agreement, at 23).

18 This built on its own proposals outlined in the 1994 discussion document *Policing in the Community*.

19 See *A Police Ombudsman for Northern Ireland* (London: HMSO, 1997).

20 *A New Beginning for Policing in Northern Ireland* (the Patten Report) at para. 4.1.
21 Patten Report at 3, para. 1.5.
22 *Ibid.* at 5, para. 1.8.
23 *Ibid.* at 6, para. 1.10, states, 'We have not tried to balance what may be politically acceptable to this group against what is reckoned to be acceptable to that.' The commission clearly sensed that this would unravel the whole carefully crafted package.
24 The RUC officially changed its name to the Police Service of Northern Ireland (PSNI) in November 2001, though it formally retains the appellation RUC in its 'title deeds'.
25 This mirrors what happened with the London Metropolitan Police following the MacPherson Inquiry into the racist murder of the young black man Stephen Lawrence.
26 The Policing Board focused on holding an organisation to account, rather than using a policing budget in a much broader way, with the RUC/PSNI being only one aspect of providing a policing service. As Patten stated, 'The title "Policing Board" is deliberate. We see the role of the new body as going beyond the supervision of the police service itself, extending to the wider issues of policing and the contributions that people and organisations other than the police can make towards public safety' (Patten Report at 29, para. 6.10).
27 Maurice Hayes, *A Police Ombudsman for Northern Ireland?* (Belfast: Stationery Office, 1997). The Ombudsoffice was envisaged as a wholly independent investigatory body for dealing with complaints against the police. These findings were fully endorsed by the Patten Commission: 'this Commission as a whole fully aligns itself with Dr Hayes's recommendations and believes that a fully independent Ombudsman operating as he envisaged in his report should be a most effective mechanism for holding the police accountable to the law' (Patten Report at 37, para. 6.41). The commission further called for 'full implementation of his report'. Given that legislation had already been passed to establish the office, this must be taken as signalling that the Police (Northern Ireland) Act 1998 did not fully implement Hayes as promised. The powers of the Ombudswoman have proved a key site of contention in terms of the push to have Patten fully implemented, and further legislative provisions were enacted in this regard in 2003 following talks at Weston Park
28 See, for instance, Peter Mandelson, MP, statement to the House of Commons during the second reading of the Police (Northern Ireland) Bill 2000, 29 June 2002.
29 Although the SDLP did eventually take their seats on the Policing Board, Sinn Féin agreed to do so only at its 2007 *ard fheis* (annual conference). This is in the context of undertakings to devolve criminal justice and policing responsibility from Westminster to the Northern Ireland Assembly and, more controversially, 'security' policing responsibility being transferred to

MI5, thus taking these issues beyond the remit of post-Patten accountability structures such as the Policing Board and the Police Ombudsoffice.

30 This plan was revised after much lobbying in August 2001 but several problems identified in the first draft by human rights organisations, like the CAJ, were not resolved before reissuing.

31 Patten Report, at para. 19.4.

32 Constantine is a North American with substantial police experience behind him.

33 This was imparted during an initial meeting with the CAJ soon after his appointment.

34 Oversight Commissioner, *Overseeing the Proposed Revision of the Policing Service in Northern Ireland*, 12 September 2001.

35 Hugh Orde, speech at the SDLP conference on the Future of Policing, Wellington Park Hotel, Belfast, March 2003.

36 Following a high-water mark of six women on the second Policing Board, the new board announced in May 2007 has four women among its nineteen members, and party political affiliation continues to appear as no bar to taking up a place as an 'independent' member. The DPPs have had a more balanced gender composition since their establishment.

37 See CAJ Commentary on the Policing Board (2004).

38 See www.nipolicingboard.org.uk.

39 See Mary O'Rawe and Linda Moore, 'Police complaints in Northern Ireland: leaving the past behind?' in A. J. Goldsmith and C. Lewis (eds), *Civilian Oversight of Policing: Governance, Democracy and Human Rights* (Oxford: Hart, 2000), for a more detailed discussion of previous government policy to 'apply British solutions to Northern Irish problems'.

40 Especially as a number of staff simply transferred from the old ICPC to the supposedly 'all new' Ombudsoffice.

41 Dated 12 December 2001.

42 Garda handling of the case has also come in for criticism in terms of whether they had intelligence that was neither handed over to the RUC nor otherwise acted upon prior to the bombing. The Gardaí are beyond the scope of this chapter but clearly have their own questions to answer on a range of fronts – not least, things done and not done in the name of state security.

43 Now legislated for as District Policing Partnerships (DPPS) Police (Northern Ireland) Act 2000.

44 See Jonathan McCambridge, 'Policing farce goes on', *Belfast Telegraph*, 15 June 2006, p. 1.

45 Report 16, June 2006, available at www.oversightcommissioner.org/reports/default.asp?page=reports.

46 Figures in respect of religious composition and gender taken from Written Ministerial Statement of Paul Goggins to Parliament, 5 March 2008 and the NI Policing Board Gender Action Plan 2008 at 2 respectively. The percentage of civilian rather than uniformed Catholics in the police work force has increased only 3 per cent since 1999, to 15.5 per cent in January 2006, and

evidence suggests a disproportionate attrition rate for Catholics leaving the PSNI in the period 2001–06.

47 Although a Historical Enquiries Team has been set up to reinvestigate where possible over 2,000 unsolved conflict-related murders, there are concerns about how effective this process will be in revealing the full truth, particularly about murders by members of the security forces. This does, however, provide an example of how eventually the past comes knocking and the door has to be answered. This is evidenced too in the recommendations by the Cory Report in 2004 to establish public inquiries into a number of controversial killings, though these too have been dogged by continued obfuscation and controversy. A debate on other truth recovery processes and mechanisms is continuing to impact on the broader society and on the peace-building project more generally, with the Eames/Bradley process its most recent official incarnation.

48 19th Report of The Oversight Commissioner, 31 May 2007, available at www.oversightcommissioner.org/reports.

49 See M. O'Rawe, 'Human rights and police training in transitional societies: exporting the lessons from Northern Ireland', *Human Rights Quarterly* 27:3 (2005), pp. 943–68.

50 As succinctly stated on a banner on the road into the nationalist village of Toomebridge, 'Where those who make the law break the law in the name of the law, there is no law.'

51 For example, policing, emergency legislation and the criminal justice process were parcelled out to three separate bodies, which then made a virtue of not consulting each other or sharing their findings. See Review of the Criminal Justice System in Northern Ireland (March 2000), available at www.nio.gov.uk.

52 See Angela Hegarty, 'The government of memory: public inquiries and the limits of justice in Northern Ireland', *Fordham International Law Journal* 26 (2003), pp. 1148–92, for a discussion of this phenomenon in respect of the Bloody Sunday tribunal.

Part II
Social identities

7

Religious change and persistence

Claire Mitchell

Northern Ireland is still a distinctly religious society. Whether one comes from the city or the country, is a Catholic or a Protestant, lives in a housing estate or a tree-lined suburban avenue, religious symbols and messages are all around. Churches, shrines, gospel halls, statues, religious posters, signs pinned to trees and religiously themed murals pepper the public landscape. Public buildings and institutions such as schools and village halls display religious images and hold religious events. Inside houses, religious objects – Bibles, crucifixes, religious paintings, memory cards, framed Bible verses – are collected, displayed and kept in drawers. Orange parades, children's Bible camps, novenas and pilgrimages structure the annual calendar of events for many people.

Of course, a visitor to Northern Ireland may miss these things. It is possible to keep to the main shopping areas, converse with non-religious Northern Irish people, absorb the growing arts scene in Belfast and leave with the impression that Northern Ireland has now become a secular society. Many students living in south Belfast may experience this other Northern Ireland. People who have grown up in Northern Ireland may not notice the religious symbols and ideas that are embedded in everyday life. After all, people in Northern Ireland do not much like to talk about their religion outside close circles of friends, if at all. Along with politics, religion is a sensitive topic.

However, any sociologist, anthropologist, historian or political scientist seeking to understand society in Northern Ireland will sooner or later be confronted with these religious realities. Anyone who observes the physical environment, talks to people who live in Northern Ireland, looks around their homes, reads the region's literature, poetry and newspapers, listens carefully to the language used by politicians and analyses the media portrayal of events and the actors involved, will soon detect religious overtones. This is the case for both Catholics and Protestants, and even sometimes those who say they have no religion. Of course, religion is not important for Catholics and Protestants in exactly the same way.

Nor is religion the same as it was even in the recent past. The first question that this chapter asks therefore is: how religious is contemporary Northern Irish society, and in what ways? It answers mainly by looking at survey data about religious practice and belief.

But there is much more to say about religion in Northern Ireland than just examining how many people go to church and believe in God. To fully understand the importance of religion we must look to the roles it plays in social and political life. From the Catholic Church's involvement in education to the Protestant preachers active in politics, religion is intimately tangled up with how Northern Ireland is organised. Some have argued that this has a very significant impact on community relations and conflict.[1] On the other hand, others maintain that religion is irrelevant to conflict: it only provides the labels of identity, and these labels really mark out competing *ethnic* groups.[2] The chapter therefore asks to what extent religion is involved in social and political life in Northern Ireland? Finally, it asks whether social divisions really have anything to do with religion? Both these questions explore what Northern Ireland was like during violent conflict, and whether the situation is any different 'after the troubles'.

How religious is contemporary Northern Irish society, and in what ways?

While the pattern of religious change in Northern Ireland is complex and varied, the region clearly continues to exhibit high levels of religiosity. First of all, we can look at religious affiliations and see that only 14 per cent of the population of Northern Ireland claim to have 'no religion'. Given that less than 1 per cent of the population claim to be members of minority religions, this leaves almost 86 per cent identifying as Catholics or Protestants. Of these, 40 per cent are Catholics and 46 per cent are Protestants.[3]

But religious identity is not just about ticking a box designated 'Protestant' or 'Catholic' in the census. After all, individuals may use religious labels but have no active form of belief or practice. However, religion is also frequently practised in Northern Ireland. This becomes apparent when we examine levels of church attendance, which indicate that 54 per cent of people go to church regularly.[4] The group with the lowest attendance is those aged eighteen to twenty-four, only 20 per cent of whom attend weekly. In contrast, 69 per cent of those over sixty-five years old attend weekly. Clearly, then, there is a generational decline in attendance. Overall, however, Northern Ireland has the fourth highest church attendance out of thirty-three western and eastern European countries surveyed in 2004.[5]

Amongst Catholics, church attendance has dropped considerably since

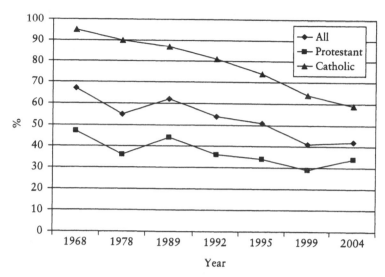

Figure 7.1 Trends in weekly church attendance rates, 1968–2003
Source: Adapted from T. Fahey et al., 2005. See Note 5.

1968, when 95 per cent went to mass every week (see Figure 7.1). However, Catholics are still the most frequent church attenders in Northern Ireland. In 2005, 68 per cent of Catholics attended mass regularly, with 56 per cent of this group going once a week or more.[6] Compared with other European societies, this is an extremely high level of churchgoing. Fewer Protestants, 51 per cent, attend church regularly, with 38 per cent of this group going once a week or more. The number of Protestant churchgoers fell only a little over the period of the conflict. In 1968, 46 per cent of Protestants attended weekly.[7] Overall, in the present, only 14 per cent of Protestants and 6 per cent of Catholics never attend church at all.

There are also indications churchgoing is strong among the under-eighteens, due in no small part to continuing parental compulsion. Sixty-five per cent of teenagers between the ages of fifteen and seventeen surveyed in 2003 claim to attend religious services regularly (once a month or more), and 44 per cent at least weekly.[8] Seventy-three per cent of Catholic teenagers and 54 per cent of Protestant teenagers are regular attenders, with 52 per cent and 34 per cent respectively attending at least weekly. Therefore it would appear that, whilst religious practices are lowest amongst young adults between eighteen and twenty-four, before the age of eighteen religion remains an important aspect of socialisation. This is important because whilst people may reject religious beliefs and practices in young adulthood, they sometimes return to the ideas of their upbringing later in life.

Table 7.1 Religious beliefs

Belief in ...	Protestants	Catholics	No religion	Total
God[a]	77	83	37	76
Heaven	75	87	20	75
Hell	64	70	22	62
Miracles	46	73	11	53
Regular prayer	63	84	25	67

Source: Northern Ireland Life and Times Survey, 1998
Note: [a] These figures include those who answered they have no doubt that
God exists (51%) and those who have doubts but believe (25%). Other
options include 'Believe sometimes' (10%), 'Do not believe in a personal God'
(6%) 'Do not know if there is a God' (4%), and 'Do not believe in God' (4%).
A similar question format is used for belief in heaven, hell and miracles.

People in Northern Ireland also have high levels of religious belief (see
Table 7.1). About three-quarters of the population believe in God, whilst
only 4 per cent of people say they do not believe in God at all. Three-
quarters of people in the region believe in heaven. Slightly fewer, 62 per
cent, believe in hell and 53 per cent in miracles. But, still, these levels of
belief are high overall. Catholics exhibit somewhat higher levels of religious belief than Protestants. It is interesting to note that 37 per cent of
those who say they have 'no religion' actually believe in God and a further
quarter pray regularly. This subgroup reflects what Davie has termed
'believing without belonging'.[9] This is where people continue to hold religious beliefs long after active religious participation such as churchgoing
has stopped. Davie argues that 'believing without belonging' is the dominant characteristic of British religiosity. In Northern Ireland many more
people attend church than in other parts of the United Kingdom, but certainly the 'no religion' believers can be described in Davie's terms.

It is important to note that stated religious beliefs in surveys do not tell
us much about how certain beliefs are held or what types of belief they
are. For example, if a Catholic woman says she believes in God and in
heaven, she may also believe in horoscopes, read self-help books, be
interested in Buddhism and she may not believe that the Pope is infalli-
ble or that the Catholic Church is the 'one true Church'. This is sometimes called 'cafeteria Catholicism', or 'religion *à la carte*' – where
individuals mix and match ideas, beliefs and practices to form personal
religions.[10] Whilst, historically, mainstream religions have often incorporated aspects of local culture and practices, it is certain that Catholics
in Northern Ireland are now less orthodox than in the past. Inglis notes
the decline in Catholics attending confession and argues that individual

conscience is becoming more important than traditional Catholic doctrine.[11] As Boal *et al.* note, younger and more educated Catholics are more religiously liberal than their elders. So, although Catholicism is still strong in Northern Ireland, individual Catholics are slowly becoming more individualised and less orthodox in their beliefs.[12]

Among Protestants there are somewhat different patterns of change. Boal *et al.* found that half of Belfast's Protestant churchgoers were religiously conservative, and only a quarter could be classed as liberal.[13] To be conservative, one had to agree that the Bible was the inspired word of God and that one had to have had a conversion experience. Whilst younger Catholics were liberalising, Boal *et al.* found that younger churchgoing Protestants were no more liberal than their elders. Although fewer young Protestants overall attend church than those in older age groups, and fewer young Protestants attend church than young Catholics, where they *do* attend church, Boal *et al.* suggest, they are slightly more conservative than the older generations.[14]

Conservative Protestants are an interesting religious group in Northern Ireland. These are Protestants who believe in the authority of the Bible, and that people must be 'saved' and enter into a new relationship with Jesus Christ.[15] The conservative Protestant grouping consists of overlapping subgroups of fundamentalist, evangelical and born-again Christians.[16] It is a growing global religion, strong in the United States, Southern and Central America, sub-Saharan Africa and Asia.[17] All three strains of conservative Protestantism have a long-standing following in Northern Ireland and show no signs of secularising.

Thirty-two per cent of the population in Northern Ireland identify as fundamentalist, evangelical or born-again – or as a combination of these.[18] There is some evidence that their numbers are growing, although it is probably safer to say that numbers do not seem to be declining.[19] There are indications that conservative Protestant Churches are picking up members at the expense of main-line Protestant denominations, although there are plenty of conservative Protestants within main-line denominations also.[20] Conservative Protestantism is popular among younger people as well as among older people. Of the 15 per cent of under-thirty-fives who identify most strongly as conservative Protestants, 82 per cent attend church at least weekly.[21] A further interesting feature of conservative Protestants is their distinctive views on morality. Whilst people with no religion and mainstream Protestants are becoming slightly more liberal about divorce, homosexuality and abortion, conservative Protestants have retained a distinctive traditional position.[22] This group flout the assumptions of the secularisation thesis and are a good example of religious persistence in modern societies.

Overall, contemporary Northern Ireland has relatively high levels of religious affiliation, practice and belief. Whilst there have been significant religious changes since the 1960s, Northern Ireland remains one of the most religious regions in the Western world. Among Catholics, individual conscience is becoming more important than traditional Catholic doctrines. Whilst church attendance amongst Catholics is falling, it remains high, unsurprisingly especially among older people. Among mainstream Protestants there has been a decline in membership, but levels of religious belief have remained high. Conservative Protestants are maintaining strong numbers and are carving out an ever more distinctive niche for themselves on account of their high levels of moral conservatism. The 'no religion' grouping has been slowly growing, but has failed to make the dramatic increases that some predicted. So the pattern of religious change is varied and shows much continuity as well as change.

To what extent is religion involved in social and political life in Northern Ireland?

But it is not enough to show that many people in Northern Ireland still attend church and believe in God. Sociologists need to explore whether religion has any *social* significance. After all, it could be that religious beliefs are important for private individuals but do not play any real public role. Sociologists of religion often describe this scenario as religious privatisation, or 'invisible religion'.[23]

In fact in Northern Ireland religion is far from socially invisible. It is deeply entangled with social and political life in a variety of ways. Whilst individuals have their own private faith and beliefs, religion plays key public roles that are difficult to ignore. This takes different forms for Catholics and Protestants. For Catholics, religion derives its social significance from the Church's involvement in public life, and the fact that many Catholics regularly attend church. For Protestants, religion is sometimes more overtly political in that religious leaders are actively involved in unionist party politics. For both Catholics and Protestants, religion structures major aspects of life – not just birth, marriage and death but also where you go to school, your friendship networks, where you live and sometimes where you work. This section explores the entanglement of religion in public life whilst the following section goes on to ask whether social divisions and conflict are *really* about religion at all.

Firstly, it is important to note the extent of social separation by religion in Northern Ireland. Only 5.5 per cent of children overall are educated in 'integrated' schools.[24] This means that an overwhelming majority of children go to schools whose pupils are drawn more or less exclusively from one religious community or the other. Most Catholic children go to schools that are organised and run by the Catholic Council for Maintained Schools (CCMS). Most Protestant children go to state-maintained schools that are not run by the Protestant Churches but which do typically have a distinct religious ethos.

The situation is not as simple as different schools teaching different religious doctrines and specific versions of history. In fact Gallagher found that there is little difference in school curricula.[25] Rather, separate education matters because it constructs a clear social boundary from an early age. And different school ethos gives social divisions certain meanings.[26] Whereas wreaths are laid in Remembrance Day services in Protestant schools and daily assemblies often involve singing traditional Protestant hymns, Catholic schools concentrate on Irish historical commemorations and Catholic religious rituals, and teachers prepare Catholic children for the sacrament of First Communion and Confirmation. Lambkin found in the mid-1990s that children's knowledge of the other communities' religion is weak, and that many religious and historical myths fill in gaps of knowledge about the 'other side'.[27] In fact Lambkin found that schoolchildren thought that religion was very important and, unlike adults, believed that the conflict was caused by religion. As such, segregated education tends to deprive schoolchildren of significant social contact with those of a different religion, and can also add to the perception that the divide is religious in nature.

Who we go to school with often influences who we are friends with. These friendship networks can last long after school years and may have an important influence on relationships throughout a person's life. Even when a neutral space is entered where both Catholics and Protestants are present, such as a university, people will not necessarily engage deeply outside their pre-existing social groups. Even if they do, they often return home to areas that are religiously demarcated. In my experience lecturing on Northern Irish society at Queen's University Belfast I have observed that it can be difficult for local students to have meaningful conversations about religion, politics and identity – often because they do not wish to offend anyone else, or mark themselves out as belonging to one group or the other.

Another offshoot of schooling and friendship networks is choice of partner.[28] People in Northern Ireland tend to be strongly endogamous – to marry within their own group. Writing at the beginning of the troubles, Rose[29] reported that only 5 per cent of marriages were mixed, and this figure remained constant throughout the 1980s and 1990s.[30] More recent survey evidence finds that 12 per cent of partnerships are now between people of differing religious identifications.[31] Put another way, 90 per cent of Catholics and 87 per cent of Protestants have a partner of the same religion. This led Moxon-Brown to argue that in Northern Ireland endogamy is the single most important factor in maintaining group boundaries.[32] Harris also made this point in her study of Ballybeg, where she found that endogamy was at the heart of the community divide because of the importance of kinship ties.[33] Having kinship networks solely within one's own community means that it is often difficult to get to know people from another community well.

Housing patterns exacerbate social separation by religion. On the eve of the outbreak of the recent troubles in 1969 Poole and Boal found that only 32 per cent of the population of Belfast lived in streets that had some degree of mixing between Catholics and Protestants.[34] This figure has since fallen, and in most electoral wards in Belfast fewer than 10 per cent of the inhabitants in a given area belong to the 'other' religion.[35] However, it must be underlined that Belfast is the most segregated part of Northern Ireland.[36] Working-class areas are also more segregated than middle-class areas. Worryingly, residential segregation in the most disadvantaged housing estates in Belfast has continued to increase despite the peace process, and there is a perception that in some of these areas that community relations have worsened.[37] Social contact has often been cut off by the presence of physical barriers such as 'peace' walls that separate one community from another. Hence an individual's experience of religious segregation in Northern Ireland is heavily influenced by social class.

The discussion above outlines the extent of social division defined by religion in Northern Ireland. Whilst people are slowly becoming more open to the idea of mixed marriages, and the middle classes enjoy a degree of mobility, Northern Ireland remains very socially divided along religious lines. But this does not yet tell us what roles *religion itself* actually plays in organising social and political life for Catholics and Protestants. In fact it is unsurprising that, in the context of these social divisions, Churches have ended up catering almost exclusively for one community or the other.

The Catholic Church in particular plays a significant part in structuring social activities for many Catholics. Morrow *et al.*[38] argue that 'in the absence of a State to which many Catholics owe their unconditional allegiance, the Church has become the main institutional organiser'. Alternative networks of business, media, hospitals, sport and, importantly, education were established by Catholics and soon became the focus of an alternative political identity. Indeed, the education system is the most significant source of social involvement for the Catholic

Church. Whilst there are fewer clerical teachers in schools than in the past, the role of the Church in school management remains substantial. Concerns that the religious aspects of education would not be provided adequately for in integrated schools lie in large part behind the Catholic Church's continued insistence on segregated education.[39] In addition to education, the Church continues to be involved in charities such as Trocaire or St Vincent de Paul. It runs preparatory marriage courses and offers marriage guidance and pregnancy counselling. In addition, it is involved in youth work and runs many other social clubs and cultural activities.

Of course, in the 2000s the Church is not the only institution organising social life for Catholics. People are now much less likely to structure their social lives around solely parish activities. For the still large proportion of Mass attenders the Church may only be one of many agencies competing for their loyalty. Having said that, for many Catholics the Church is still the focal point of a sense of community. For example, in interviews I found young Catholics describing the church as a meeting place and Mass as a social occasion. Others described the church as a community centre and talked of priests as social workers.[40] This creates a positive association of the Church with public service and indicates that, whilst individual Catholics may be making up their own minds about their beliefs, the Church can continue to play an important role in creating ideas of Catholic 'community' and belonging.

In contrast to its prominent role in social life, the Catholic Church has not been overly involved in party politics. Its involvement has diminished further since the 1998 Agreement and the decline in violent conflict. No priests are Sinn Féin or SDLP politicians, and the Church is not officially involved in politics. However, as O'Connor once remarked, 'it would be difficult not to notice how nice they are about each other'.[41] Perhaps in order to retain its influence, the Church has always tried to articulate mainstream nationalist political views and has regularly spoken up on behalf of the 'Catholic community'. Members of the clergy, such as Fr Alex Reid, have occasionally been involved in behind-the-scenes negotiations between politicians and paramilitaries. So the Church has been seen as a respectable and trustworthy representative of nationalism. Another example is where clergy were trusted to verify IRA acts of decommissioning weapons. However, the Catholic Church is now much less politicised than at the height of the 'troubles' when priests joined civil rights protests and visited hunger strikers. The politics of peace have meant that the Catholic Church is increasingly taking a political back seat.

The situation is rather different within unionism. Protestant clergy are much more likely to be involved in unionist party politics. The Reverend

Ian Paisley, the Free Presbyterian Church and the Democratic Unionist Party (DUP) are the best-known examples. These two organisations are not synonymous and many individuals belong to one and not the other.[42] However, there is a clear overlap between the organisations. As Bruce[43] points out, in the period between 1972 and1980 64 per cent of DUP activists belonged to the Free Presbyterian Church, and many of the remainder to other conservative Protestant congregations. Many current DUP MLAs belong to Paisley's Free Presbyterian Church, whilst others are members of smaller conservative Protestant denominations such as Elim, Baptist and Free Methodist.[44]

The DUP is also adapting to change in contemporary Northern Ireland, however. It has in recent years tried to present itself as a party with more secular policies, no longer for example having sabbatarianism at the heart of its agenda.[45] Individuals in the DUP clearly acknowledge the limits of the social acceptability of a conservative Protestant message and appear to have initiated something of a PR drive to cut down religious references in the political sphere. However, there are limitations on how far the DUP can transform itself. Current political issues such as same-sex partnerships and adoption rights have seen them assume a strict morally conservative stance. As Smith argues in the context of the United States, evangelicalism easily adapts to political change and engages with whatever issues modernity throws up.[46] Playing down sabbatarianism does not necessarily make the DUP more secular. In fact it would seem likely that members of the DUP will continue to advocate morally and socially conservative policies in the future.

The Orange Order represents another aspect of the public significance of Protestantism. Since its inception in 1795 the Orange Order has been committed to a classic brand of Reformed Protestantism, opposed to biblical error and concerned with promoting scriptural truth. It forbids members to marry a Catholic or attend Catholic religious services. The influence of Orangeism extends beyond its actual membership. From the 1790s to the 1970s, the Order represented an important network in forming the opinions of ordinary Protestants – exerting pressure on senior unionist party officials, formulating opinions at local lodge meetings and then transmitting these to local politicians.[47] By 2005, however, it seemed that the relationship between the Orange Order and the Ulster Unionist Party (UUP) was loosening – the Order severing its link because it felt the UUP was becoming too secular.

However, whilst the Orange Order may have tried in this case to flex its religious muscles, there are indications that its strength is waning. Although the Order claims to have 100,000 members, Jarman estimated that the number had fallen nearer to 40,000 by the late 1990s.[48] Violence and disruption surrounding controversial parades during the late 1990s and 2000s further damaged its popularity. The urban and fairly secular 'blood and thunder' flute band parades are now more popular than the rural and more religious Orange Order parades,[49] and are better known for the proliferation of Buckfast[50] than Bibles.

Protestant Churches have also not been as actively involved in community life as the Catholic Church. Although Protestant clergy often sit on schools' boards of governors and may also be employed to teach religious education, there are few 'Protestant' schools run by Protestant Churches to parallel Catholic educational provision. (An exception is the handful of small Free Presbyterian primary schools.) The Protestant Churches do offer a variety of activities – church choirs, mothers' groups, crèches, Sunday schools and various recreational, sporting and fund-raising activities.[51] There are a variety of para-church organisations, festivals and events that bring especially conservative Protestants together from time to time. However, with more than fifty Protestant denominations in Northern Ireland, these activities have not been important for bringing Protestants together as an imagined community, rather they have been more important within particular congregations or subgroup traditions, for example among 'spirit-filled' charismatics. Indeed, interviews find most Protestants underlining their sense of a lack of overarching religious community.[52]

Finally, an important role that both Catholic and Protestant Churches have played is in providing support for communities in conflict. At the height of political violence, Churches often became involved in the struggles of their members – whether this was praying from the pulpit for those who suffered discrimination,[53] counselling the hunger strikers and their families,[54] denouncing the latest IRA bomb in a sermon or burying the victims of violence in funeral services.[55] This meant that clergy were seen to be at the heart of their community's struggles. Of course, none of the Churches was ever significantly involved in paramilitary politics, and Churches have more often than not promoted peace. Some of the key figures and organisations working for reconciliation in Northern Ireland have been religious. However, working in a conflict-ridden society meant that clergy needed to engage with the reality of violence. When loyalist and republican combatants have been killed, the churches have generally provided religious funerals for them, which created the perception that they were sympathetic to the goals of their organisations.

Of course, as the political climate changes so too does the brief of the clergy. The fewer the victims of violence the less churches are required by their flocks to be a place of sanctuary and the less clergy are expected to address sensitive political issues. This means that by default the Churches are called upon to play less political roles in contemporary Northern Ireland. However, it is much too soon to argue that the Churches are now irrelevant in providing sanctuary and political guidance. For example, a Catholic priest, Fr Aiden Troy, played a crucial role during the Holy Cross School disputes in 2001 and 2002. Father Troy walked every day for three months with 225 schoolgirls to Holy Cross Primary in the Ardoyne, an interface area of Belfast, escorted by the security forces as loyalists tried to block their path. A number of Protestant clergy remain actively engaged with loyalist paramilitaries in the quest for conflict transformation. The low-level conflict that persists in Northern Ireland, along with continuing segregation, means that the churches will probably be called upon to play these mediating roles for some time to come.

The question we asked at the beginning of this section was: to what extent is religion involved in social and political life in Northern Ireland? After examining the evidence, we must conclude that religion in Northern Ireland is not simply privatised or invisible. It continues to have a palpable social and political presence. The religious boundary continues to pervade many areas of life, from schooling to friendships, to marriages and housing. Whilst there is more openness to religious mixing and there are more neutral social spaces, there is also evidence of polarisation in some interface areas. Moreover, the churches in Northern Ireland continue to play important public roles. The Catholic Church is a particularly important part of social organisation, not least in the realm of education. The influence of the Protestant Churches is more publicly visible in party politics, especially in the DUP. In addition, the Churches do still tend to represent and speak up for their members in public life. However, their involvement in politics is less intense in the present because of the changing political situation. Although communities are still polarised, a reduction in violence and the number of victims as well as progress on fundamental issues such as civil rights have meant that there is less immediacy in the Churches' involvement in politics.

Do social divisions really have anything to do with religion?

So far we have established that people in Northern Ireland are still rather religious, and that religion continues to be publicly important. But there is still a piece of the jigsaw missing. We have not yet explored whether conflict in Northern Ireland was ever really about religion, and whether social divisions in the present have any religious components. Is it possible that religion could be publicly important without being a factor in conflict? Plenty of other factors shape social life and division in Northern Ireland. It could be argued that social class has a much greater impact on people's opportunities and experiences than does religion.[56] Indeed, most of the violent conflict and now low-level violence is based in the least well-off parts of Northern Ireland – areas that also happen to have the lowest levels of church attendance. Others have argued that ethno-nationalism is the most significant social division, and that Protestants and Catholics are in dispute because of territory and political identity.[57]

Certainly, social divisions in Northern Ireland are not *primarily* about religion. Divisions are based on overlapping political, cultural and economic as well as religious factors. But for many years religion was viewed only as a marker of ethnic differences.[58] Partially this was because academics wanted to present the conflict in Northern Ireland as a thoroughly modern one. Very often observers outside Northern Ireland had characterised the conflict as a holy war, with two communities stuck in the past, and social scientists wanted to challenge this stereotype. It was also a time when the secularisation thesis was popular in the sociology of religion, and the focus was on the *decline* of religion's social significance.[59] However, with Islam and evangelicalism growing in the modern world, and actively engaging in politics, the climate is very different today and many commentators have begun to reassess what roles religion may have played in conflict, as well as in contemporary Northern Ireland.[60] This literature concentrates on the ways that religion helps construct identities for Catholics and Protestants in a divided society.

Firstly, religious practices have been used to construct a sense of community in Northern Ireland. This has been particularly important for Catholics, for whom, as we have seen, the level of religious attendance is higher. Even if many Catholics do not have orthodox religious beliefs, there is a strong tendency to use the Church to foster communal identity. For example, one young Catholic couple, the Murphys, described to me their concerns over raising their children in the Catholic Church. Neither of them attends church, and they do not particularly like traditional Catholic doctrine. In fact they describe their religion as 'Murphyism', based on their own questions and ideas. However, they also say that they would prefer their children to grow up with a sense of Catholic identity, so they know where they belong in Northern Ireland. In order to create this Catholic identity the parents send their children to a Catholic school, where they will take the holy sacraments of First Communion and Confirmation. Furthermore, they say that they will probably start to bring their children to church to familiarise them with these rituals.

One interpretation of the Murphys' story is that they are simply using religion to mark out a secular ethnic identity. However, there is much more to it than that. To provide the children with a Catholic Irish identity, Church structures are utilised. The children will become familiar with Catholic religious doctrine, symbolism and ritual. When they attend church to familiarise themselves with the ceremonies they will come into contact with religious teaching and customs. Whilst the parents and children may not agree with everything they hear or see, ritual creates an atmosphere where people may feel bonded to one another. They also help define who is not part of the group – in other words, who are Protestants. Moreover, these different social spaces are saturated with religious ideas and images that can often be used to ascribe values or qualities to the in-group and the out-group. In this way we can see how religious practices in Northern Ireland can help reproduce social divisions, rather than transform them. Here, religion is much more significant than a mere boundary marker. It is also more significant for Catholics than for Protestants. This is due to both the tendency of Protestants to attend church less frequently and the fragmentation between different Protestant denominations.

Where religion is more important for constructing a sense of identity and community for Protestants is through religious beliefs and religious ideas. Sometimes religious beliefs can help individuals understand their own place in society and social change. They may provide comfort, explanation, justification, and, for those who believe the Bible to be true, religious beliefs can provide guidelines for social action. It is not the case, however, as Hickey argues, that theological teachings completely dictate the actions of believers.[61] Rather, individuals can creatively and strategically adapt beliefs in line with wider political change. In fact we find that religious beliefs are just as politically significant after the 1998 Agreement as they were during violent conflict, but in somewhat different ways.

An example of the relationship between religious beliefs and politics, and religion's adaptation to change, is dispensationalist 'end times' theology. Many conservative Protestants in Northern Ireland believe that the biblical book of Revelation predicts the sequence of events leading to the end of the world. It predicts that conditions will worsen for Bible believers, who will face persecution and be challenged by the antichrist. Some conservative Protestants believe that recent political changes in Northern Ireland, in particular the Good Friday Agreement, are 'a sign of the times' that indicates the imminent second coming of Christ. Generally this has led to increased emphasis on private spirituality and gaining conversions, and has not yet been channelled politically.[62] It provides perhaps a telling example of how religious beliefs can help shape identities and social relations.

Another doctrine that has been politically influential in Northern Ireland is anti-Catholicism. Anti-Catholicism takes many theological forms, and has a variety of political manifestations, from encouraging strong unionist opposition to a united Ireland to encouraging withdrawal from the public sphere.[63] In a strong form, anti-Catholicism combines teachings that popery enslaves its followers, that it is superstitious, conformist and opposed to individual freedom. In Protestantism salvation is achieved through faith alone, which means that there is a relationship between the individual and God. Thus traditional Protestant theology holds that 'superstitions', such as prayers to Mary and the saints, insignia and medals, as well as the role of priests as intermediaries with the divine, are not only a waste of time but are idolatrous. Ideas that Catholicism is fundamentally wrong, and that individual Catholics are deluded at best or damned at worst, have informed Ulster Protestant identity for centuries, including Ian Paisley and his followers today.

But one does not have to be a strict Protestant believer for anti-Catholic ideas to be influential in explaining social relations in Northern Ireland. It depends on an individual's socialisation. Those who gained familiarity with teaching on the perils of Catholicism as children can often find anti-Catholic gut feelings difficult to discard. For example, otherwise secular Protestant interviewees can be found describing Protestantism as a personal choice, a way of life and a source of freedom, as opposed to Catholicism which they describe as a strict, brutal and indoctrinating.[64] Whilst these ideas are not strictly speaking theological, they are informed by religious doctrines that have filtered through into commonsense understandings of social life in Northern Ireland. These ideas often create stereotypes of Protestants as free and Catholics as unfree, which in turn influences the way people think about and act towards each other. This can feed back into social relations.

Religious ideas are not a significant resource for the construction of Catholic identity. There are some connections between republicanism and millenarianism[65] and a religious resonance to concepts of martyrdom, sacrifice and redemption that run through nationalist and republican history. But overall, because Catholicism is a ritually and liturgically oriented faith, there is less personal familiarity with theology among Catholics. Interestingly, Catholic identity is often framed as a negation of fervent religion, contrasting laid-back Catholic normality with Protestant inflexibility and fundamentalism. Interviews find Catholics presenting Protestant religion as aggressive, noisy and extreme, in contrast with a self-presentation of Catholics as open and tolerant.[66] In this way 'anti-Protestantism' is a much more subtle phenomenon than anti-Catholicism, lacking the latter's stark religio-political language and imagery. But that is exactly the point. Anti-Protestantism may be described as the construction of boundaries around humility versus arrogance, openness versus intolerance, which point to Protestants as 'worse' than Catholics. This often leads to a stereotype of the Protestant group being formed in a way that does not distinguish between members. Indeed, these mutual stereotypes persist just as strongly in contemporary Northern Ireland as they did during violent conflict, and show little immediate sign of transformation.

In these ways, religion plays an important role in constituting social divisions in Northern Ireland, rather than simply just marking them out. Religion can give meanings to Protestant and Catholic identities and to the boundary. While, of course, conflict has not been in the past, and is not now, primarily about religion, religion carries significant, and often different, social meanings for both Protestants and Catholics. Religious rituals, beliefs and ideas often help individuals identify and attribute value to differing social groups. Engaging in religious practices creates a separate social space for each group, and also generates meanings of what it is to belong to that group, as opposed to the other group. These meanings are of course not always theological – although sometimes they are – but are often based on religious practices and ideas that are derived from religious doctrine. As such, religion is an essential part of identification processes in contemporary Northern Ireland and it is at least as much about the social as about the spiritual.

Conclusion

Individuals in Northern Ireland continually adapt their religious beliefs and practices to a changing social and political climate. At the same time, the social and political climate in Northern Ireland is partially constructed from religious resources. Some social groups, in particular Catholics, are becoming more individualised in their expression of faith. But, for many, the Catholic Church is still a focal point for the imagination of identity, the practice of community and for socialisation. Nationalist politicians are still reluctant to offend the Church, which remains a powerful social actor. However, the Catholic Church has lost some of the political influence it had during conflict, where it could speak up for the views of its 'community' and publicly underline its influence. Religious ideas also continue to be a significant resource for the construction of identity, even for some non-churchgoing Protestants. The DUP now dominates unionist politics and retains a distinctive religious ethos. This ethos is increasingly oriented towards moral conservatism, rather than anti-Romanism, which both reflects the views of, and tries to provide leadership to, a numerically important group of conservative Protestants.

Some of these religious adaptations reflect global religious trends – such as the morally traditional views of conservative Protestants, and individualisation among Catholics. Other changes show religion adapting to specific social and political developments in Northern Ireland – such as the interpretation of the 1998 Agreement as a sign of the 'end times'. What has remained constant, however, is the continuing identification of Catholics by Protestants, and Protestants by Catholics, as the primary social 'other' to define themselves against. This is perpetuated by entrenched religious segregation in all stages of the life cycle, as well as continuing political conflict and low-level violence that fuel suspicion of the other group and make social stereotypes difficult to transform. For these reasons, religion is likely to form an important dimension of social relations in Northern Ireland for the foreseeable future.

Notes

1 D. Morrow, D. Birrell, J.Greer and T. O'Keefe, *The Churches and Inter-community Relationships* (Coleraine: Centre for the Study of Conflict, 1991); J. Fulton, *The Tragedy of Belief: Division, Politics, and Religion in Ireland* (Oxford: Clarendon Press, 1991); J. Fulton, 'Religion and enmity in Northern Ireland: institutions and relational beliefs', *Social Compass* 49:2 (2002), pp. 189–202.

2 J. McGarry and B. O'Leary, *Explaining Northern Ireland* (Oxford: Blackwell, 1995).

3 Northern Ireland Census of Population, 2001. Question marks remain over the reliability of census data in Northern Ireland. In the 1981 census there were significant amounts of non-co-operation from nationalists and republicans, although it is not possible to say how far it skewed the figures. Whilst tensions around the census have eased, anecdotal evidence suggests a significant number of people continue to refuse to give their religious affiliation. In the present period this may be the case for some Protestants, perhaps fearing 'reverse discrimination'.

4 Monthly or two to three times a month. Northern Ireland Life and Times Survey (NILTS), 2005. These data are available at www.ark.ac.uk/nilt/.

5 T. Fahey, B. C. Hayes and R. Sinnott, *Conflict and Consensus: A Study of Attitudes and Values in the Republic of Ireland and Northern Ireland* (Dublin: Institute of Public Administration, 2005), pp. 45–6.

6 NILTS, 2005.

7 R. Rose, *Governing without Consensus* (London: Faber, 1971).

8 Young Northern Ireland Life and Times Survey (YNILTS), 2003. These data are available at www.ark.ac.uk/nilt/.

9 G. Davie, *Religion in Britain since 1945: Believing without Belonging* (Oxford: Blackwell, 1994).

10 R. W. Bibby, *Fragmented Gods: The Poverty and Potential of Religious Growth in Canada* (Toronto: Irwin, 1987), pp. 62–85.

11 T. Inglis, *Moral Monopoly: The Rise and Fall of the Catholic Church in modern Ireland*, second edition (Dublin: University College Dublin Press, 1998).

12 F. Boal, M. Keane and D. Livingstone, *Them and Us? Attitudinal Variation among Churchgoers in Belfast* (Belfast: Institute of Irish Studies, Queen's University Belfast, 1997).

13 *Ibid.*

14 *Ibid.*

15 Interestingly, 6 per cent of Catholics identify as evangelicals, 3 per cent as born again and 8 per cent as fundamentalist. (These are sometimes overlapping identifications.) The evangelical and born-again identifications probably tap into the small but significant Catholic charismatic renewal movement in Northern Ireland, whilst the slightly higher number of fundamentalist Catholics is more likely to reflect a conservative, traditional Catholicism. (NILTS, 2004.)

16 Pentecostalists and charismatics are often included as subgroup variations. For an overview of the definition and measurement of conservative Protestant subgroups see R. L. Woodberry and C. Smith, 'Fundamentalism *et al.*: conservative Protestants in America', *Annual Review of Sociology* 24 (1998), pp. 25–56.

17 D. Martin 'The evangelical Protestant upsurge and its political implications', in P. L. Berger (ed.), *The Desecularisation of the World* (Washington DC: Ethics and Public Policy Center, 1999), pp. 37–50.

18 In addition to identifying as Protestant and Christian, 6 per cent identify as born-again only, 3 per cent as evangelical only and 3 per cent as fundamentalist only. Nine per cent identify as born-again and evangelical, whilst a further 8 per cent identify as born-again, evangelical and fundamentalist. None is both evangelical and fundamentalist without identifying also as born again. Interestingly, a further 3 per cent identify as Protestant and fundamentalist but do not identify themselves as Christians. (NILTS, 2004.)

19 J. D. Brewer, 'Are there any Christians in Northern Ireland?' in A. M. Gray, K. Lloyd, P. Devine, G. Robinson and D. Heenan (eds), *Social Attitudes in Northern Ireland: The Eighth Report* (London: Pluto Press, 2003), pp. 22–38.

20 *Ibid.*

21 This 15 per cent includes those who identify as born again, evangelical and fundamentalist, and as born again and evangelical. A further 9 per cent of the under-thirty-fives identify with one of these labels. Of these, the born-agains display the highest levels of religiosity and the fundamentalists are the least religiously observant. (NILTS, 2004.)

22 C. Mitchell and J. Tilley, 'The moral minority: evangelical Protestants in Northern Ireland and their voting behaviour', *Political Studies* 52:4 (2004), pp. 585–602.

23 T. Luckman, *The Invisible Religion* (New York: Macmillan, 1967).

24 Northern Ireland Council for Integrated Education, annual report, 2006 (in preparation).
25 A. M. Gallagher, 'Social identity and the Northern Ireland conflict', *Human Relations* 42:10 (1989), pp. 917–35.
26 J. Darby and S. Dunn, 'Segregated schools', in R. D. Osborne, R. J. Cormack and R. L. Miller (eds), *Education and Policy in Northern Ireland* (Belfast: Queen's University and University of Ulster, Policy Research Institute, 1987), pp. 85–98.
27 Children's views were recorded as part of an investigation of a curriculum development project in the mid-1990s designed to investigate the connections between religion and politics in Northern Ireland. (B. Lambkin, *Opposite Religions Still? Interpreting Northern Ireland after the Conflict*, Aldershot: Avebury Press, 1996.)
28 R. O'Leary and F. Finnas, 'Education, social integration and minority-majority group intermarriage', *Sociology* 36:2 (2002), pp. 235–54. M. Hornsby-Smith, *Roman Catholics in England: Studies in Social Structure since the Second World War* (Cambridge: Cambridge University Press, 1987).
29 Rose, *Governing without Consensus*.
30 E. Moxon-Browne, 'National identity in Northern Ireland', in P. Stringer and G. Robinson (eds), *Social Attitudes in Northern Ireland: The First Report* (Belfast: Blackstaff Press, 1991), pp. 23–30; E. Moxon-Browne, *Nation, Class and Creed in Northern Ireland* (Aldershot: Gower Press, 1983).
31 NILTS, 2005.
32 Moxon-Browne, 'National identity in Northern Ireland'.
33 R. Harris, *Prejudice and Intolerance in Ulster: A Study of Neighbours and Strangers in a Border Community* (Manchester: Manchester University Press, 1972).
34 M. Poole and F. Boal, 'Religious residential segregation in Belfast in mid-1969: a multi-level analysis', in B. D. Clark and M. D. Gleave (eds), *Social Patterns in Cities*, Special Publication 5 (Belfast: Institute of British Geographers, 1973), p. 14.
35 J. Tonge, *Northern Ireland: Conflict and Changes*, second edition (London: Pearson Education, 2002), p. 109.
36 J. Whyte, *Interpreting Northern Ireland* (Oxford: Clarendon Press, 1990), p. 34.
37 P. Shirlow and B. Murtagh, *Belfast: Segregation, Violence and the City* (London: Pluto Press, 2006).
38 Morrow *et al.*, *The Churches and Inter-community Relationships*, p. 122.
39 G. Fraser and V. Morgan, *In the Frame: Integrated Education in Northern Ireland – the Implications of Expansion* (Coleraine: Centre for the Study of Conflict, 1999).
40 A full discussion of this theme can be found in C. Mitchell, *Religion, Identity and Politics in Northern Ireland: Boundaries of Belonging and Belief* (Aldershot: Ashgate Press, 2005).

41 F. O'Connor, *In Search of a State: Catholics in Northern Ireland* (Belfast: Blackstaff Press, 1993), p. 290.
42 S. Bruce, *God save Ulster: The Religion and Politics of Paisleyism* (Oxford: Clarendon Press, 1986).
43 S. Bruce, *The Edge of the Union: The Ulster Loyalist Political Vision* (Oxford: Oxford University Press, 1994), p. 23.
44 Of the thirty MLAs that were elected from the DUP in 2003 or defected to the party later, seventeen belonged to Paisley's Free Presbyterian Church, six to other conservative Protestant denominations (three Elim, two Baptist and one Free Methodist), six to the Presbyterian Church and one to the Church of Ireland (Mitchell, *Religion, Identity and* Politics, p. 51). This information is not available for the MLAs elected in 2007.
45 N. Southern, 'Ian Paisley and evangelical Democratic Unionists: an analysis of the role of evangelical Protestantism within the Democratic Unionist Party', *Irish Political Studies* 20:2 (2005), pp. 127–45.
46 C. Smith, *American Evangelicalism: Embattled and Thriving* (Chicago: University of Chicago Press, 1998).
47 A. Buckley and C. Kenny, *Negotiating Identity: Rhetoric, Metaphor and Social Drama in Northern Ireland* (Washington DC: Smithsonian Institution Press, 1995).
48 N. Jarman, *Material Conflicts: Parades and Visual Displays in Northern Ireland* (Oxford: Berg, 1997), p. 94.
49 J. Witherow, 'The 'war on terrorism' and Protestant parading bands in Northern Ireland', *Quest* 1:1 (2006), available on line at www.qub.ac.uk/sites/QUEST/Issue1/Tableofcontents/.
50 An inexpensive and potent tonic wine.
51 Morrow *et al.*, *The Churches and Inter-community Relationships*.
52 Mitchell, *Religion, Identity and Politics in Northern Ireland*.
53 F. Burton, *The Politics of Legitimacy: Struggles in a Belfast Community* (London: Routledge, 1978).
54 Of course it should be remembered that the Hunger Strikes presented a serious dilemma for Catholic clergy, who remained ambiguous as to whether the strikes should be seen as suicide, which is a sin in Catholic doctrine. For discussion see P. O'Malley, *Biting at the Grave: The Irish Hunger Strikes and the Politics of Despair* (Belfast: Blackstaff Press, 1990).
55 Morrow *et al.*, *The Churches and Inter-community Relationships*.
56 See, for instance, Smyth and Cebulla, Chapter 9 in this volume.
57 McGarry and O'Leary, *Explaining Northern Ireland*; K. A. Cavanaugh, 'Interpretations of political violence in ethnically divided societies', *Terrorism and Political Violence* 9:3 (1997), pp. 33–54.
58 By the late 1990s Hayes and McAllister argued that an 'academic consensus' now hung around the idea that religion functioned merely as a badge of ethnic difference in Northern Ireland. See, for instance, B. C. Hayes and I. McAllister, 'Ethnonationalism, public opinion and the Good Friday Agreement', in J. Ruane and J. Todd (eds), *After the Good Friday Agreement:*

Analysing Political Change in Northern Ireland (Dublin: University College Dublin Press, 1999), pp. 30–48. This argument is found in a plethora of studies from that time, for example McGarry and O'Leary, *Explaining Northern Ireland*; P. Clayton, 'Religion, ethnicity and colonialism as explanations of the conflict in Northern Ireland', in D. Miller (ed.), *Rethinking Northern Ireland* (London: Longman, 1998), pp. 40–54; L. Fawcett, *Religion, Ethnicity and Social Change* (London: Macmillan, 2000).

59 D. Martin, *A General Theory of Secularization* (New York: Harper & Row, 1979).

60 Mitchell, *Religion, Identity and Politics in Northern Ireland*; J. Ruane and J. Todd, *Dynamics of Conflict and Transition* (Cambridge: Cambridge University Press, forthcoming); G. Ganiel, *Conserving or Changing? The Theology and Politics of Northern Irish Fundamentalist and Evangelical Protestants after the Good Friday Agreement*, IBIS Working Paper 20 (Dublin: Institute for British–Irish Studies, 2002).

61 J. Hickey, *Religion and the Northern Ireland Question* (Dublin: Gill & Macmillan, 1984).

62 Ganiel, *Conserving or Changing?*; Mitchell, *Religion, Identity and Politics in Northern Ireland*

63 J. D. Brewer, *Anti-Catholicism in Northern Ireland, 1600–1998* (London: Macmillan, 1998).

64 Mitchell, *Religion, Identity and Politics in Northern Ireland*.

65 Allen Feldman, *Formations of Violence: The Narrative of the Body and Political Terror in Northern Ireland* (Chicago: University of Chicago Press, 1991).

66 For an extended discussion of anti-Protestantism based on this interview data see Mitchell, *Religion, Identity and Politics in Northern Ireland*.

8

Gender and ethno-nationalist politics

Fidelma Ashe

Northern Irish society has been referred to as 'terrorism's laboratory'.[1] This particular characterisation of the region reflects how the specific dynamics of this politically antagonistic society offer researchers an arena to explore the causes, effects and dynamics of ethno-nationalist antagonism and conflict resolution. Subsequently the political conflict in Northern Ireland has produced a massive amount of academic literature. However, much mainstream, or 'malestream', scholarship in Northern Ireland has sidelined issues of gender inequality and gender power.

This 'patriarchal monologue' on Northern Irish politics has been challenged by feminist writers and activists. Feminists have engaged in groundbreaking studies that have made the category of gender power visible in Northern Irish society and have succeeded in pushing issues of gender on to the political and intellectual agenda in the region. The recent acknowledgement of the category of gender in research on Northern Ireland politics is reflected in the inclusion of a 'gender chapter' in this book. However, the addition of feminist work to contemporary academic surveys of Northern Irish politics raises political and practical issues for the feminist scholar.

This chapter, therefore, begins by examining the problems that emerge from the inclusion of a discussion of gender politics in this type of book. It then genders the Northern Irish conflict by examining three aspects of ethno-gender politics: ethno-gender ideologies or discourses, ethno-gendered inequalities and gendered practices of resistance within an ethno-nationalist society. The chapter concludes by returning to the issue of feminism and mainstream scholarship and considers the continuing importance of feminist research within the context of Northern Irish politics.

Ethno-nationalism and gender: separate spheres?

A range of feminist studies of Northern Irish politics have exposed how gender ideologies are fully intertwined with issues of inequality and the political conflict.[2] One effect of this research has been that contemporary scholarship often includes gender issues in the broad analysis of Northern Irish society.[3] While the former exclusion of gender from academic work on Northern Ireland greatly concerned feminist writers and activists, the contemporary inclusion of gender in examinations of politics in Northern Ireland has brought new concerns. Zalewski has argued that the now obligatory chapter on women/feminism in academic texts on Northern Ireland society means that gender issues are included in discussions of the region while simultaneously marginalised and contained within a specific chapter, usually dedicated to examining the position of women in an ethnically divided society.[4] This creates the impression that gender and feminism have little explanatory value beyond tracing and charting 'women's issues'. Zalewski contends that this means that gender becomes treated as a separate sphere of politics in relation to the ongoing ethno-nationalist antagonism in Northern Ireland. She claims that feminist work and feminist frameworks can be applied to Northern Irish politics in a broader fashion. For example, feminist theory can be utilised to analyse dimensions of ethno-nationalist conflict. Therefore she highlights how gender politics extend beyond the concept of 'women's issues'.

What Zalewski is suggesting is that feminism is recognised by mainstream scholarship in Northern Ireland only in relation to a specific set of issues that affect women such as poverty, the feminisation of the economy or domestic violence. Feminist interventions in Northern Irish society and politics that go beyond these issues, she argues, are still ignored. For example, feminist theories of identity, group conflict and democracy continue to be viewed as having little analytical use by mainstream scholars. Moreover, the category of gender affects all aspects of society, including national boundaries, political violence, programmes for peace, culture and history.[5] As Sharoni observes, 'the narrow definition of "women's issues" has been used to justify women's exclusion from domains that men have sought to maintain as their own primary positions of social and political power'.[6] Indeed, if we examine the other issues analysed in this particular text it is clear that gender plays a role in each of the political arenas examined by the other authors. Yet, as Zalewski notes, feminism's explanatory and analytical value is bounded in a distinct, separate chapter.

Zalewski's observations raise important concerns about the effects of the relatively new inclusion of gender issues in mainstream academic work. Bearing these concerns in mind, this chapter attempts to illustrate the connection between ethnic conflict and gender power, albeit from a marginal and bounded location. As mainstream scholarship has traditionally viewed gender as peripheral to the conflict in Northern Ireland, this chapter draws on feminist scholarship to expose how explanations of the ethnic conflict that ignore gender are always partial. This particular discussion of gender attempts to trouble the idea that gender politics in Northern Ireland are only about charting women's issues – issues that for feminists are of vital importance but not their only concern. It does not reflect the full potential of feminist analytical frameworks in Northern Ireland. What it does do, though, is draw on feminist work in the region to bring the category of gender into 'the story' of the nationalist conflict in Northern Ireland.

Other issues also need consideration when writing a chapter on gender and Northern Ireland. Given the confines of space, there is the further difficulty of attending to the complex theoretical and political debates that have emerged between feminists in the region.[7] A related concern is that any examination of gender in Northern Ireland would seem to require some recognition of how wider feminist debates about the concept of 'woman', difference, the objectives of feminist theory, and feminist political practice impact on feminists' work in deeply divided societies.[8]

Clearly it would be impossible to consider the full complexity of feminist research and activism in Northern Ireland in this kind of discussion. This chapter, therefore, does not afford many issues relating to gender identities and the study of gender politics sufficient treatment. For example, the issue of sexuality is given scant attention. However, it does attempt to give a flavour of the dynamics of the field of gender politics in Northern Ireland, while illustrating its centrality to ethno-nationalism. The section that follows begins this task by attempting to illustrate how gender discourses and nationalist discourses are thoroughly interconnected in the constitution of nationalist aspirations, communities and identities.

Gender, ethno-nationalism and the politics of conflict

Writers in the area of nationalism have argued that nationalism is not some kind of primordial identity but rather a modernist narrative about identity and belonging.[9] Nationalism and nationalist identity, according to this perspective, do not simply exist but have developed through complex historical, social and economic forces in the modern period. This opens up an analytical space for exploring how national identity is constituted through social forces rather than through kinship or some innate drive to identify with a national community.[10]

Nationalism is equated with the idea that a people have the right to determine their form of government. However, nationalism is much more than the basic political aspiration to self-government. The idea of a distinct nation and a distinct national people is underpinned by a complex set of discourses about the character of the nation and the nation's people. Writers such as Finlayson believe that these discourses actually produce the idea of a separate, distinct nation and constitute the idea that there is a unified national people with specific characteristics.[11] Finlayson contends that nationalism does not simply reflect and articulate a pre-given nation and organic national people. Instead, he claims, nationalism can be understood only when it is recognised as always part of 'a discursive articulation of particular social formations'.[12] His analysis of nationalism suggests that cultural narratives and social institutions create the idea that there is a national people naturally bounded to a national territory through history, culture and shared bonds.

Feminists have been keen to chart the role of gender in the constitution of the nation and national identities.[13] Gendering nationalism has certainly been a concern for feminists in Northern Ireland. The rest of this section draws on feminist work in the region to expose how gender is not secondary to ethno-nationalism in Northern Ireland but is integral to its production and operation.

Feminist studies have illustrated how both principal ethno-religious communities in Northern Ireland have developed gendered discourses about nationhood and national identity. Contemporary feminism suggests that gender identity is not biologically or psychologically determined.[14] It suggests that human identity is a product of social discourses, institutions and practices. In other words, society, not nature, produces gender identity in its different historical and social forms.[15] Nationalism is a set of discourses involved in the production of gender identities. In the case of Northern Ireland, Irish nationalism has drawn more explicitly on gender symbolism than unionism.[16] In Irish literature and myth a number of female figures symbolise the 'capture' of the Irish nation by a foreign power, for example Cathleen ni Houlihan and Dark Rosaleen.[17] Like many others, Irish nationalism's most common representation of the nation is as a mother. Mother Ireland is symbolised as captured, raped or pillaged by the enemies of the Irish nation.[18] Notions about female, and even more specifically maternal, vulnerability, innocence and goodness give the allegory of the nation as woman its emotional and sentimental force.[19]

The other dominant representation of femininity in Irish nationalism is the Virgin Mary. Like Mother Ireland, Mary the mother of God represents womanly goodness and womanly suffering. The relationship between Irish nationalism and Catholicism has meant that Mary has been one of the dominant female icons in Irish nationalism.[20]

Traditionally Irish women were encouraged to identify with Mary, suffering mother and paradoxically chaste virgin.

Warner argues that the 'cult of the Virgin' at once confirms femininity as asexual while at the same time 'proclaiming motherhood as the ideal role for women'.[21] These icons set up the norms of femininity for women in Irish nationalist cultures. Such paragons of Irish femininity suggest that certain forms of behaviour are normal, functional, moral and natural for women in the nationalist community. As Innes notes, the iconography of the Mother of God and Mother Ireland 'provided models' for Irish women to identify with, and these models of femininity were valorised by nationalists.[22] In terms of the development of Irish nationalism, these ideals of femininity were reflected in the structuring of gendered roles and power within the nationalist group, with men dominating political and cultural life.

Irish mythology offered nationalists an alternative gendered iconography. In contrast to the passive female figures that dominated nationalist representations of women, figures like Fedelm, the warrior princess of ancient Irish myth, or Granuaile, a pirate and leader of men in sixteenth-century Ireland, would have provided more active female icons. The historical veneration of passive female figures in Irish nationalist discourses illustrates how nationalist ideology invents the ideals of femininity in particular and selective ways.

As suggested above, Irish nationalism, like nationalisms in general, positions men as the defenders or liberators of the Irish nation. It therefore has a tradition of generating notions about the need for manly courage and sacrifice in the face of foreign domination. While the constitution of men's role within the nation has received less attention, it tends to revolve around the hegemonic manly ideals of bravery, courage, sacrifice and, most important, the physical protection of the nation.[23] The constitution of 'national manhood' around these hegemonic ideals in the Irish context is illustrated by Patrick Pearse's vision of Irish manhood. Pearse, one of the leaders of the Irish nationalist rebellion in 1916, set up a model of Irish manhood that revolved around the ideal of an active male warrior modelled on Cuchulain.[24] In Celtic legend Cuchulain was an exceptional warrior with extraordinary speed, stamina and beauty who defended Ireland from its enemies. Pearse portrayed Cuchulain as a 'hero who fights for his country and dies a Christ-like redeemer and Messiah'.[25]

Discussing nationalism more generally, Nagel notes how terms 'like honour, patriotism, cowardice, bravery and duty are hard to distinguish as either nationalist or masculinist, since they seem so thoroughly tied to both the nation and to manliness'.[26] Nationalism, as feminist writers have noted, is an arena for the 'accomplishment' of hegemonic masculinity.[27] In Irish nationalism the warrior identity has been marked as *naturally* male. Ethno-gendered discourses in Northern Ireland have therefore entrenched male power in the Irish nationalist/republican community. Men assume public and military roles with all the power that positioning implies. A later section reveals how this constitution of men and women's roles has been continually troubled, challenged and subverted.

Unionism does not use the same gendered imagery as Irish nationalism/republicanism.[28] However, its cultural practices and imagery are also highly masculine. Irish nationalism is organised around masculine institutions such as the GAA, whereas unionism organises around different male institutions and practices such as the Orange Order.[29] Unionist organisations are dominated by men, as is political life in the unionist community. For example, Racioppi and O'Sullivan See write that the Orange Order marches are 'organised exclusively by male orders, generally dominated by male bands, the marches constitute expressions of *male* loyalism . . . most women participate by bringing children to the march, by providing lunches, and by cheering on their menfolk'.[30] They claim that the dominant femininity during the marches operates around supporting men's cultural and political leadership. Like physical force republicanism, loyalist paramilitary groups are male-dominated and few women in the unionist community have taken up roles as combatants.[31]

In their prescribed primary role of mother, women, however, undertake vital functions for the ethno-nationalist project. Yuval-Davis and Anthias have pinpointed the five main functions women in nationalist communities fulfil. They claim that women act as the biological producers of the national people; reproduce ethnic boundaries; participate in the ideological reproduction of the collective community and act as transmitters of its culture; signify ethnic differences and participate in 'national, economic, political and military struggles'.[32]

Men, on the other hand, are expected to sacrifice their lives for the nation and take up positions of power within the community. However, like women, men are divided not only by nationality but also by class and age. For some young working-class men, nationalism and the 'failure' of politics have led them to identify with militaristic and violent models of masculinity. When we talk about male power we need to take into account men's dominant political and military positions in the community but we must also take into account the effects of the power of nationalist identifications on people's interpretations of their roles as gendered subjects, their political interests and political activities.

Nationalism gives working-class men a certain kind of power but it also encourages them to assume forms of ultra-masculinity, including violence and the sacrifice of life and liberty in the national cause. While ethno-gendered discourses in Northern Ireland certainly impact nega-tively on the social and political position of women, ethno-nationalism also impacts negatively on men. However, there has been very little aca-demic work carried out on masculinity in the region.[33] The disinterest of scholars in the region in the concept of manhood is occurring in an inter-national context of bourgeoning research on the politics of masculinity in a range of social science disciplines. The sidelining of the category of manhood in research on ethno-nationalism in Northern Ireland exposes the continued tendency of Northern Irish scholarship to sideline issues of gender in investigations of the region.[34]

Given the lack of enquiries into the effects of nationalism on male iden-tity, the next section concentrates in more detail on the effect of ethno-nationalism on women's positioning in Northern Irish society as constituted through ethno-gender networks of power and the effects of political violence.

Nationalism, gender and inequality

The inequalities that women experience in Northern Ireland are similar to those experienced by women in other Western European countries. Coulter surveys gender inequality in Northern Ireland in the spheres of education, employment and the domestic division of labour. In addition, he charts how ethno-religious identity and social class impact on women's employment and education.[35]

If the formal arena of politics is examined, there is a clear power dif-ferential between men and women in Northern Irish society which is reinforced by the political situation in the region. As suggested above, ethnic conflict supports the male monopolisation of power and reduces the importance of issues of gender and sexual inequalities to that of peripheral political issues. Until recently the dominance of the conflict has meant that political parties have not been particularly interested in addressing issues of gender equality. Rooney has also exposed how women exercise little influence over party political culture in Northern Ireland.[36]

Societies where there is a high level of ethno-nationalist conflict often exacerbate the problem of women's political underrepresentation. The impact of nationalist conflict on women's political representation in Northern Ireland was illustrated in the outcome of the devolutionary ini-tiative in the United Kingdom. With the exception of Sinn Féin, political parties in Northern Ireland were much more resistant to improving women's representation during the devolutionary initiative compared with Scotland and Wales.[37] In the first elections to the United Kingdom's new devolved institutions, which took place between 1998 and 1999, 37 per cent of members elected to the new Scottish Parliament and 40 per cent of members elected to the Welsh Assembly were women. In contrast, only 13 per cent of those members returned to the Northern Ireland Assembly were women. In the 2003 elections to devolved institutions in the United Kingdom, the representation of women in the Scottish Parliament increased to 39.5 per cent. And in the Welsh Assembly the proportion of women returned actually rose to 50 per cent. While the representation of women in the Northern Ireland Assembly grew, it remained pitifully low at a mere 16.7 per cent.[38]

Women have, however, exerted pressure from within the political parties on the issue of gender and this pressure combined with the intervention of the Northern Ireland Women's Coalition has forced the political parties to consider issues relating to gender inequality. The new attention to gender inequality is not substantial enough, though, to create significant change in the positioning of men and women in Northern Irish society. To achieve this, a more radical engagement with the issue of gender equality will be required by all the political parties.[39]

Outside the structures of formal political power, women's ethno-nationalist positioning in Northern Ireland is characterised by different forms of gender disciplining. This has been most prevalent perhaps in the arena of 'body politics'. Both unionism and Irish nationalism have traditionally taken an interest in women's moral behaviour.[40] While the Protestant Churches have no equivalent symbolism to the Virgin Mary, like Catholicism they promote conformity to a rigid code of sexual behaviour.[41] Nagel has argued that in nationalist societies women's behaviour represents the nationalist group's distinctive culture. As exalted mothers of the nation, women's behaviour must be impeccable and transgressions may be punished.[42]

More broadly, the influence of religious values in Northern Ireland has resulted in significant resistance to campaigns and policy changes focused around issues such as gay rights, abortion, contraception and protection against domestic violence.[43] While the largest Irish nationalist party, Sinn Féin, has undergone considerable modernisation in terms of issues relating to sexual and reproductive rights, the protests of some members of the DUP against legislation allowing gay couples to engage in civil ceremonies in December 2005 illustrates the continued political resistance to sexual equality in Northern Ireland.

Issues of sexual autonomy and reproductive freedom tend to cut across different classes of women. However, dimensions of women's inequality in Northern Ireland are affected by women's class position. The political conflict has had a particular impact on the everyday lives of women living in working-class communities. As working-class areas often become the focus of ethnic conflict and violence, the line between the home and the street sometimes becomes fluid.[44] Homes become the target of violence and the security of family members is jeopardised, especially during travel in and out of ethnically segregated housing estates. Furthermore, during the period of the troubles, many women's partners were imprisoned or killed in the conflict.[45] This left women to bring up families in very difficult circumstances. Feminists, however, have illustrated how the circumstances that 'the Troubles' created for women opened spaces for women's political activities.[46] Furthermore, the ethnic conflict has produced a number of female-led protests, including the peace marches of the late 1970s and, more recently, the campaign by the McCartney family to bring to justice those who murdered Robert McCartney in January 2005. The next section examines gendered resistances in Northern Ireland and explores how traditional ethno-nationalist constitutions of gender roles and identities have been troubled and subverted.

Nationalist conflict and gender resistance

The traditional gender ideologies that have characterised ethno-nationalism in Northern Ireland have been challenged in a multitude of ways at both the micro and the macro level of politics. This section examines three forms of gendered resistance to gender power in Northern Ireland: organised feminism, military femininity and resistances based around traditional female identities.

Organised feminism was relatively slow to develop in Northern Ireland. Its emergence was signalled by the advent of the Northern Ireland Women's Rights Movement (NIWRM) in the 1970s. This group was a coalition of trade unionist women, socialist feminists, liberal feminists, civil rights campaigners, community activists and radical and lesbian feminists.[47] The political dynamics of the NIWRM reflects one of the central issues that feminism in Northern Ireland has had to confront, that of women's different ethnic identifications.

The NIWRM was a cross-community feminist grouping that dealt with ethnic and class differences between women by attempting to prioritise unionist and Irish nationalist/republican women's shared inequalities and oppressions. In this respect the NIWRM reflected broader trends in feminism during the period of the 1970s. At the time, radical feminists had developed a form of politics around notions of female solidarity and the recognition of shared female interests among women of different classes, races and sexualities. The NIWRM attempted to minimise ethno-nationalist differences between women in Northern Ireland to cultivate women's solidarity in the face of shared male oppression.[48]

However, this solidarity was almost impossible to achieve as women disagreed about what issues feminism should address. Deep divisions emerged, for instance, around the issue of the strip-searching of republican women prisoners.[49] Nationalist women argued that strip-searching was a feminist issue, while some unionist women considered it a nationalist issue. Due to ethnic differences between women, the NIWRM fragmented. New organisations emerged such as Women against Colonialism that organised around the inequalities they experienced across their dual identities as women and as Irish nationalists/republicans.[50]

By the 1980s there was recognition that feminist theory and practice could not ignore women's nationalist identifications by aspiring to notions of shared female interests that could transcend women's complex differences and antagonistic standpoints on the national question. The experience of earlier feminist organisations suggested that any form of cross-community feminism would have to deal with ethnic differences between women in Northern Ireland. This recognition of differences between women again reflected broader developments within the feminist movement.[51]

In the 1980s feminism in general was confronting issues of excluding women's racial, class and ethnic oppression by prioritising gender inequality over other forms of oppression.[52] In Northern Ireland feminists explored ways of supporting and recognising women's different identities while at the same time trying to facilitate unified feminist strategies. Against this background 'transversalism' became popular. This is a strategy that involves women recognising their ethnic differences while working together on issues of common concern where agreement could be reached in terms of developing campaigns.[53] Transversalism has proved difficult and has tended to be the exception rather than the rule.[54] However, women within their respective communities continued to struggle for social changes that would improve their lives. Transversalism became popular again with feminists in the 1990s. As detailed below, the Northern Ireland Women's Coalition (NIWC) developed a form of tranversalism within the context of conflict resolution.

The declarations of cease-fires by the Provisional IRA and various loyalist paramilitaries in 1994 'brought a new political climate'.[55] The British and Irish governments began to prepare for the possibility of peace negotiations between the unionist and Irish nationalist/republican communities and published a text that provided a framework for these negotiations. The 'framework document' was based around the idea of facilitating an 'accommodation of the two traditions'.[56]

Feminists and community activists realised that, given the low political representation of women at the higher levels of the political parties, there was a danger that issues relating to gender inequality would be ignored in the talks. Also, if power devolved to local assemblies, there was a fear that local politicians might resist equality legislation.[57] Some women from both communities began to see that they had common gender concerns in relation to the peace process.

In response to similar concerns, Republican women organised a conference to discuss the marginalisation of women in the emerging peace process. A small group of unionist women also met to discuss the shifting political landscape from the point of view of gender inequalities.[58] Republican women made proposals to the Forum for Peace and Reconciliation concerning the rights of women, children and lesbians, and argued for the development of economic equality.

Other women organised into a cross-community political party, the NIWC, to contest elections to the peace talks. The NIWC succeeded in having two members elected. As a cross-community alliance of women, the Coalition had to deal directly with the issue of ethnic and class differences between women, while at the same time participating in a talks process that would involve it in difficult discussions about Northern Ireland's divisive political issues.[59]

To deal with differences between women, the Coalition organised around supporting a particular practice of politics rather than taking positions on controversial issues such as policing and decommissioning. Reflecting the ideals of transversalism, the Coalition attempted to find a common ground among women on certain issues, while at the same time accepting that ethno-nationalist differences between women meant that they might not reach agreement on a range of issues that divided the two communities. The Coalition supported a position of dialogue on divisive issues. By distancing itself from partisan politics, the Coalition was able to play a role in promoting dialogue between the political parties in the run-up to the signing of the Belfast Agreement in 1998.[60] Rather than assuming an exclusive concentration on the national question, the Coalition also prioritised economic and social inequalities. It succeeded in placing gender equality clauses in the Agreement, secured the appointment of a Children's Commissioner and was instrumental in the establishment of a new Civic Forum, which was designed to improve democratic processes by facilitating input by community organisations into the policy-making process.

After the signing of the Belfast Agreement the political landscape became less conducive to the NIWC. Changes in the voting system and an electoral shift towards what are often conceived as the more 'extreme' ethno-nationalist parties combined to reduce the Coalition's electoral viability. In the 2003 elections it lost its two electoral seats. Regardless of its electoral demise, the Coalition was a very significant expression of feminist politics in Northern Ireland. Evidence from other countries suggests that women's parties tend to be time-limited projects that work in transitional political circumstance to promote awareness of gender issues.[61] Academics have developed different assessments of this kind of time-limited deployment of feminism in the Northern Ireland context.[62]

The Coalition believed that it had succeeded in overcoming some of the problems of difference that had previously 'confounded the women's movement in Northern Ireland'.[63] However, writers such as Little and Bairner argue that deep differences between women's perspectives remained.[64] Little argues that the Coalition tended to avoid ethnic differences between women by sidestepping or sidelining different political positions by women on the constitutional issue, preferring to develop processes for the resolution of difference.[65] He argues that the NIWC did not deal with important issues such as security that affect nationalist women in particular. He claims that, if women are to take difference seriously, they must talk about their differences in an honest and open way. This would include incorporating the concerns of nationalist women into the NIWC agenda, which would presumably involve taking some kind of position in relation to the Irish nationalist political agenda, for example on issues such as policing. I have argued elsewhere that this kind of inclusive feminism is largely 'imaginary', as it suggests that there exists some common, binding interest among women that enables them to overcome deep ethno-nationalist divisions.[66] For example, if the NIWC had 'incorporated' the concerns of Irish nationalist women and taken standpoints on these issues, it would have almost certainly alienated unionist/loyalist women.

Porter developed a more positive analysis of the Coalition.[67] She claims that the Coalition's dialogic approach represented a more rational, progressive form of politics, able to move beyond less flexible political positions. However the identification of a particular form of politics with women rather than with 'both' genders may reinforce traditional stereotypes of women as more oriented to care, concern and dialogue than men. Bairner writes, 'to suggest that the NIWC's approach has been in some way peculiar to them, as women, is to run the risk of offering support for an essentialist conceptualisation of stereotypical female attributes such as the spirit of co-operation and the capacity to care'.[68] Bairner highlights the need to engage with men in moving gender politics forward.

Furthermore, any valorisation of the Coalition's form of politics over other deeply nationalist-identified women raises concerns about the way

different types of women's political standpoints are evaluated and prioritised by feminists and other commentators.[69] Feminism in Northern
Ireland is multi-faceted; each expression troubles gender ideologies but
also raises specific problems. While the NIWC raised awareness about
women's equality and political representation, as the above critiques
highlight, it did not circumvent the complexities of feminist strategies of
political resistance. The political and theoretical dynamics of the NIWC
require careful consideration.[70]

Almost in direct contrast to the Coalition's dialogic feminism, women
have troubled gendered ideologies in Northern Ireland by taking up the
role of combatant. Such women have been few in number but their direct
involvement in military action means that they reject traditional female
behaviour and challenge the positioning of women as primarily domestic and maternal. Combatant women have been viewed as transcending
their traditional gender identity, and their action appears to represent an
assault on the gendered discourses of nationalism. Margaret Ward's
pioneering work on women's military roles during the Irish War of
Independence exposed how combatant women troubled assumptions
about the position of women in nationalist cultures.[71] Other more contemporary studies have also exposed how 'woman' as combatant troubles traditional ideas about femininity in Northern Ireland.[72] Certain
accounts of women's military action suggest that women were given full
equality by republican men from the time women were admitted as
members to the IRA in 1972. Prior to that, women had joined Cumann
Na mBan, a women's IRA support group. Women in the organisation
were not involved in direct military conflict but played supporting roles,
for example as couriers or intelligence gatherers. In his biography the
republican commander Sean MacStiofain writes, 'some of the best shots
I ever knew were women . . . women were admitted on a basis of full
equality with men . . . .'[73]

Other accounts suggest that different gender dynamics emerged around
women's military involvement. Military action was often gendered. It is
alleged, for example, that women sometimes hid bombs in prams and that
there were incidents of women using their sexuality to lure British soldiers
into ambushes.[74] Aretxaga's study of the republican hunger strikes in the
1980s also notes that a disproportionate number of women imprisoned
at the time for involvement in paramilitary activity were young and
unmarried.[75] She claims women with this profile were more attractive
to republicans because they had not taken up traditional feminine roles
as wives and mothers. Aretxaga's study of the republican prison protests reveals further differences between perceptions of male and female
prisoners in the 1980s.[76] Lorraine Dowler's important study of women

combatants in Belfast illustrates how gender affected male Republican attitudes to combatant women.[77] While male combatants were hailed as heroes, women combatants were typically viewed as wild and unruly and their contribution was not acknowledged by the community.

Some feminists such as Edna Longley have questioned how much women's involvement in militarism actually subverts nationalism's gender ideology. In an exceptional and provocative, if contentious, analysis of contemporary nationalism in Northern Ireland she argues that the interests of women and nationalism are incompatible.[78] She argues that nationalism encourages women to join a 'death cult'. Physical force nationalism, she argues, is a male-dominated and male-defined ideology that demands 'masochistic martyrdom' and rejects the humanitarianism and connectivity of feminism.[79] Nationalist feminists would most likely retort that such a view fails to recognise the inequalities that women suffer because of their ethnic identity and is, therefore, reflective of a feminism that refuses to acknowledge different women's experiences and political standpoints.

Women have also often engaged in nationalist conflict not by transcending their feminine roles but through their domestic roles. As suggested above, nationalist conflict often means that the line between the public and private sphere becomes fluid. The home can therefore become the target of political conflict and ethnic aggression. Women have often protested when the family has been threatened and have employed the familial identities of wife, mother, sister or daughter as the basis of those protests. While such protests can reinforce women's traditional identities, they also trouble them because such protests involve women deploying their domestic identities in a political way, thereby contesting the gendered public–private divide discussed in the second section of this chapter. Nationalist mothers' defiance of a loyalist boycott of the Holy Cross school in Ardoyne in 2001 and the campaign by female relatives to expose the murder of Robert McCartney in 2005–06 are examples of this kind of resistance.[80] These women frame their protests around ideas about women's right to defend and protect members of their family, while at the same time troubling gender ideology by taking up public, political positions. The protests are usually short-lived and the long-term effects of these expressions of women's political agency on women's power in nationalist communities is debatable in the longer term.[81]

Feminist theory and Northern Irish politics

This chapter has attempted to gender the ethnic conflict in Northern Ireland. By doing so, it has tried to expose the partiality of accounts of ethno-nationalist conflict that ignore the category of gender identity. However, as suggested earlier, the potential of feminist theory is much broader than this chapter suggests. Feminism has developed a range of methodologies that can be applied to analysing ethnic conflict and conflict resolution. Zalewski has shown how quickly these methodologies have been dismissed by writers on the conflict. Some writers, however, have employed or considered the utility of feminist resources in charting and exploring the ethnic conflict in Northern Ireland.[82] For example, Norman Porter employed the work of Iris Marian Young in his analysis of unionist politics.[83] Similarly, Shane O'Neill and Adrian Little have explored the utility of feminist philosophies for developing theoretical models of politics and democracy in Northern Ireland.[84] And other commentators have sought to locate gendered identities in Northern Ireland as points of potential political disruption.[85]

This chapter has illustrated how feminist and gender politics are part of the political culture of Northern Ireland and offer conceptual resources to academics engaged in investigating the conflict. If we as an academic community are to fully understand and debate Northern Irish politics, then feminism and feminist theory must be a central part of that exploration and discussion. There is much work left to be done on gender politics and Northern Irish society. We can only hope that future academic work on the region will continue to explore gender as an important category of analysis and continue to expand and develop feminist work in that political context.

Postscript

Political negotiations between the main political parties in Northern Ireland led to an Assembly election on 7 March 2007. Eighteen women gained seats, out of a total of 108. Sinn Fein had eight women elected, gaining the highest number of women elected to the Assembly. The SDLP had four women elected, the DUP three, Alliance gained two seats for women, and Dawn Purvis, who replaced the late David Ervine as leader, won one female seat for the PUP.

In the new devolved Assembly women remain underrepresented, despite a law that enables parties to use positive discrimination to increase the number of successful women candidates in Assembly elections. Women, however, have been given ministerial posts in the new Assembly. The First and Deputy First Ministers are men. Women have filled four of the other ten Ministerial positions in the Assembly. Whether or not women MLAs will be able to work together to improve gender equality for women in Northern Ireland remains to be seen.

Notes

1 A. O'Day, *Terrorism's Laboratory: The Case of Northern Ireland* (Aldershot: Dartmouth Publications, 1995).

2 B. Aretxaga, *Shattering Silence: Women, Nationalism, and Political Subjectivity in the North* (Princeton NJ: Princeton University Press, 1997); L. Dowler, ' "And they think I'm just a nice old lady": women and war in Belfast, Northern Ireland', *Gender, Place and Culture* 5:2 (1998), pp. 159–76; C. Davis and C. Roulston (eds), *Gender, Democracy and Inclusion in Northern Ireland* (Basingstoke: Palgrave, 2000); E. Longley, *The Living Stream: Literature and Revisionism in Ireland* (Newcastle upon Tyne: Bloodaxe Books, 1994); M. Ward, *Unmanageable Revolutionaries: Women and Irish Nationalism* (London: Pluto Press, 1983).

3 A. Aughey and D. Morrow, *Northern Irish Politics* (Harlow: Longman, 1996); C. Coulter, *Contemporary Northern Irish Society: An Introduction* (London: Pluto Press, 1999); M. McGovern and P. Shirlow (eds), *Who are the People? Unionism, Protestantism and Loyalism in Northern Ireland* (London: Pluto Press, 1997), pp. 141–57.

4 M. Zalewski, 'Gender ghosts in McGarry and O'Leary and representations of the conflict in Northern Ireland', *Political Studies* 53:1 (2005), pp. 201–21.

5 F. Ashe, 'Gendering the Holy Cross School dispute: women and nationalism in Northern Ireland', *Political Studies* 54:1 (2006), 147–64; F. Ashe, 'The McCartney sisters' search for justice: gender and political protest in Northern Ireland', *Politics* 26:3 (2006), pp. 161–7; F. Ashe, 'The Virgin Mary connection: reflecting on feminism and Northern Irish politics', *Critical Review of International Social and Political Philosophy* 9:4 (2006), pp. 573–88; C. Encloe, *Bananas, Beaches and Bases: Making Feminist Sense of International Relations* (Berkeley CA: University of California Press, 1989); K. Martin 'Death of a nation: transnationalism, bodies and abortion in late twentieth-century Ireland', in T. Mayer (ed.), *Gender Ironies of Nationalism: Sexing the Nation* (London and New York: Routledge, 2000), pp. 65–88; Mayer, *Gender Ironies of Nationalism*; A. McClintock, 'Family feuds: gender, nationalism and the family', *Feminist Review* 44 (1993), pp. 61–80.

6 S. Sharoni, *Gender and the Israeli–Palestinian Conflict* (New York: Syracuse University Press, 1995), p. 78.

7 C. Coulter, *The Hidden Tradition: Feminism, Women and Nationalism in Ireland* (Cork: Cork University Press, 1993).

8 C. Roulston, 'Democracy and the challenge of gender: new visions, new processes', in Davis and Roulston, *Gender, Democracy and Inclusion in Northern Ireland*, pp. 24–48; M. Ward (ed.), *A Difficult, Dangerous Honesty: Ten Years of Feminism in Northern Ireland* (Belfast: Women's Book Collective, 1986).

9 B. Anderson, *Imagined Communities: Reflections on the Origins and Spread of Nationalism* (New York: Verso, 1983).

10 A. Finlayson, 'Ideology, discourse and nationalism', *Journal of Political Ideologies* 3:1 (1998), pp. 99–119; E. Gellner, *Nations and Nationalism* (Oxford: Blackwell, 1983).
11 Finlayson, 'Ideology, discourse and nationalism'.
12 *Ibid.*, p. 103.
13 See Encloe, *Bananas, Beaches and Bases*; A. McClintock, *Imperial Leather: Race, Sexuality and Gender* (London and New York: Routledge, 1995); N. Yuval-Davis and F. Anthias (eds), *Women–Nation–State* (Basingstoke: Macmillan, 1989).
14 For surveys see F. Ashe, 'The subject', in F. Ashe, A. Finlayson, M. Lloyd, I. Mackenzie, J. Martin and S. O'Neill, *Contemporary Social and Political Theory: An Introduction* (Buckingham: Open University Press, 1999), pp. 88–110; F. Ashe, 'Deconstructing the experiential bar: male experience and feminist resistance', *Men and Masculinities* 7:2 (2004), pp. 187–204.
15 J. Butler, *Gender Trouble* (London and New York: Routledge, 1990).
16 Longley, *The Living Stream*; R. Sales, 'Gender and Protestantism in Northern Ireland', in Shirlow and McGovern, *Who are the People?* pp. 141–57.
17 C. L. Innes, *Woman and Nation* (Hemel Hempstead: Harvester Wheatsheaf, 1993); Longley, *The Living Stream*.
18 Innes, *Woman and Nation*; Yuval and Anthias, *Women–Nation–State*.
19 Ashe, 'Gendering the Holy Cross School dispute'; Ashe, 'The Virgin Mary connection'.
20 *Ibid.*; Innes, *Woman and Nation*; M. Warner, *Monuments and Maidens* (London: Weidenfeld and Nicolson, 1985).
21 Warner, *Monuments and Maidens*, p. 38.
22 Innes, *Woman and Nation*, pp. 41–2.
23 J. Nagel, 'Masculinity and nationalism: gender and sexuality in the making of nations', *Ethnic and Racial Studies* 21:2 (1998), pp. 242–60.
24 Innes, *Woman and Nation*, p. 58.
25 *Ibid.*
26 Nagel, 'Masculinity and nationalism', p. 252.
27 R. Connell, *Gender and Power* (Cambridge: Polity Press, 1987).
28 Sales, 'Gender and Protestantism'.
29 Longley, *The Living Stream*.
30 L. Racioppi and K. O'Sullivan, 'Ulstermen and loyalist ladies on parade', *International Journal of Feminist Politics* 2:1 (2000), pp. 1–24, p. 13.
31 Sales, 'Gender and Protestantism'.
32 Yuval-Davis and Anthias, *Women–Nation–State*, p. 7.
33 Exceptions include A. Bairner, 'Masculinity, violence and the peace process', *Capitalism and Class* 69:2 (1999), pp. 125–45; A. Feldman, *Formations of Violence: The Narrative of the Body and Political Terror in Northern Ireland* (Chicago: University of Chicago Press, 1991); R. Jenkins, *Hightown Rules: Growing up on a Belfast Housing Estate* (Leicester: National Bureau Publishers, 1983). The Centre for Young Men's Study at the University of Ulster explores young working-class men's violence.

34 F. Ashe ' "Men–nation–state": what are political theorists talking about in Northern Ireland?' (under review).
35 Coulter, *Contemporary Northern Irish Society*.
36 Rooney, quoted in *ibid.*, p. 137.
37 A. Brown, T. Donaghy, F. Mackay and E. Meehan, 'Women and constitutional change in Scotland and Northern Ireland', *Parliamentary Affairs* 55:1 (2002), pp. 71–84.
38 Ashe, 'Gendering the Holy Cross School dispute'.
39 *Ibid.*; Ashe, 'The Virgin Mary connection'.
40 Morgan, 'Women and the conflict in Northern Ireland'; Sales, 'Gender and Protestantism', p. 144.
41 *Ibid.*; V. Morgan, 'Women and the conflict in Northern Ireland', in O'Day, *Terrorism's Laboratory*.
42 Nagel, 'Masculinity and nationalism', p. 245; see Coulter, *Contemporary Northern Irish Society*, p. 135, for examples.
43 Morgan, 'Women and the conflict in Northern Ireland', p. 67.
44 Aretxaga, *Shattering Silence*.
45 E. Fairweather, R. McDonough and M. McFadyean, *Only the Rivers run Free: Northern Ireland – the Women's War* (London and Sydney: Pluto Press, 1984).
46 Davis and Roulston, *Gender Democracy and Inclusion in Northern Ireland*; M. McWilliams, 'Struggling for peace and justice: reflections on women's activism in Northern Ireland', *Journal of Women's History* 6:4 (1995), pp. 13–39.
47 C. Roulston, 'Women on the margins: the women's movement in Northern Ireland, 1973–1988', *Science and Society* 53:2 (1989), pp. 219–36.
48 *Ibid.*
49 Coulter, *Hidden Tradition*; Roulston, 'Women on the margins'; Ward, *A Difficult, Dangerous Honesty*.
50 *Ibid.*
51 C. Roulston, 'Democracy and the challenge of gender: new visions, new processes', in Davis and Roulston, *Gender, Democracy and Inclusion in Northern Ireland*, pp. 164–86.
52 D. Riley, *Am I that Name? Feminism and the Category of 'Women' in History* (Basingstoke: Macmillan, 1988).
53 C. Cockburn, *The Space between Us: Negotiating Gender and National Identities in Conflict* (London: Zed Books, 1998).
54 Ashe, 'The Virgin Mary connection'.
55 K. Fearon and M. McWilliams, 'Swimming against the mainstream: the Northern Ireland Women's Coalition', in Davis and Roulston, *Gender, Democracy and Inclusion in Northern Ireland*, pp. 177–240, p. 118.
56 *Ibid.*
57 *Ibid.*
58 E. Rooney, 'Women in Northern Irish politics: difference matters', in Davis and Roulston, *Gender, Democracy and Inclusion in Northern Ireland*, pp. 164–86, p. 171.

59 Fearon and McWilliams, 'Swimming against the mainstream'.
60 *Ibid.*
61 M. Ferree, B. Risman, V. Sperling, T. Gurikova and K. Hyde, 'The Russian women's movement: activists, strategies and identities', *Women in Politics* 20:3 (1999), pp. 83–109.
62 A. Bairner, 'Masculinity, violence and the peace process'; A. Little, 'Feminism and the politics of difference in Northern Ireland', *Journal of Political Ideologies* 7:2 (2002), pp. 163–77; E. Porter, 'Women and politics in Northern Ireland', *Politics* 18:1 (1998), pp. 25–32; E. Porter, 'Participatory democracy and the challenge of dialogue across difference', in Davis and Roulston, *Gender, Democracy and Inclusion in Northern Ireland*, pp. 141–63.
63 Fearon and McWilliams, 'Swimming against the mainstream', p. 117.
64 Bairner, 'Masculinity, violence and the peace process'; Little, 'Feminism and the politics of difference in Northern Ireland'.
65 Little, 'Feminism and the politics of difference', p. 172.
66 Ashe, 'The Virgin Mary connection'.
67 Porter, 'Women and politics in Northern Ireland'; Porter, 'Participatory democracy and the challenge of dialogue across difference'.
68 Bairner, 'Masculinity, violence and the peace process', p. 139; see also Ashe, 'The Virgin Mary connection'.
69 Ashe, 'The Virgin Mary connection'; Rooney, 'Women in Northern Irish politics'.
70 Ashe, 'The Virgin Mary connection'.
71 Ward, *Unmanageable Revolutionaries*.
72 Dowler, ' "And they think I'm just a nice old lady" '.
73 Quoted in E. Shannon, *I am of Ireland: Women of the North Speak Out* (Amherst MA: University of Massachusetts Press, 1997), p. 112.
74 *Ibid.*, p. 114.
75 B. Aretxaga, 'Dirty protest', *Ethos* 23:2 (1995), pp. 123–48.
76 *Ibid.*
77 Dowler, ' "And they think I'm just a nice old lady" '.
78 Longley, *The Living Stream*.
79 *Ibid.*, p. 192.
80 Ashe, 'Gendering the Holy Cross School dispute'; Ashe, 'The McCartney sisters' search for justice'.
81 *Ibid.*
82 Zalewski, 'Gender ghosts in McGarry and O'Leary and representations of the conflict in Northern Ireland'.
83 N. Porter, *Rethinking Unionism* (Belfast: Blackstaff Press, 1996).
84 Little, 'Feminism and the politics of difference in Northern Ireland'; S. O'Neill, *Impartiality in Context: Grounding Justice in a Pluralist World* (Albany NY: New York University Press, 1997).
85 Bairner, 'Masculinity, violence and the peace process'.

9

The glacier moves? Economic change and class structure

Jim Smyth and Andreas Cebulla

The relationship between the economy and class structure in Northern Ireland has not been a topic of sustained discussion. Apart from studies of poverty and exclusion, little research exists on the determinants of social class and the effects of economic change on the social structure. Instead, research on Northern Ireland focuses overwhelmingly on the causes and consequences of ethno-religious differences and the resultant conflict.[1] Clearly, the political has been historically 'over-determined', that is, the political system was used to reinforce ethno-religious differences and ensure the unionist monopoly of political power in Northern Ireland for almost half a century. But this over-determination, which manifested itself in blatant discriminatory practices, should not disguise the reality of class difference, a reality which existed for and within both communities. For example, the education system, based historically upon selection, acts to reinforce class differences and does so irrespective of ethno-religious allegiance[2].

This chapter argues that the over-determination of the political in the arena of class formation and reproduction in Northern Ireland has lost most of its previous salience. This is not simply because of the collapse of unionist political cohesion, but also because of the changing landscape of the global economy and the position of the United Kingdom in general and Northern Ireland in particular as subordinate elements within this system. The coherence of unionism as an all-class alliance and a political project has been fatally eroded. The internal cohesion of unionism depended upon the tacit and overt support of the British state and the constitutional convention that the Westminster parliament could not intervene in the internal affairs of the North. This allowed the Stormont regime to regulate internal affairs to the advantage of the monolithic Unionist Party and its supporters. The demands of the civil rights movement from 1968 onwards, by challenging the sectarian practices of the local state, finally forced Britain to adopt a policy of direct intervention, a policy which led to the reconfiguration of the political landscape and a fragmentation of unionism. In class terms, this intervention created a space for a new Catholic middle class to emerge.

Enforced political realignments were compounded by economic change. The economic and social landscape of the Northern Ireland that existed in the late 1960s has been fundamentally transformed in the intervening decades. After the Second World War the social and economic life of the region was dominated by the irreversible decline of the two pillars of economic activity: the manufacture of textiles and the industrial cluster centred around the shipbuilding industry. Efforts to transform the textile industry by capitalising on the branch plant expansion of the British synthetic fibre industry ended in failure, and as the peace process began to unfold in the mid-1990s the once mighty shipbuilding sector was consigned to history, with plans later unfolding to develop a post-industrial theme park on the site of the yards.

The post-war reconstruction of the European economies around Fordist principles of balancing mass production and mass consumption had profound social consequences, as part of the settlement was the introduction of welfare state measures and increasing government intervention in the management of society and the economy. The advent of welfarism was not welcomed by the two principal power brokers in the north, the Unionist Party and the Catholic Church, as both instinctively realised that increasing state intervention in health, welfare and education would undermine their power.

The gradually increasing social mobility which resulted from economic and social change became the basis of the indigenous civil rights movement and demands for reform of the sectarian practices which underpinned unionist power. It was in this sense that the political was 'over determined': the political reality of the local state was the need to keep the unionist alliance together through the exclusion of the minority from strategic political and economic sectors even if it entailed conflict with the ultimate paymasters in London.

The resultant internal war may have distorted and delayed inevitable change but could not materially deflect the remorseless march of deindustrialisation and social change that spread across the world in the wake of the oil crises of 1973–74. The local economy was locked into a now familiar trajectory as traditional heavy industry closed its doors, to be replaced by service industries, and a flexible and feminised work force displaced the male, and mainly Protestant, industrial worker. Old political alliances and certainties were disintegrating everywhere, while in Northern Ireland a resurgence of ethno-political antagonism fuelled a bloody internal war that drove the two principal communities further apart.

In hindsight it is clear that the hugely successful politically inspired strike of loyalist workers in 1974 was the last gasp of the dying beast of the unionist class alliance and the final meaningful attempt of unionism to use the streets to resist change. Apart from anything else, the link between workplace, residence and political allegiance was irretrievably shattered as the tide of economic change began to transform not only the economy but the nature of social space and particularly the urban space of Belfast. As the traditional Protestant working class was displaced to the suburbs the terraces they left behind were swiftly gentrified and the city centre, slowly but surely, became an arena of consumption and no longer a contested political space. The persistence of internal war acted as a brake on the speed of social and economic change, distorting both employment and investment patterns as well as constraining the ambit of urban restructuring. Massive state investment, particularly in housing, went some way to correct the imbalance between the north and other regions of the United Kingdom, and the expansion in public-sector employment helped alleviate the traditionally high levels of unemployment within the nationalist community.

Economic development in the post-conflict years

In the 1990s the Northern Ireland economy experienced what appeared to be a fundamental turn-round in fortunes. After decades as the ailing economy of the United Kingdom the region's fate appeared to change. Employment expanded and, for the first time in the region's history, unemployment began to fall to levels close to that in Britain.[3] Most notable was Northern Ireland's ability to ride out the 1992 recession, which hit Britain hard and led to the country leaving the European exchange rate mechanism in spectacular fashion. Whereas employment in Britain briefly dropped and then stagnated for some years after 1992, it continued to grow steadily in Northern Ireland. By the spring of 2004 the total number of employees in employment in Northern Ireland stood at 678,000, compared with just 493,000 in 1983. Employment in Northern Ireland had increased by 37 per cent in little over a decade, compared with a rise of just 17 per cent in the United Kingdom as a whole.

Just as elsewhere in the United Kingdom, much of the growth in jobs was in part-time employment, which increasingly was being taken up by men as well as women. However, whereas from the late 1990s slower growth in employment in Britain reflected productivity improvements, in Northern Ireland employment expanded parallel with the total hours worked, creating more jobs and working more hours.[4] This expansion was driven by capacity utilisation. Northern Ireland appeared to leave behind the economic straitjacket that had inhibited employment growth and sustained high levels of unemployment. But it did so at a cost: in the first half-decade of the current millennium Northern Ireland economic productivity fell further behind Britain's. This fundamental weakness of the economy was highlighted as far back as 1957 by Isles and Cuthbert,[5] who noted the:

> . . . two general conditions which differentiate the provincial sector of the economy from the rest. These are, firstly, the lower general level of employ-ment, proportionately to the labour force, which involves heavier unem-ployment and therefore proportionately more people who earn no income at all; and, secondly, the relatively narrow industrial structure, which restricts the number of openings for the employment of capital and labour at rates of earnings equivalent to those in Great Britain, and which thereby depresses the income of those who do earn.

Removing the shackles of the low-wage, low-productivity economy has been the continued challenge for Northern Ireland. The economy has remained dominated by an agricultural sector that is, strangely, both large and small at the same time, depending on how one chooses to look at it. While agriculture accounts for only 4 per cent of regional employment it also provides nearly one-third of the region's VAT-based enterprises – compared with 8.5 per cent in the United Kingdom. This sector is essen-tial to the revenue-raising capacity of the local state, not because of its size and economic strength but because of the weakness of the service sector. Less than 50 per cent of VAT-based businesses in Northern Ireland are in services, compared with over 70 per cent of businesses in the United Kingdom.[6] Tertiarisation of the economy is happening in Northern Ireland, just as it has been happening elsewhere in the industrialised world, but, literally, it does not pay off – at least, not for the regional state, which has been unable to build its fiscal resources on the strength of an expanding service sector and, particularly, on business services.[7]

Northern Ireland remains the United Kingdom's most specialised and least diversified regional economy. Some 40 per cent of its work force is employed in industries that, as a proportion of total employment, are substantially larger than equivalent industries elsewhere in the United Kingdom. This is not least due to the large share of employment contributed to the regional economy by the public sector, retailing and membership organisations. Many of the latter emerged as a result of the civil conflict, representing grass-roots and community-based organisa-tions concerned with social and economic development. A particular feature of the remaining overrepresented industries is that they operate in low-value service and manufacturing sectors and, for that reason, do not contribute in the same way to the region's aggregate industrial output as they do to employment. The failure to engage in high value-added production may not just weaken their international competitiveness by maintaining wages and salaries at low levels but also has detrimental effects on wealth creation.

Despite efforts to strengthen Northern Ireland's industrial base in the 1970s and into the 1990s, the region's industries have remained largely disconnected and unembedded in the local economy, both in terms of the trading and sourcing of goods[8] and in terms of local investment in research and development.[9] Even efforts to anchor Northern Ireland in the once burgeoning IT and call centre operations sector appear to have faltered, as employment in these areas declined from 12,000 in 2001 to 9,000 in 2005, very much counter to UK trends.[10]

Although the service sector in Northern Ireland has been expanding and has taken a more visible role as a potential driver of economic development, many of the key sectors that have shaped regional restructuring in parts of Britain have remained slow to develop and remain relatively underdeveloped in the regional economy. This applies, in particular, to banking and business services and to real estate. Whereas these sectors have been instrumental to the changing economic fortunes of the major English regions, they are struggling to make an impact on the internal Northern Ireland economy and, more important, to forge linkages beyond the region. To the present day, banking, finance and insurance contribute only some 7.5 per cent of employment in Northern Ireland, compared with 15.5 per cent in the United Kingdom, increasing their share of employment since 1984 by a mere fifth, compared with two-thirds in the United Kingdom. Instead the main growth area in services in Northern Ireland has been the retail sector, expanding, in particular, in Belfast and the region's larger towns, often initiated and funded by government intervention.[11]

Changes in employment patterns have reflected these economic developments. Employment growth in the ten years leading up to the new millennium remained firmly anchored in security-related occupations such as the police, the prison service and the Royal Irish Regiment, which had been a major source of employment – especially for members of the Protestant community – throughout the conflict. Whereas growth in sectors such as retail, professional and technical offered new employment opportunities, they continued to operate within the inherited structures of the local economy: a legacy of low productivity and a lack of embeddedness which continued to fall short in offering service and manufacturing industries of the type and quality required to become part of the supply chain of major actors in the regional economy. Moreover, they often offered wages lower than the UK average, not so much at the lower level of employee qualifications as at the medium and, in particular, higher level of skills.

The political economy of containment and adjustment

It is of course difficult to quantify precisely the effects of internal war on the Northern Irish economy. It remains reasonable nonetheless to assume that the conflict acted as a major disincentive to foreign investors[12] at a time when industrial and fiscal policies pursued south of the border – in particular, low corporation tax and generous grants – more than offset the infrastructural deficit there, eventually leading to a massive influx of multinational capital. Little has changed in this respect since the beginnings of the process of political settlement in Northern Ireland in the mid-1990s. In fact there has been a falling level of inward investment since 1995, and multinational corporations continue to be more attracted to the Irish Republic, which has the advantage, among other things, of a low corporation tax of 12.5 per cent as opposed to the 21–28 per cent rate in the United Kingdom. A 2005 study concluded that, adjusted for size, the south attracts twenty times more foreign investment than the north and that the main reason is the lower rate of corporation tax.[13] Northern Ireland's low-wage advantage that helped to attract multinational capital in the 1960s has since turned into a disadvantage as, following the fall of the Iron Curtain and the emergence of the Asian Tiger economies, footloose industries look farther afield to place their investments. Whereas the Republic of Ireland can compete for mobile capital on the basis of well qualified and flexible human capital, no such distinct assets are available to the North of Ireland. There have been repeated demands from political parties, employer organisations and trade unions for a reduction in corporation tax, which many seem to view as a panacea for the economic ills of the region. Any decision to lower corporation tax would be made in London, and would have profound implications for other regions of the United Kingdom and the principle of a unified taxation system. It is difficult to see the Treasury making any concessions in this area.

While internal strife may have accelerated the decline in manufacturing employment in the 1970s and 1980s, the simultaneous growth in public-sector jobs, which itself was to a considerable extent induced by the conflict, compensated for much of the loss in secondary industry jobs. Between 1970 and 1985 the British subsidy of the Northern Irish economy rose from under £100 million to £1.6 billion at 1980 prices.[14]

While in the late 1960s the subvention came to about 7 per cent of total expenditure, by 1985 it comprised 33 per cent of the total. Since the 1980s total annual transfer payments from the UK government to Northern Ireland have accounted for between one-third and two-fifths of the total revenue generated in Northern Ireland.[15] Writing in 1988, Rowthorn and Wayne[16] noted that:

> It would be little exaggeration to describe Northern Ireland in the late 1980s as a workhouse economy. A large part of its population is unemployed. Those who are not are chiefly engaged in servicing or controlling each other – through the provision of health, education retail distribution, construction security and social services. Relatively few people within the province are engaged in the production of tradable goods and services, which can be sold outside.

Rowthorn and Wayne's critique of the local economy still has resonance and relevance nearly two decades later. The basic weakness of the economy, which was underscored by the former Northern Ireland Secretary of State, Peter Hain, has, if anything, been amplified in recent years.[17] The particular paradox that besets the economy in the north is that it is geographically part of an island economy, but politically part of the United Kingdom, with separate political institutions but limited economic autonomy. The intention of the framers of the Government of Ireland Act 1920 was that the north should make a net contribution to the British exchequer and not be a burden on central funds. This provision – called the 'imperial contribution' – although abandoned in 1938, had significant consequences in that, for accounting purposes, the Northern Irish economy is treated as a separate entity, unlike other regions of the United Kingdom.

Although initially expected to pay its way, Northern Ireland consistently failed to do so and soon became dependent for its existence on a financial subsidy from London. During the 1970s the existing *ad hoc* arrangements were transformed into a crucial part of the British state's strategy to contain civil conflict through an attempt to equalise living and working conditions through public spending on housing, social services and a vast expansion of employment in the public sector.

It has been argued that the level of public subsidy has had a negative effect on the ability of the region to adjust to the demands of a global economy by inhibiting the development of a competitive private sector and absorbing much of the graduate work force into the high-wage public sector, which has the effect of driving up wages generally.[18] Others see the particular circumstances of Northern Ireland as meriting higher public spending. Specific social and economic problems such as a large agricultural sector, high levels of exclusion and social need and a collapsing infrastructure demand higher public expenditure. While this argument has some force, Northern Ireland's public sector, which employs over 30 per cent of the region's work force, appears inflated by international comparison.

Across the border, the need to deal with equally difficult social, economic and infrastructural problems is being tackled by a public sector which is considerably smaller at less than 20 per cent of the work force. Within the OECD, the share of public jobs in total employment is generally lower than 20 per cent, with no country exceeding 25 per cent. Furthermore, Northern Ireland's public administration is estimated to account for up to 60 per cent of regional GDP and is, by far, the largest and, given its size, a disproportionate contributor to regional wealth. By comparison, public administration in the Republic of Ireland accounts for just 35 per cent of GDP.

A number of factors have led to the emergence of an inflated service sector characterised by relatively poor productivity. The expansion of the public sector was, to a large extent, driven by political considerations such as the need to create alternative employment opportunities to counteract the precipitous decline in industrial employment and to address the exclusion of the minority from significant sectors of employment. In addition, the exigencies of internal war led both to an expanded security sector and, from the late 1980s onwards, the creation of job opportunities for (former) paramilitaries to deter them from further involvement in political violence.

The social effects of economic change

The changing structure of the labour market has been a key manifestation of the shifting fortunes of the two principal ethno-religious communities in Northern Ireland. Underlying labour market restructuring were also significant and important demographic shifts. According to the 2001 population census, the age profile of the two communities is diverging, to the benefit of the nationalist minority. Of those in the sixteen to thirty-five-year age cohort, 51 per cent are Catholic, which has both economic and political consequences. At the other end of the age profile, Protestants make up 63.3 per cent of those approaching retirement age. The composition of the economically active work force is another significant indicator: 57.3 per cent Protestant to 42.7 per cent Catholic. The census also shows that the number of Protestants in employment has fallen marginally (0.6 per cent), while the number of Catholics has risen by 1.7 per cent. The historic trend in the composition of the labour force is also significant.

Since 1990 overall Catholic representation has increased by 6.5 percentage points, from 34.9 per cent in 1990 to 41.4 per cent in 2004. During this period there was a net increase of 37,739 Catholic full-time employees, while for Protestants the net increase was 2,109.[19]

The central trend for the future will be increasing labour market activity on the part of a younger Catholic population which seems to be more adept at entering 'new' occupations. There is also evidence that a significant number of undergraduates – 34 per cent of the total in 2001/02 – choose to study in England or Scotland, and of this body of students only 28 per cent return to Northern Ireland after graduation. Although the reasons for this trend are unclear, it has been suggested that Protestants are twice as likely to study in England or Scotland, and most of those who choose to do so do not return.[20] This trend has tended to reinforce the pattern of increasing participation of Catholics in professional, managerial and white-collar occupations, particularly in the state sector.

The decline of manufacturing industry accelerated with the 'third phase' of globalisation during the 1990s and had, as we have seen, a dramatic effect on the economy of Northern Ireland.[21] This impact also had a political and social dimension particular to the region in that the bulk of manufacturing employment was Protestant, as Catholics were traditionally excluded from this, and other, sectors of the economy. The overall trend towards increased Catholic participation in the work force was further reinforced by the transition to a service economy which went hand in hand with the decline of manufacturing. The introduction of equality legislation in Northern Ireland effectively imposed a legal obligation on both the public and the private sector to increase the number of Catholics in employment, although a policy of positive discrimination was not part of the legislation.

Against a background of industrial decline, the main effect of the legislation was to help increase the number of Catholics employed in the public sector and to contribute significantly to increasing the size of the (non-productive) Catholic middle class. The size of the managerial and professional class has remained relatively constant at about 25 per cent of the work force, but the Catholic share of these occupations has risen by 10 per cent since 1990. In contrast, the size of the Protestant middle class has fallen.[22] A paradox of the Protestant near-monopoly of industrial employment was that Catholics were in a position to make the transition to a service economy more easily because of a combination of equality legislation, a younger work force and the lack of an industrial background.

During the decades of civil unrest after 1970 the contraction of employment in industry was to some extent offset by the expansion of

the security sector, which benefited the Protestant community in employment terms.[23] In 2002 almost one-third of all Protestant males working
in the public sector were employed in security and defence.[24] The number
employed in this sector – over 17,000 – is set to decline drastically over
the next few years as British army bases close, the home battalions of the
Royal Irish Regiment are disbanded and general levels of security are
lowered. There is also likely to be a knock-on effect in terms of supply
and maintenance contracts.

In effect, both communities are affected by structural economic change
and government policy, if in different ways. The decline in traditional
manufacturing industry has disproportionately affected the Protestant
community, as have the cutbacks in security-related employment. The
imminent reorganisation of the public sector may well see a contraction
of employment and employment opportunities enjoyed by the minority
in recent decades. Unlike in the Republic of Ireland, little alternative
employment is available from inward investment.

Poverty and exclusion

Regional economic changes in the 1980s and 1990s, which culminated
in rising employment and decreasing unemployment, brought with them
alterations in Northern Ireland's social structure and, in particular, the
extent and nature of social disadvantage. Research into the extent of
poverty and deprivation in the North concluded that:

> well over a quarter of Northern Ireland's households – 29.6 per cent – were
> poor in 2002/03. A further 2.1 per cent of households were judged to have
> recently risen out of poverty – that is, they lacked three or more necessities
> but had relatively high incomes. Another 12.1 per cent could be described
> as vulnerable to poverty in that their incomes were relatively low but they
> did not currently lack three or more necessities.[25]

A comparison with similar estimates for Britain in 1999 reveals a
greater risk of poverty and vulnerability to poverty, but also *less possibility of exiting poverty* in Northern Ireland.[26] Overall, the risk of
poverty and social exclusion remains higher in Northern Ireland than
in Britain or the Irish Republic. However, within Northern Ireland,
the nature of the risk of poverty and the sections of the population at
greatest risk of exclusion has changed. Comparing the composition of
the population of individuals on a low income between 1990 and 1994
with those on a low income between 1999 and 2002, Dignan[27] observes
a significantly increased risk of low income in households with only
one worker and in households with no workers owing to sickness and

disability. The proportion of one-worker households on a low income increased from 27 per cent in the early 1990s to 33 per cent in the early 2000s. Likewise, the proportion of no-worker households owing to sickness or disability and on a low income increased from 48 per cent to 57 per cent during that same period. By contrast, the low-income risk of retired households without workers decreased from 34 per cent to 29 per cent.

These shifts illustrate the changing nature of the risk of poverty in the context of regional economic growth, which, not atypically, coincides with a growing risk of poverty, including in-work poverty, often as a result of diverging income trends and changes in dependence on state welfare payments. Similar shifts can be observed for the two main ethno-religious groups. Applying their measure of poverty and social exclusion, Hillyard *et al.*[28] estimate that 36 per cent of Catholic households and 25 per cent of Protestant households are 'poor'. Because of the larger number of Protestant households in the Northern Ireland population, the Catholic and Protestant households contributed very similar shares to the total number of poor and excluded households: 48 per cent and 47 per cent respectively. The remaining 5 per cent of poor households were of no religious affiliation, or their religious affiliation could not be determined. Using a purely income-based measure of poverty, and focusing only on those who declared their religion, Dignan's findings[29] deviate somewhat from Hillyard *et al.*'s. He estimates that, by the early 2000s, 55 per cent of people in households on a low income were Catholics, compared with 45 per cent being Protestants.

Between the early and the late 1990s the proportion of Catholics in the Northern Ireland population increased by two percentage points, while the Protestant share decreased by the same amount. Dignan's study reveals that, at the same time, Catholics became less likely to be at risk of low income: the proportion of Catholics on a low income decreased by three percentage points, to 38 per cent, in 2001/02. The reverse happened to Protestants, whose risk of low income increased by two percentage points to 25 per cent. As a result of a growing population share and a declining risk of low income, the share of Catholics among those on a low income declined from 58 per cent to 55 per cent between the beginning and the end of the 1990s. By contrast, the relative decline in the Protestant population and its increased risk of low income caused the latter's share among the low-income population to increase from 42 per cent to 45 per cent. At the same time the proportion of workless households[30] declined by a larger margin among Catholics (by 4.8 percentage points to 33.6 per cent in 2003) than among Protestants (by 2.4 percentage points to 35.8 per cent).[31]

The changing pattern of poverty can be seen in shifts in educational attainment in the two communities. It can be broadly argued that 'Catholic men have caught up with their Protestant counterparts at almost every level of education'[32] and, indeed, the numbers from both communities gaining an A grade in the transfer test taken at age eleven – which offers access to the relatively prestigious and academically successful grammar schools – and the numbers completing third-level education are broadly comparable. But when these figures are controlled for class a different picture emerges. In schools with a high percentage of pupils in receipt of free school meals only 16.9 per cent of Protestant pupils get an A as opposed to 26.4 per cent in similar Catholic schools. According to government statistics, of the fifteen local government wards with the worst educational attainment, thirteen are in Protestant working-class areas.[33] However, pupils from Catholic secondary schools are more likely to leave school without qualifications than comparable Protestant pupils, and far fewer pupils from Catholic secondary schools (18.4 per cent) go on to further education than those from Protestant schools (28.5 per cent).[34]

It is difficult to interpret the statistics on education and to decode the underlying reasons but one thing is clear: the main determinant of educational achievement is not religion but class, the effects of which are filtered *differently* through the two parallel educational systems. More Protestant working-class pupils fall out of the system altogether but those who do go on to secondary school have a better chance of gaining a third-level qualification, while Catholic working-class pupils are more likely to leave secondary school without any qualification. The overall tendency would seem to be moving towards 'equality of misery' for a substantial section of both communities but the movement into poverty is more pronounced for Protestants, a tendency which is already having political consequences.

Conclusion

During the first phase of globalisation the economy of Northern Ireland was in a position to benefit from imperial expansion and was organised in such a way as to reward those loyal to the Union and exclude those of nationalist leanings. Although practices of ethno-religious exclusion were not legally sanctioned, such practices were in tune with the imperialist jingoism of the period. With the establishment of Northern Ireland the fortunes of the local economy were subservient to those of the central state, and the unionist regime was in the anomalous position of having considerable political and administrative power but negligible economic independence.

Economic stagnation and political inertia defined the inter-war period, because of the global economic recession and from fear of destabilising a profoundly dysfunctional political system. When socio-economic change began to take place in the aftermath of the Second World War the impetus came from welfare state legislation implemented from London. The unintended consequence of this legislation was to benefit the minority population and lead to the emergence of a Catholic white-collar middle class employed mainly in the public sector. The internal structures of exclusion, condoned and extended by the Stormont regime, were challenged by the underlying political message of post-war social democracy and by structural economic change.[35] The tenacity of internal divisions and the failure to confront them was partly instrumental in the tragic slide to internal war, but acted simply to delay and distort the impact of globalisation.

Whether by accident or design, the response of the British state to a crumbling economy and serious civil conflict was to increase public expenditure and create an alternative source of employment and consumption. Structural change was inevitable as the economy followed a standard global trajectory from a declining industrial economy to a service economy: the role of the state was to take up the slack caused, in part, by the effects of internal war on inward investment. The result was an inflated public sector, which had the effect, in combination with other factors, of eroding the ethno-religious imbalances that characterised the labour market under the unionist regime at Stormont, as well as sustaining relatively high levels of consumption and disposable income. These changes have benefited the Catholic middle classes by opening up new employment opportunities, particularly in the public sector. The propensity of Protestant university students to both study in the United Kingdom and remain there after graduation has reduced labour market competition to the benefit of Catholic graduates.

Although the lot of the Catholic middle class has seen substantial improvement, the same cannot be said for the Catholic working class. The Church-administered education system has failed them and, although unemployment has fallen, many of the jobs that have become available are part-time and unskilled. The Protestant middle class remains intact, if shrinking and aging, and no longer dominates the public sector and the professions. Elements of the Protestant working class are becoming increasingly marginal as their traditional sources of employment disappear, although apart from isolated and somewhat incoherent protests little organised resistance to these changes seems to be emerging.

Essentially, the labour market has been depoliticised, but at the cost of failure to make the transition to a knowledge-based economy and to attract high-tech investment. With the ending of the IRA campaign the British government has issued a stark warning that levels of public expenditure cannot be maintained. The former Secretary of State for Northern Ireland, Peter Hain, made this abundantly clear in an interview in early 2006:[36]

> There is no prospect of the *status quo* prevailing – millions of pounds being paid out for people not to do their jobs. . . . I don't think people have woken up to the fact that the economy is not sustainable in its present form in the long term. We have got to become more competitive, less dependent upon a bloated public sector with huge state subsidies.

There is something of 'back to the future' about this statement. As early as 1957, as has been pointed out above, Isles and Cuthbert identified the fundamental weakness of the local economy in the combination of a narrow industrial base and low productivity. The industrial base crumbled in the 1970s, to be replaced – mainly for political reasons – by an inflated state sector which had the negative effect of draining talent away from more productive and technologically progressive industries. During the 1970s and 1980s much effort was expended on the attempt to revive the industrial sector, but to little avail. Neither the education system nor state policy was directed at developing modern knowledge-based industry.

There is yet a further echo in Hain's warning. In 1974, at the height of the Ulster Workers' Strike against the ill fated Sunningdale agreement, the then Prime Minister, Harold Wilson, made his famous 'sponging' speech, in which he commented:

> British taxpayers have seen the taxes they have poured out, almost without regard to cost . . . going into Northern Ireland. They see property destroyed by evil violence and are asked to pick up the bill for rebuilding it. Yet people who benefit from all this now viciously defy Westminster, purporting to act as though they were an elected government; people who spend their lives sponging on Westminster and British democracy and then systematically assault democratic methods. Who do these people think they are?[37]

Although the political context has changed irrevocably, the message is the same: Westminster is intent on relieving itself of the burden of subsidising the north, particularly in a situation where a return to political violence seems unlikely and an essentially hegemonic neo-liberal ideology dictates reduced public expenditure.

Notes

1 For a discussion of this lacuna see C. Coulter, 'The absence of class politics in Northern Ireland', *Capital and Class* 69:3 (1999), pp. 77–100; P. Shirlow

and I. Shuttleworth, '"Who is going to toss the burgers?" Social class and the reconstruction of the Northern Ireland economy', *Capital and Class* 69:3 (1999), pp. 27–46.

2 C. Coulter, *Contemporary Northern Irish Society: An Introduction* (London: Pluto Press, 1999).

3 By 2000 the unemployment rate stood at 5.7 per cent, which compared favourably with a UK rate of 4 per cent. Unemployment continued to fall from 4.6 per cent in 2004 to 3.4 per cent in 2005 while the UK rate stood at 4.9 per cent in December 2005. Against that, the activity rate is the lowest of all UK regions, at 70.8 per cent. See *Northern Ireland Labour Force Survey, Historical Supplement* (Belfast: HMSO, 2005); First Trust Bank, *Economic Outlook* (Belfast: FNB, 2005); UK Office for National Statistics.

4 C. Allen, G. Gudgin and A. Webb, 'Hours worked: what can they tell us about the Northern Ireland labour market?' *Labour Market Bulletin 18*, November (Belfast: Department for Employment and Learning, 2004), pp. 71–81.

5 K. Isles and N. Cuthbert, *An Economic Survey of Northern Ireland* (Belfast: HMSO, 1957), p. 5.

6 J. Gillan, 'Structure and growth' in Department of Enterprise, Trade and Investment (DETINI), *The Northern Ireland Economic Bulletin 2005* (Belfast: DETINI, 2005). The turnover threshold for payment of VAT is around £30,000. Enterprises below the threshold because of their small size fall outside the VAT net.

7 Department of Enterprise, Trade and Investment, *Northern Ireland Index of Services (Experimental), Quarter 3, 2005* (Belfast: DETINI, 2006).

8 N. Hewitt-Dundas, B. Andresosso-O'Callaghan, M. Crone, J. Murray and S. Roper, 'Selling global, buying local? What determines the sourcing patterns of multinational plants in Ireland?' *Regional Studies* 39 (2005), p. 225–39.

9 Arthur D. Little Ltd, *Research and Development Business Expenditure in Northern Ireland: Final Report to the Department of Enterprise, Trade and Investment* (Belfast: DETI, 2004).

10 G. Heckley, 'Offshoring and the labour market: the IT and call centre occupations considered', *Labour Market Trends*, September 2005, pp. 373–85.

11 A. Cebulla, *Urban Policy in Belfast: An Evaluation of the Department of the Environment's Physical Regeneration Initiatives* (Belfast: Department of the Environment for Northern Ireland, 1994); A. Cebulla, J. Berry and S. McGreal, 'Evaluation of community-based regeneration in Northern Ireland: between social and economic regeneration', *Town Planning Review* 71:2 (2000), pp. 169–89.

12 S. Fothergill and N. Guy, *Branch Factory Closures in Northern Ireland*, NIERC Report 5 (Belfast: Northern Ireland Economic Research Centre, 1990).

13 Goodbody Stockbrokers, 2005.

14 B. Rowthorn and N. Wayne, *Northern Ireland: The Political Economy of Conflict*, Cambridge: Polity Press, 1988), p. 98.

15 D. Heald, *Funding the Northern Ireland Assembly: Assessing the Options*, NIEC Research Monograph 10 (Belfast: Northern Ireland Economic Council, 2003); G. Hutchinson, 'Public expenditure in the regional economy of Northern Ireland: has the growth of the 1970s been sustained?' *Journal of the Statistical and Social Inquiry Society of Ireland* 28:1 (1998/99), pp. 1–25.

16 Rowthorn and Wayne, *Northern Ireland*, p. 98.

17 In an interview in the *Irish Echo* (15 December 2005) the Secretary of State commented that the Northern Ireland economy was 'not sustainable in the long term' and stressed that cross-border economic linkages were the way forward.

18 J. Bradley, *An Island Economy: Exploring the Long-term Consequences of Peace and Reconciliation on the Island of Ireland* (Dublin: Stationery Office, 1996).

19 These figures are extracted from the *Monitoring Report* of the Equality Commission, 2004. It should be noted that the figures exclude small private-sector concerns (eleven to twenty-five employees).

20 DEL, 2003. These figures should be interpreted with caution. On the other side of the equation, those who study in the north have a high propensity (97 per cent) to stay. The figure for Scotland is 85 per cent. If any region does actually suffer from a 'brain drain' it is Wales: 38 per cent study outside the region and few return. For those educated inside Wales only 59 per cent remain after graduation.

21 Modern globalisation can be divided into three periods. The first period, driven by British imperial expansion in the latter half of the nineteenth century, led to the early industrialisation of the north-east of Ireland and its integration into the imperial economy. The second phase, from the 1970s, led to the collapse of the traditional industrial base of Northern Ireland as heavy industry relocated outside the West. The third and current phase saw the emergence of the knowledge-based economy and the rise of India and China as potential economic superpowers.

22 Equality Commission for Northern Ireland, *Monitoring Report: A Profile of the Northern Ireland Workforce* (Belfast, Equality Commission, 2002, 2005), www.equalityni.org.

23 Rowthorn and Wayne, *Northern Ireland*, p. 112.

24 Equality Commission, *Monitoring Report*.

25 P. Hillyard, G. Kelly, E. McLaughlin, D. Patsios and M. Tomlinson, *Bare Necessities: Poverty and Social Exclusion in Northern Ireland: Key Findings* (Belfast: Democratic Dialogue, 2003), p. 29.

26 In making this comparison, allowance must be made for changes in the risk of poverty and social exclusion in Northern Ireland during the intermittent years between 1999 and 2002/03, when the British and Northern Ireland surveys were conducted. There are no comparable data based on the

consensual method of measuring poverty and social exclusion. However, a number of studies using a range of alternative poverty measures have highlighted the small but steady decline in the prevalence of poverty in both Northern Ireland and Great Britain: G. Palmer, J. Carr and P. Kenway, *Monitoring Poverty and Social Exclusion* (York: Joseph Rowntree Foundation, 2004); H. Sutherland, T. Sefton and D. Piachaud, *Poverty in Britain: The Impact of Government Policy since 1997* (York: Joseph Rowntree Foundation, 2003); Department for Social Development, *Households below Average Income, Northern Ireland, 2003–2004* (Belfast: DSD, 2004; T. Dignan, *Low Income Households in Northern Ireland, 1990–2002* (Belfast: Equality Directorate Research Branch, Office of the First Minister and Deputy First Minister, 2003). Given their findings, it is unlikely that the poverty and exclusion gap between Northern Ireland and Britain narrowed substantially between these years.

27 Dignan, *Low Income HouseholdsIreland*. Dignan's analysis uses the Northern Ireland Continuous Household Survey (CHS). In order to increase the number of cases for more detailed analysis the data were pooled for three periods: 1990/91–1993/94, 1997/98–1998–99 and 1999/00–2001/02.

28 Hillyard *et al.*, *Bare Necessities*.

29 Dignan, *Low Income Households*.

30 Workless households are households where no one is in employment.

31 *Office of the First Minister and Deputy First Minister Indicators of Social Need for Northern Ireland* (Belfast: OFMDFM, no date). Downloaded 23 December 2005 from www.research.ofmdfmni.gov.uk/hbai.pdf.

32 O'Leary and Yaojun Li (2006), p. 6.

33 See *Irish Times*, 5 April 2006, for a report on a government initiative to tackle this problem.

34 B. Osborne, and I. Shuttleworth, *Fair Employment in Northern Ireland: a Generation on* (Belfast: Blackstaff Press, 2004), pp. 74 ff.

35 See Jim Smyth, 'Moving the immovable: the civil rights movement in Northern Ireland', in L. Connolly and N. Hourigan (eds), *Social Movements in Ireland* (Manchester: Manchester University Press, 2006).

36 *Sunday Times*, 15 January 2006.

37 R. Fisk, *The Point of No Return: The Strike which Broke the British in Ulster* (London: André Deutsch, 1975), p. 138.

10

Whiteness, racism and exclusion: a critical race perspective

Paul Connolly and Romana Khaoury

> The peace process has allowed us to snap out of the trance of the two tra-
> ditions, that mutual obsession of nationalists and unionists, the hypnotic
> focus of a cobra and a mongoose about to attack each other. As the shouts
> and din of ancient quarrel begin to subside, we hear other voices. In Ireland
> today there are atheists, Jews, Sikhs, Buddhists, socialists, Chinese,
> Travellers, blacks, Muslims, gays, asylum seekers, feminists, and others, all
> of whom locate themselves outside the two traditions and are entitled to
> parity of esteem and equality of treatment.[1]

There is certainly a tendency, as illustrated in the quotation from Paddy
Logue above, to view the marginalisation of race issues within Northern
Ireland as largely an unintentional consequence of the conflict between
the two principal ethno-political traditions in the region. Nationalists
and unionists have been so obsessed with fighting one another, so the
argument goes, that they simply have had no time to consider the voices
of others. With the paramilitary cease-fires and the onset of the peace
process, it is felt that things are now changing. Space is increasingly
emerging within the social and political agenda to consider the needs and
experiences of others, including those of black and minority ethnic
people living in the region.

We want to argue in this chapter, however, that there is a danger with
arguments such as these, as they tend to underplay the significance of race
within Northern Ireland. Rather than the marginalisation of race issues
being a by-product of the divisions that exist between the unionist and
nationalist traditions, we want to show in this chapter that it has actually been a constitutive element of those traditions. By drawing upon
Critical Race Theory (CRT), it will be argued that, while it may often go
unrecognised, race is a fundamental element of the social identities and
lives of people in Northern Ireland. The historical (and continued) marginalisation of race issues within the region is, therefore, not simply an
oversight or the result of thoughtlessness but is actually a reflection of the
way in which white, settled people's power and privilege within Northern

Ireland has become a normalised and taken-for-granted aspect of life here. Recognising this, in turn, raises important questions about how we might best understand the nature of racism within the region and whether, as Barnor Hesse has suggested, the existing focus on institutional racism with its emphasis on the largely 'unintentional' and 'unwitting' nature of racism is entirely appropriate.[2]

The chapter begins, therefore, with a brief outline of CRT and the critique of whiteness therein before using it as a basis from which to examine the research literature on racism in Northern Ireland. It will be shown that there has been a tendency within existing research to frame black and minority ethnic people's experiences within the region with the concept of institutional racism. What we will argue is that, while this has been extremely useful in drawing attention to the structural aspects of racial discrimination, it also tends to make a distinction between the practices and processes of racial discrimination and the white, settled majority population. By reviewing the findings of a range of studies, we want to suggest that rather than racism being simply the result of unthinking behaviour and ignorance, it is actually a routine and normalised part of life in Northern Ireland. We will argue that there is a need to move beyond the existing limited focus on institutional racism towards a more fundamental naming and interrogation of whiteness as it is constructed and practised by differing majority groups and traditions within the region.

Critical Race Theory and the rise of whiteness studies

Stemming from the field of critical legal studies, CRT has its origins in the 1970s and the concerns being raised at that time about the slow progress being made in the United States with regard to racial reform.[3] While it is still largely a body of work located within the United States, it is now beginning to be taken up and applied in other contexts, most notably in relation to race and education in the United Kingdom.[4] CRT is a particularly useful framework with which to begin thinking about race issues in Northern Ireland because of the way that it problematises race and places a concern with racism at the heart of the analysis. According to Delgado and Stefancic, while CRT embodies a wide range of research and scholarship it tends to be underpinned by at least five core principles. The first is that racism is not an abnormal or aberrational aspect of society but is ordinary and routine; it is seen as 'the usual way society does business' and thus tends to be the common, everyday experience of black and minority ethnic people.[5] Second, there is recognition that racism serves important purposes, both psychic and material, and thus there is little incentive among the majority white population to challenge it.

Third, CRT adopts a social constructionist approach to race and is thus concerned with interrogating the processes by which particular groups of people become racialised over time and why. As Delgado and Stefancic explain:

> [R]ace and races are products of social thought and relations. Not objective, inherent, or fixed, they correspond to no biological or genetic reality; rather, races are categories that society invents, manipulates, or retires when convenient. People with common origins share certain physical traits, of course, such as skin colour, physique, and hair texture. But these constitute only an extremely small portion of their genetic endowment, are dwarfed by that which we have in common, and have little or nothing to do with distinctly human, higher-order traits, such as personality, intelligence, and moral behaviour. That society frequently chooses to ignore these scientific facts, creates races, and endows them with pseudo-permanent characteristics is of great interest to critical race theory.[6]

Following on from this social constructionist approach is, fourth, recognition that race is not a fixed category but one that changes both over time and from one context to the next. Thus, differing groups will become racialised and excluded at different times and for different reasons. Moreover, the ways in which race as a social process impacts upon black and minority ethnic people will vary according to context and will be fundamentally informed by factors such as gender and social class. It is in recognition of this that there is a strong emphasis within CRT on the notion of intersectionality (i.e. examining the interrelationships between race, gender and social class as they impact upon people's lives) and an anti-essentialist approach.

The fifth and final key principle underpinning CRT is an emphasis on the unique voice of black and minority ethnic people. As Delgado and Stefancic concede, this sits in 'uneasy tension' with the previous anti-essentialist principle. However, there remains a need to foreground and prioritise the experiences and perspectives of black and minority ethnic people as, collectively, they are in a unique position to understand the nature and effects of racism and, through their narratives, to provide new and challenging ways to understanding existing systems and social relationships.

In the context of Northern Ireland, this overarching approach to thinking about race provided by CRT helps us to move beyond some of the limitations associated with the notion of institutional racism mentioned in the introduction. While there remains an emphasis on identifying and problematising the role of institutions and structures in maintaining and reproducing racial inequalities, CRT requires us to go beyond this. In particular, it helps us recognise the normal and ordinary nature of racism and the psychic and material investment that members of the majority white, settled population tend to have in it. One of the key ways in which this understanding has been developed within CRT over recent years has been in relation to the increasing focus placed on critically interrogating whiteness.[7] In this sense, the power of whiteness as a racial identity can be seen not only in terms of its ability to impose itself as the central reference point by which all other groups are 'Othered' and measured against but also, crucially, by the way that it is so normalised and taken for granted that it can remain unstated and unrecognised. As Wicomb has explained, 'white is an empty signifier, both everything and nothing . . . being invisible to itself it cannot acknowledge its existence . . . it can only articulate itself in terms of the markedness of black, the contrast which supplies the meaning of white as the norm'.[8]

Whiteness, therefore, has become the means by which race is capable of being, at one and the same time, both normal, ordinary and endemic and yet also unrecognisable and unknowable. In places such as the United States this is achieved, as Frankenberg has argued, through the continual 'slippages' between discourses on race, nation and culture that 'continue to "unmark" white people while consistently marking and racialising others'.[9] Thus, for example, whiteness has come to represent what it means to be such things as: American,[10] working-class[11] and also a woman.[12] This has then become the measure against which the differences of others are identified and judged. Ultimately, it is only here that glimpses can be gained of the nature of whiteness itself as depictions of the 'other' offer some understanding of what it therefore means to be white.[13] As Aanerud has explained, for example, the many discourses that constitute 'the exotic, the promiscuous, the earthy and accessible female other' come, by definition, to define white female sexuality. Similarly, the construction of black and minority ethnic people as lazy and 'welfare scroungers' also come, by default, to define the white working class as 'decent', 'hard-working' and 'honourable'.[14]

Of course, in the context of Northern Ireland, things are more complex still. There is no one majority white population around which discourses on whiteness can be constructed. Rather, the majority white and settled population is divided politically and ethnically between two overarching traditions – unionism and nationalism – as the opening quotation to this chapter alluded to. The scale of these divisions and the level of violence associated with them have meant that both traditions have been actively involved in their competing projects of nation-building. Rather than the majority white population being characterised by a largely unstated and elusive ethnic identity, the conflict in Northern Ireland has thus produced at least two main majority ethnic groups[15] with strong, explicit and opposing notions of whiteness. As with all other forms of whiteness, however, the power of these particular versions lies in their ability to be permeated by race without ever needing to acknowledge it. This is an argument that we intend to develop through the remainder of this chapter.

Northern Ireland and institutional racism

Within this context set by CRT, it is now worth examining what we currently know about race and racism in Northern Ireland. Northern Ireland is an overwhelmingly white, settled population. Data from the 2001 census estimate that there are only around 14,300 minority ethnic people living in the region, representing just 0.8 per cent of the total population. Within this, the largest minority ethnic groups are the Chinese (4,100), followed by South Asians (2,500), Irish Travellers (1,700) and African Caribbeans (1,100). In terms of settlement patterns, each of these main minority ethnic groups tends to be fairly evenly distributed. Around a third of the Chinese, South Asian and African Caribbean populations and a quarter of the Irish Traveller population reside in the two principal urban areas of Belfast and Derry/Londonderry, with the remainder living in rural and semi-rural areas. In addition, while it is more difficult to quantify, given the transient nature of their populations, there are increasing numbers of mainly European migrant workers in Northern Ireland[16] as well as refugees and asylum seekers.[17]

Until relatively recently there has tended to be a strong denial that racism is a problem or even a significant political issue in Northern Ireland.[18] Such has been the extent of this denial that it was not even thought to be necessary to extend the core provisions of the Race Relations Act 1976 that outlawed racial discrimination to the region until some twenty years later via the implementation of the Race Relations (Northern Ireland) Order 1997. While a long time coming, the order has at least helped to raise awareness of issues of race and racism in Northern Ireland and to begin to place them on the political agenda. Perhaps as important for advancing race equality issues in the region has been the equality provisions introduced through the Northern Ireland Act 1998. These provisions formed part of the 'Good Friday Agreement', aimed at addressing the causes of the conflict in Northern Ireland and establishing a political settlement. Part of the Agreement involved the introduction of new legislation that placed a statutory duty on all public authorities to ensure equality of opportunity and promote good relations. This was supported by the requirement that each public authority must produce an Equality Scheme detailing how precisely it intends to meet these statutory duties and to submit it to the newly established Equality Commission for Northern Ireland for approval. While the primary impetus for these developments was undoubtedly to address relations between the two main majority ethnic traditions in the region, it also covered many other aspects of inequality including, most important for this present chapter, 'race'.

Since the late 1990s, therefore, Northern Ireland has witnessed an important shift, symbolically at least, in relation to an increased legal and political will to begin addressing racism and discrimination in the region. It is likely that this change has served to increase awareness of race issues among policy makers as well as their willingness to recognise and begin to address some of them. All this, in turn, has been supported by a growing body of research evidence that has helped to document black and minority ethnic people's experiences and needs and to begin mapping out the key issues that require attention.[19] Two key themes have tended to underpin this work: an emphasis on institutional racism as implicated in the provision of public services to black and minority ethnic people in the region and the more specific issue of racist harassment. It is worth briefly considering each of these two themes.

In relation to institutional racism, a growing number of studies have emerged since the mid-1990s that have examined how well black and minority ethnic people's needs are being addressed by a range of public services, including education, health, housing, social security, training and employment.[20] Within this work, a common framework that has tended to be used to make sense of the services being provided has been the notion of 'institutional racism'. This was defined most significantly in the Macpherson Report as:

> the collective failure of an organisation to provide an appropriate and professional service to people because of their colour, culture or ethnic origin. It can be seen or detected in processes, attitudes and behaviour which amount to discrimination through unwitting prejudice, ignorance, thoughtlessness, and racist stereotyping which disadvantage minority ethnic people.[21]

There are too many detailed and specific insights into the nature of institutional racism within Northern Ireland provided through this body of work to be able to include them all here. However, there are four core issues that have tended to emerge across a range of studies and service areas[22] that give a flavour of the findings that have arisen from this work. These are: the problems presented by the 'language barrier' and, more specifically, the difficulties faced by black and minority ethnic people who speak little or no English attempting to access services; the lack of information provided to black and minority ethnic communities, leading to low awareness and thus take-up of particular services; the lack of race awareness training provided to staff across a range of services, leading to some staff responding to black and minority ethnic people in ways that are inappropriate, insensitive and/or condescending; and the tendency for particular services not to recognise and attempt to meet the specific cultural and dietary needs of differing black and minority ethnic communities.

All four of these key issues tend to reflect the emphasis placed within the notion of institutional racism on those policies and practices that, however unintentional and unwitting, tend to collectively disadvantage black and minority ethnic communities. Thus the fact that particular service providers have tended not to make interpreters routinely available may well not be because a senior manager within that organisation purposely wishes to exclude particular black and minority ethnic communities from their services. Rather, it is quite likely that there may just not have been the demand for interpreters historically and the continued lack of interpreters is simply due to the thoughtlessness of service providers unaware of the needs of specific communities.

These core arguments concerning institutional racism would appear to be equally applicable to the growing number of migrant workers that have arrived in Northern Ireland over recent years.[23] Such patterns of inward migration have been steadily increasing, particularly since 2004, when ten new countries joined the European Union. Some of the impact of inward migration has been studied by McVeigh and Fisher, who found that it has tended to lead to rural regeneration and the retention and development of a number of industries that, without migration, would have collapsed.[24] While the experiences of many migrant workers arriving in Northern Ireland have been positive, this has not been the case for everyone. Indeed, some have encountered racial prejudice and discrimination across a range of areas and have also found it difficult accessing some public and private services.[25]

Overall, while this increasing recognition of and emphasis on the notion of institutional racism has been a welcome development, there remains little evidence of any substantial efforts having been made to begin addressing it.[26] While the establishment of positive responsibilities through equality legislation may have ensured minimum standards being set and adhered to within public services, these alone have not been enough to begin effecting real change. Indeed, a recent report on racist violence and criminal justice in Northern Ireland has indicated that the response of various government agencies remains profoundly lacking.[27] The key findings from this report would seem to replicate the experiences of minority ethnic communities in relation to many other service areas within Northern Ireland in that, while there has indeed been some movement at policy level, the challenge remains very much one of translating it into practice on the ground.

Perhaps the key problem to draw out from the developments outlined above is that they do tend to undermine the construction of institutional racism as essentially the result of ignorance. With the increasing political recognition of race issues and media coverage of racist attacks, as well as the many legal and policy developments that have taken place over the last decade as outlined above, it is becoming increasingly difficult to continue to claim that people in Northern Ireland remain as ignorant as before around issues of race. Indeed, the type of intransigence that is now being identified through research and the lack of will by those on the ground to make a significant effort to begin to tackle racial discrimination suggest that the white majority population may not be entirely benign.

This point takes us on to the second key theme that has underpinned research in Northern Ireland over the last ten years, namely that of racist harassment.[28] This tendency of institutional racism to construct the majority white and settled population within Northern Ireland as essentially benign (albeit thoughtless and ignorant) certainly sits uneasily with the routine experiences that members of the black and minority ethnic communities have of racist harassment in the region. One of the earliest and most comprehensive studies conducted in Northern Ireland on racist harassment was Irwin and Dunn's survey of 1,176 black and minority ethnic people published in 1996. They found that a significant proportion of their minority ethnic respondents had been verbally abused (44 per cent), experienced criminal damage to their property (29 per cent) and been physically abused (10 per cent).[29] Within these overall trends, Irwin and Dunn found that the Chinese community was the most likely to experience harassment, with 65 per cent reporting that they had been verbally abused and 52 per cent that they had experienced criminal damage to their property.[30] This higher level of harassment can, partly, be explained in terms of their greater contact with the general public through Chinese restaurants and takeaways. Beyond this, racist harassment has been found to take place in a variety of contexts, including schools,[31] housing,[32] the workplace[33] and also in a range of public places such as in city centres, shops, train stations, on buses and in the street.[34]

Moreover the number of incidents of racist harassment reported to the police has increased steadily. Attacks on migrant workers, particularly

Eastern Europeans, have become a significant problem over recent years with an increasing number of reports of migrant workers being badly beaten and their homes attacked.[35] A number of incidents have been reported of migrant workers being burnt out of their homes that have attracted high levels of media attention and resulted in Northern Ireland being branded the 'race hate capital of Europe'.[36]

Such routine and persistent levels of racist harassment certainly bring into question the tendency to place too much emphasis on the unwitting and unintentional nature of racism in the region. Moreover, and even beyond these explicit acts of violence towards black and minority ethnic people, there is evidence that race remains a powerful yet unstated aspect of the collective conscience in Northern Ireland. Consider, for example, the following two quotes provided by two African Caribbean women interviewed as part of Connolly and Keenan's study of racist harassment in the region:[37]

> Even if they don't say something, they don't say anything to you, but it's the looks. Sometimes the way they can just look at you. You know, like, drop dead . . . The elderly people, yes. Or they would just bump into you, you know what I mean? They don't say anything, it's the way they look at you or push you.

> I just feel, if there is anything, if there is anything that comes out to me about being in this country, it's that . . .racism. It's not really overt racism, it's covert. Things like they'd [*local people*] see me, and people that I've talked to have said it, they wouldn't necessarily see me as a person, they'd see me as a black girl, you know. That's the first thing people see.

Racial attitudes and identities in Northern Ireland

What these findings on racist harassment suggest is that it may not be entirely appropriate to continue to work simply within the interpretative framework of institutional racism, with its emphasis on the unintentional and unwitting nature of racial prejudice and discrimination. As suggested earlier, one of the consequences of this approach is to create the impression that a distinction can be made between the white, settled majority population – who are constructed as essentially race-neutral and benign but possibly thoughtless and ignorant – and the practices and processes of racial discrimination. However, given the underlying intransigence among the majority white population in relation to addressing racial exclusion and discrimination and also the widespread nature of racist harassment in the region, it is at least questionable whether such a distinction can be made. To explore this further, it is worth looking a little more closely at the attitudes and identities of the majority white population in Northern Ireland to see if we can begin to ascertain how central race is to their everyday lives.

In relation to racial prejudice, there have been a number of attitudinal studies conducted in Northern Ireland over the last ten years exploring people's attitudes to race. In comparing people's attitudes over that period, Gilligan and Lloyd have drawn attention to a trend for people to both claim that they are personally more prejudiced now than ten years ago and also that racial prejudice is generally more of a problem now than it used to be.[38] As regards this latter point, while 34 per cent of respondents in 1994 felt that people in general would mind ('a little' or 'a lot') if a suitably qualified Chinese person was appointed as their boss, this steadily increased to 55 per cent in 2004.[39] As Gilligan and Lloyd suggest, however, it is not possible to determine whether these trends reflect real shifts in the levels of racial prejudice in the region or just an increasing awareness of it. Perhaps a slightly more valid measure to use to compare changes over time is the more specific question of how a respondent would feel personally if they were to have a Chinese boss. This question has been asked in six separate surveys between 1994 and 2004 and, as Gilligan and Lloyd report, the proportion of respondents reporting that they would mind 'a little' or 'a lot' has tended to show no overall trend; simply fluctuating between 11 and 19 per cent over this period.[40]

Because of the tendency for respondents to under-report socially undesirable attitudes such as this, it is difficult to read too much into the actual percentage figures provided. Moreover, because of the subjective nature of such attitudinal surveys, there is no objective way of determining whether racial prejudice has actually increased or decreased over this period. Perhaps the main point to draw out from all of this is that with up to one in five respondents willing to admit that they would mind if a Chinese person was appointed as their boss, then it is clear that race is a social reality in Northern Ireland that has the potential to shape people's attitudes in the region. To gain more of an insight into how significant race actually is to the majority white population in Northern Ireland, it is interesting to compare levels of racial and sectarian prejudice. The only study that has done this to date is Connolly and Keenan's survey of a stratified random sample of 1,267 adults in the region.[41] While it was conducted in 2000 and is therefore a little dated, it is the only study that has explicitly compared attitudes in this way and so is worth briefly considering here. As part of the survey, respondents were asked how willing they would be to mix with individuals from particular minority ethnic groups as well as those from the other main majority ethnic group to themselves (i.e. Catholics or Protestants). The findings are shown in Table 10.1.

Table 10.1 Percentage of respondents stating that they would be unwilling to
accept members of other ethnic groups

'I would not willingly accept the following person as . . .	% of respondents agreeing with the statements in relation to the following ethnic groups				
	African Caribbean	Chinese	Asian	Irish Traveller	Protestant/ Catholic[a]
citizens of Northern Ireland who have come to live and work here'	18	16	20	45	10
residents in my local area'	26	25	27	57	15
a colleague at my work'	35	34	36	66	19
a close friend of mine'	42	41	43	70	26
a relative by way of marrying a close member of my family'	54	53	54	77	39

Source: P. Connolly and M. Keenan, *Racial Attitudes and Prejudice in
Northern Ireland* (Belfast: Northern Ireland Statistics and Research Agency,
2000), p. 18.
Note: [a] 'Protestant' if the respondent, identified themselves as Catholic and
'Catholic' if the respondents identified themselves as Protestant.

As can be seen, around a quarter of respondents stated that they were
unwilling to accept African Caribbean, Chinese and Asian people as residents in their local area, while around a third of respondents were
unwilling to accept them as colleagues at work. Although attitudes
towards these three groups were very similar it can be seen that much
more negative attitudes tended to be expressed towards Irish Travellers,
with over half of respondents not wanting them as residents in their local
area and around two-thirds not wanting an Irish Traveller as a colleague
at work. However, and in the context of the present chapter, the most significant finding relates to how these attitudes compare with those associated with the sectarian divide. As can be seen, respondents were more
likely to state that they were unwilling to mix with those from black and
minority ethnic communities compared with those from the other main
ethno-religious tradition. Again, while it would be inappropriate to focus
on the precise percentage figures involved, this is arguably an important
finding nonetheless. It is widely accepted that Northern Ireland is fundamentally structured along sectarian lines. What this finding hints at is
that, in relative terms, Northern Ireland is likely to be also fundamentally

structured and informed by race, given that levels of racial prejudice appear to be more substantial than sectarian prejudice in the region.

Of course, it would be rash to draw too many conclusions from the findings of this one study. Fortunately, another attitudinal study that has approached the issue of race from a different angle also tends to confirm this overall picture that race is an underpinning element of social life in Northern Ireland. This study, undertaken by Connolly, involved asking a representative sample of 380 white respondents in Northern Ireland to rate how important a number of elements were to their sense of identity.[42] A wide range of elements were listed, including their gender, occupation, political beliefs, educational background, ethno-religious persuasion (i.e. 'being Protestant' or 'being Catholic'), area of residence, the music they listen to, the clothes they wear, their educational background and also their race (i.e. explained to respondents as: 'being White'). For each variable they were asked to state whether it was 'very important', 'quite important', 'not very important' or 'not at all important' to their sense of identity. The respondents' answers were then analysed to ascertain whether any underlying pattern existed in relation to how they rated each of the elements. In other words, did respondents tend to rate particular variables together in the same way?

The results of the procedure, known as a factor analysis, are provided in Table 10.2. For those unfamiliar with this type of research method, the findings are explained in more detail elsewhere.[43] For now the key point to note is that the analysis found that the answers provided by respondents could be grouped into five main factors. In other words, the analysis found that there were five main underlying identities (called factors) that tended to influence people's ratings of these individual variables. These five factors and the key variables that tend to be grouped together within each factor are shown in Table 10.2. The strongest factor, and the one of most interest in relation to this present chapter, is factor 1. As can be seen, it tends to represent what we would associate with the classic Northern Ireland identity in terms of its emphasis on neighbourhood, nationality, politics and being Catholic/Protestant. What the analysis shows is that those who tend to rate one of these variables strongly also tend to rate the others strongly as well. The most interesting aspect of factor 1, however, is the fact that race is listed alongside all these other variables. The key point to draw out from this, therefore, is that this classic Northern Irish identity would also seem to be fundamentally racialised. In other words, evidence presented here clearly suggests that for those who rate being Protestant/Catholic as important to how they see themselves alongside their nationality, politics and local neighbourhood are also equally likely to rate their racial identity as important as

Table 10.2 Factor analysis of the items that respondents felt were important to them in relation to their identity[a]

Factor	Variables most closely related to the factor[b]	Proportion of the answers by respondents across the sample that the factor can account for (%)
1	Neighbourhood Social class background Racial identity Being Protestant/Catholic Nationality Political beliefs	24.6
2	Clothes Star sign Music Social activities	14.2
3	Political beliefs Religious faith Exercise Family	8.1
4	Age Gender	6.6
5	Educational background Occupation	6.3

Notes: [a] Principal axis factoring with oblique rotation.
[b] Only variables with factor loadings of 0.5 or higher are listed here.

well. Thus, while it may tend to be left unstated, 'being white' does appear to be a fundamental aspect of the two main majority ethnic traditions associated with Northern Ireland.

The final point to note about racial prejudice and the significance of race for people's sense of identity is that they have been found not to be the preserve of any particular subsection but tend to be found right across the population. In relation to the above factor analysis, for example, a respondent's age, gender, social class background and whether they were Catholic or Protestant were all found to be poor predictors of who was more likely to express an identity associated with factor 1.[44] Moreover, as part of the large-scale survey of racial attitudes conducted by Connolly and Keenan that was described earlier, a measure of racial prejudice was included comprising the sum of responses to six different statements.[45] This was then used to ascertain how well a person's levels of racial prejudice could be predicted using other variables, namely: age, gender, religion, social class and area of residence. As before, what the analysis found was that all of these variables were very poor predictors of how racially prejudiced a person would be.[46]

Interrogating whiteness in Northern Ireland

What the above empirical studies suggest, therefore, is that there is a need for much more critical research with the aim of beginning to name and interrogate whiteness in Northern Ireland and thus to draw attention to the ways in which it tends to be a normal and ordinary aspect of life here. As regards the two main majority ethnic traditions in Northern Ireland, a useful starting point would be to examine the historical development of these respective traditions and to begin to problematise the role of race within this. For unionists, for example, their tradition is associated historically with Scottish and English Protestant settlers who were mobilised by Britain from the 1600s onwards as part of its plantation strategy to maintain and extend control over the island of Ireland.[47] They settled largely in the north-eastern corner of Ireland that became the island's main industrial and trading centre, particularly in the production of linen, cotton and ships.[48] From the very beginning, therefore, the unionist collective identity tended to be informed by this sense of having to defend itself against the threat of the native Irish.[49] Moreover, this sense of defensiveness and the need to protect their 'heritage' continued on after the partition of Ireland and led the leaders of the newly created unionist majority within Northern Ireland to strive to create 'a Protestant Parliament for a Protestant State' as the then Northern Ireland Prime Minister James Craig stated in 1933.[50]

At the very heart of the unionist tradition and its collective identity, therefore, has been this desire to defend its Protestant heritage. This can be seen most obviously in relation to Orange marches that tend to celebrate the ascendancy of Protestantism in the region. However, it is also reflected in many political murals in Protestant areas that tend to be much more militaristic, commemorating key battles fought and won historically and signalling the continued need to be vigilant and to be prepared to take up arms to defend what is seen as their birthright. Given this emphasis on the defence of a tradition that has clear lines of descent, it is not surprising to find that the unionist identity has been fundamentally racialised. As the findings reported above have shown, while it has largely gone unrecognised and need not be stated, there is clearly an underpinning sense that being part of the unionist tradition has, to date, been predicated on being white.

Similar processes have also been evident in relation to the nationalist tradition. Historically, it has been a sense of identity born out of the resistance to British colonial exploits in Ireland and this in turn has tended to encourage the creation and maintenance of a strong sense of Irish national identity. This sense of national identity has, itself, often relied upon stirring images of a romantic, mystical and essentially rural Ireland. This emphasis on land and resistance is, for example, a popular theme of political wall murals found in some nationalist areas in Northern Ireland, with Ireland tending to be constructed as ancient and spiritual, the Celtic mythological figure of the belligerent Cuchalainn appearing with some regularity.[51] Moreover, this elevation of the rural in such depictions of Ireland and consequent constructions of Irishness is not coincidental but is arguably a central part of the project of establishing the Irish nation as a natural entity and thus, as has been argued, seeking to confer on it a moral authority much greater than the current (imposed) political structures associated with Northern Ireland.[52] As Coulter explains further:

> The essential splendour of the landscape of Ireland finds echoes in the nature and experience of its people. The Irish are held to comprise an ancient national community. Various murals seek to establish the connections between the present inhabitants of the island and previous generations. References are made both to fragments of Celtic mythology and to rather more literal incidents from Irish history. In part the murals seek to establish the authenticity of the nation. The Irish are portrayed as a people who have been defined by, and survived, the eventful passage of history. . . . Feelings of Irishness have been sustained through many centuries and, therefore, possess a moral value greater than that of other ontological states of rather more recent vintage.[53]

Not surprisingly, therefore, the active process of nation building that took place particularly following the partition of Ireland in the 1920s both in relation to the newly independent Irish state in the south and among the now politically isolated minority Catholic population in the north not only tended to be built upon a strong rural idyll but also tended inevitably to be exclusionary, constructing Irishness as an homogeneous identity that was essentially Catholic and nationalistic as well as rural.[54] Moreover, the timeless depiction of Irishness and the continued evocation of an ancient and mystical past ensured that such an identity tended to remain essentially white. It is within this context that the strong negative reactions to Irish Travellers can be located. In this respect, it would have been reasonable to assume that levels of prejudice against Irish Travellers would have been less among members of the nationalist tradition as compared with unionists, given the indigenous nature of Irish Travellers and their associations with rural Ireland. MacLaughlin suggests one explanation for this apparent paradox in relation to the project of nation building within Ireland with its emphasis on modernisation, social progress and, importantly, the acquisition of land.[55] As he argues, the traditional and nomadic ways of life of Irish Travellers came to be distinctly at odds with such a project:

Thus nationalism in Ireland as elsewhere in Europe stressed the links between 'people' and 'Mother Ireland'. Moreover it did so in such a way as to suggest that this was an entirely natural, organic, even sacred relationship. Anyone who threatened that relationship, particularly those who 'tarnished' it through association with vagrancy or nomadism, had no place in the nation-state. 'Tinkers' were perceived as a people without either a history or a homeland, serious deficiencies indeed in a country where attachment to land could reach primal proportions, and where political recognition and respectability was sought in an international arena where claims to nationhood could be seriously jeopardised through 'racial inferiority' or association with nomadic cultures and practices.[56]

Interestingly, this argument has been developed further by some who have claimed that this attempt to build a modern Irish nation has not included a direct challenge to the colonial 'othering' of the Irish in general as uncivilised and backward but rather has been characterised by a simple transference of that discourse on to Irish Travellers. As ní Shuinéar has argued, for example, it is in this sense that Travellers are seen as 'the descendants of those victims of colonial policy – famine, evictions, land clearances – who (unlike "us") stayed down when they were pushed down, and ceased to experience history. Travellers are [therefore] essentially Irish peasants in a timewarp.'[57]

Conclusion

Overall, and as outlined in this chapter, there is now ample evidence that racism is a significant problem for Northern Ireland. The key issue is how this can be best theorised and understood. As has been shown, much of the research to date has been framed by the concept of institutional racism. This concept has not only been applied to the experiences of existing black and ethnic minority communities in the region but has also been found to be equally applicable to the increasing numbers of migrant workers arriving in Northern Ireland. The notion of institutional racism has certainly played an important role in drawing attention to the structural and routine nature of racial discrimination. With its emphasis on unintentional and unwitting processes and practices it has also been extremely useful politically in allowing racism to be problematised without necessarily holding any particular individuals responsible. However, what we have argued in this chapter is that there are also dangers in placing too much emphasis on this way of conceptualising racism in the region. More specifically, it encourages us to separate out issues of race and racism from the majority white and settled population. In this way, race can be considered to be an irrelevance for the majority of white people in Northern Ireland. Not only

can it then be argued that race has little meaning for members of the majority white and settled population but also that any part they do play in
maintaining and reproducing racial inequalities is simply the result of
thoughtlessness and ignorance.

What we have attempted to do in this chapter is to challenge this way
of thinking about race in Northern Ireland. By reconsidering existing
research evidence from a critical race perspective, we have suggested that,
far from race having little meaning for the majority white population, it
actually represents one of the key ways in which it is constituted. As
shown, while it may tend to go unrecognised and unstated, race is a fundamental aspect of how people construct their sense of identity and,
moreover, has tended to underpin the historical development of the two
main majority ethnic traditions within the region.

Given this, while there remains a need to continue to analyse and
understand the institutional aspects of racism as they operate for different black and minority ethnic groups within Northern Ireland, we want
to conclude by arguing that there is a need to also begin identifying and
problematising the ways in which race tends to underpin all aspects of
life here. This, in turn, requires us to begin naming and interrogating
whiteness as it is constructed and reproduced among specific groups
across time and place. Some possible ways in which this process may
begin is through much more critical research into the historical development of the two main majority ethnic traditions in the region and the
salience of whiteness within this. Even from the brief discussion of the
historical development of these 'two traditions' provided above, it is clear
that while it may be largely unrecognised and unstated, 'being white'
does appear to have been a constitutive and founding element for both
of these overarching traditions. Moreover, the evidence presented here
from a number of attitudinal studies certainly suggests that current identities predicated on being Catholic/Protestant and on nationality, politics
and the local neighbourhood remain fundamentally racialised.

Clearly, more work is now required not only in helping to understand
how race has been implicated in the historical development of the various
ethno-religious traditions in Northern Ireland but also, crucially, how
whiteness is currently being constructed and reproduced by differing elements of the population in the region. Moreover, while the attitudinal
research considered in this chapter tends to suggest that there is little to
distinguish between ordinary members of the two main majority ethnic
traditions in terms of the significance of race to their competing senses of
identity, there are differences evident in the current approaches taken by
nationalist and unionist politicians and also the leaders of loyalism and
republicanism in relation to their responses to race issues in Northern

Ireland. As yet, however, there is very little research that has been undertaken or published on this area and, unfortunately, it lies well beyond the scope of this chapter.

Perhaps the key point to conclude on is that the more that we can begin to name and interrogate whiteness in the ways outlined above the more we can begin to address racism at its source. As CRT has stressed, there is nothing objective or natural about the racialisation of particular groups within society. Similarly, and within the context of Northern Ireland, there is nothing necessary nor essential about the current tendencies for the main traditions in the region to be underpinned by whiteness. In critically interrogating whiteness it is possible to begin to create alternative and more inclusive ways of being nationalist or unionist and also, by extension, to begin constructing a more inclusive society more generally.

Notes

1 P. Logue (ed.), *Being Irish: Personal Reflections on Irish Identity Today* (Dublin: Oaktree Press, 2000), p. xviii.
2 B. Hesse, 'Discourse on institutional racism: the genealogy of a concept', in I. Law, D. Phillips and L. Turney (eds), *Institutional Racism in Higher education* (Stoke on Trent: Trentham Books, 2004).
3 See: K. Crenshaw, N. Gotanda, G. Peller and K. Thomas (eds), *Critical Race Theory: The Key Writings that Formed the Movement* (New York: New Press, 1995); R. Delgado and J. Stefancic (eds), *Critical Race Theory: The Cutting Edge* (Philadelphia: Temple University Press, 2000); R. Delgado and J. Stefancic, *Critical Race Theory: An Introduction* (New York: New York University Press, 2001).
4 See, in particular D. Gillborn, 'Education policy as an act of white supremacy: whiteness, critical race theory and education reform', *Journal of Education Policy*, 20:4 (2005), pp. 485–505.
5 Delgado and Stefancic, *Critical Race Theory*, p. 5.
6 *Ibid.*, p. 7.
7 See, for example, R. Dyer, *White* (London: Routledge, 1997); R. Frankenberg (ed.), *Displacing Whiteness: Essays in Social and Cultural Criticism* (Durham NC: Duke University Press, 1997).
8 Z. Wicomb, 'Five Afrikaner texts and the rehabilitation of whiteness', *Social Identities*, 4:3 (1998), pp. 363–83, p. 371.
9 R. Frankenberg, 'Introduction: local whitenesses, localising whiteness', in Frankenberg, *Displacing Whiteness*, p. 6.
10 R. Frankenberg, *White Women, Race Matters: The Social Construction of Whiteness* (London: Routledge, 1993).
11 D. Roediger, *The Wages of Whiteness: Race and the Making of the American Working Class* (New York: Verso, 1990).
12 H. Carby, 'White woman, listen! Black feminism and the boundaries of sisterhood', in Centre for Contemporary Cultural Studies (eds) *The Empire*

Strikes Back: Race and Racism in 70s Britain (London: Hutchinson, 1982).

13 Dyer, *White*.

14 R. Aanerud, 'Fictions of whiteness: speaking the names of whiteness in US literature', in Frankenberg, *Displacing Whiteness*, p. 41.

15 The term 'majority ethnic groups' is used here to refer to the Protestant and Catholic traditions respectively. This term is used to stress the fact that ethnicity is not the preserve of minority groups but that everyone has an ethnic identity. In this sense, 'majority ethnic groups' is meant to be used alongside the more commonly used term 'minority ethnic groups'. Using such terms helps to focus our attention on the socially constructed nature of all identities and traditions. In relation to the present chapter, this is particularly useful as a means of problematising the identities of the majority white population that have tended to be normalised and taken for granted. It is recognised, however, that there are clearly limitations to describing Protestants and Catholics as two majority ethnic groups, given the major and significant divisions that exist within each of them. However, this limitation is equally applicable to describing any group as an ethnic group. It will, therefore, be useful for some purposes but not others.

16 See: K. Bell, N. Jarman and T. Lefebvre, *Migrant Workers in Northern Ireland* (Belfast: Institute for Conflict Research, 2004); D. Holder and R. Khaoury, *Racial Attitudes and Prejudice towards Migrant Workers* (Belfast: Animate, 2005).

17 See: V. Tennant, *Sanctuary in a Cell* (Belfast: Law Centre, 2000); R. McVeigh, *Northern Ireland a Place of Refuge? Asylum Seekers and Refugees in Northern Ireland* (Belfast: Refugee Action Group, 2002).

18 See: D. Mann-Kler, *Out of the Shadows: An Action Research Report into Families, Racism and Exclusions in Northern Ireland* (Belfast: Barnardo's, 1997); P. Hainsworth (ed.), *Divided Society: Ethnic Minorities and Racism in Northern Ireland* (London: Pluto Press, 1998); P. Connolly *'Race' and Racism in Northern Ireland: A Review of the Research Evidence* (Belfast: Office of the First Minister and Deputy First Minister, 2002).

19 For an overview see Connolly, *'Race' and Racism in Northern Ireland*.

20 For an overview see *ibid*.

21 W. Macpherson, *The Stephen Lawrence Inquiry*, Cm 4262-I (London: Stationery Office, 1999), Section 6.45.

22 These four themes were identified in the review of research undertaken by one of the present authors. See Connolly, *'Race' and Racism in Northern Ireland*, pp. 45–56.

23 See, for example, D. Holder and C. Lanao, *Estudos sobre discriminação na comunidade portuguesa da Irlanda do Norte* (Dungannon: STEP and Animate, 2006).

24 R. McVeigh and C. Fisher, *An Economic Impact Assessment of Inward Migration into the Dungannon, Craigavon and Cookstown Council Areas* (Dungannon: Animate, 2006).

25 Holder and Lanao, *Estudos sobre discriminação na comunidade portuguesa*; D. Holder and R. Khaoury, *Racial Attitudes and Prejudice towards Migrant Workers: A Survey of Staff in Statutory Agencies in the Cookstown, Dungannon and Craigavon Areas* (Dungannon: STEP and Animate, 2005).

26 P. McGill and Q. Oliver, *A Wake-up Call on Race: Implications of the Macpherson Report for Institutional Racism in Northern Ireland* (Belfast: Equality Commission, 2002).

27 R. McVeigh, *The Next Stephen Lawrence? Racist Violence and Criminal Justice in Northern Ireland* (Belfast: NICEM, 2006).

28 See, for example: G. Irwin and S. Dunn, *Ethnic Minorities in Northern Ireland* (Coleraine: Centre for the Study of Conflict, University of Ulster, 1997); Mann-Kler, *Out of the Shadows*; K. Chahal and L. Julienne, *'We can't all be white!' Racist Victimisation in the UK* (London: Joseph Rowntree Foundation, 1999); P. Connolly and M. Keenan, *The Hidden Truth: Racist Harassment in Northern Ireland* (Belfast: Northern Ireland Statistics and Research Agency, 2000); N. Jarman and R. Monaghan, *Analysis of Incidents of Racist Harasment recorded by the Police in Northern Ireland* (Belfast: Institute of Conflict Research, 2003); N. Jarman and R. Monaghan, *Racist Harassment in Northern Ireland* (Belfast: Institute for Conflict Research, 2004).

29 Irwin and Dunn, *Ethnic Minorities in Northern Ireland*, p. 101.

30 *Ibid.* See also A. M. Watson and E. McKnight, 'Race and ethnicity in Northern Ireland: the Chinese community', in P. Hainsworth (ed.), *Divided Society: Ethnic Minorities and Racism in Northern Ireland* (London: Pluto Press, 1998).

31 See: M. Gorman, *Travellers in Newry: An Assessment and Consultation Report* (Belfast: Save the Children Fund (Northern Ireland), 1986); Mann-Kler, *Out of the Shadows*; P. Connolly and M. Keenan, *Opportunities for All: Minority Ethnic People's Experiences of Education, Training and Employment in Northern Ireland* (Belfast: Northern Ireland Statistics and Research Agency, 2000).

32 Northern Ireland Housing Executive, *Housing Needs of the Chinese Community* (Belfast: NIHE, 1995).

33 Connolly and Keenan, *Opportunities for All*.

34 Connolly and Keenan, *The Hidden Truth*; Jarman and Monaghan, *Racist Harassment in Northern Ireland*.

35 See: Bell *et al.*, *Migrant Workers in Northern Ireland*; Holder and Khaoury, *Racial Attitudes and Prejudice towards Migrant Workers*.

36 A. Chrisafis, 'Racist war of the loyalist street gangs', *Guardian*, 10 January 2004, www.guardian.co.uk/race/story/0,11374,1120113,00.html (accessed 19 September 2006).

37 Connolly and Keenan, *The Hidden Truth*, p. 23.

38 While only 11 per cent of respondents believed themselves to be at least 'a little prejudiced' in 1994, this rose to 25 per cent in 2005. See C. Gilligan and K. Lloyd, *Racial Prejudice in Northern Ireland*, Research Update (Belfast: ARK, Northern Ireland Social and Political Archive, 2005), p. 1.

39 *Ibid.*, p. 2.
40 *Ibid.*, p. 3.
41 P. Connolly and M. Keenan, *Racial Attitudes and Prejudice in Northern Ireland* (Belfast: Northern Ireland Statistics and Research Agency, 2000).
42 P. Connolly, ' "It goes without saying" (well, sometimes): racism, whiteness and identity in Northern Ireland', in J. Agyeman and S. Neal (eds), *The New Countryside? Ethnicity, Nation and Exclusion in Contemporary Rural Britain* (Bristol: Policy Press, 2005).
43 *Ibid.*
44 A score for each respondent was calculated on the basis of how strongly they related to the first factor. An attempt was then made to ascertain how well one could predict a person's score, using multiple regression analysis. It was found that age, gender, religion and social class were actually very poor predictors of whether a person had acquired this particular ethno-religious (and racialised) identity or not.
45 Connolly and Keenan, *Racial Attitudes and Prejudice*.
46 This particular regression analysis was conducted subsequently to the publication of the original report. For further details see Connolly, ' "It goes without saying" ', pp. 34–5. What the analysis found was that even when all these variables were taken together they could account for only 11.3 per cent of the variation in people's scores. In other words, nearly 90 per cent of the variation in levels of racial prejudice across Northern Ireland remained unaccounted for.
47 J. Darby, 'Conflict in Northern Ireland: a background essay', in S. Dunn (ed.), *Facets of the Conflict in Northern Ireland* (London: Macmillan, 1995).
48 R. Munck, *The Irish Economy: Results and Prospects* (London: Pluto Press, 1993).
49 Darby, *Conflict in Northern Ireland*.
50 Cited in R. McVeigh and R. Lentin, 'Situated racisms: a theoretical introduction', in R. Lentin and R. McVeigh (eds), *Racism and Anti-racism in Ireland* (Belfast: Beyond the Pale Publications, 2002), p. 20.
51 *Ibid.*, p. 211.
52 *Ibid.*, p. 213.
53 C. Coulter, *Contemporary Northern Irish Society* (London: Pluto Press, 1999), p. 213.
54 See: J. MacLaughlin, 'Nation-building, social closure and anti-Traveller racism in Ireland', *Sociology* 22:1 (1999), pp. 129–51; McVeigh and Lentin, 'Situated racisms'.
55 MacLaughlin, 'Nation-building'. See also B. Fanning, *Racism and Social Change in the Republic of Ireland* (Manchester: Manchester University Press, 2002).
56 MacLaughlin, 'Nation-building', p. 138.
57 S. ní Shuinéar, 'Othering the Irish (Travellers)', in Lentin and McVeigh, *Racism and Anti-racism in Ireland* (Belfast: Beyond the Pale Publications, 2002), p. 187.

Part III
Cultural practices

11

Still taking sides: sport, leisure and identity

Alan Bairner

According to the seventh edition of the *Lonely Planet* guide to Ireland:

> Belfast is buzzing. Massive investment combined with optimism engendered by the peace process have transformed the city into a boom town, and its old bombs and bullets reputation has given way to a designer Belfast, typified by hip hotels like TENsq and Malmaison, elegant restaurants like Roscoff and Michael Deane, and the trendy boutiques that line Lisburn Road.[1]

Other places fare less well. 'Poor old Larne,' for example, 'is a little lacking in the charm department.'[2] Of Newcastle the authors write, 'nice setting, shame about the main street – on summer weekends it's a garish, traffic-choked strip of raucous amusement arcades and fast-food outlets'.[3] Craigavon, Lurgan and Portadown do not even merit a mention. That said, it is often the case that countries and regions are judged by what is happening in their major city and undeniably on that basis there appears to be a widely accepted view that Belfast, and by implication Northern Ireland as a whole, are undergoing a rapid process of transformation.

Writing in 2002 in support of Belfast's bid to become the 2008 City of European Culture (an honour won subsequently by Liverpool), poet and critic Tom Paulin asserted, 'It is our faith in the emergence of a new, wholly peaceful culture that makes us support Belfast as the City of European Culture 2008.'[4] More recently, novelist Glenn Patterson was moved to comment, 'it's not just the fact of change that is new in Belfast, it's the speed'.[5] How different such descriptions are from that penned by Paul Theroux[6] in the early 1980s:

> I knew at once that Belfast was an awful city. It had a bad face – mouldering buildings, tough-looking people, a visible smell, too many fences. Every building that was worth blowing up was guarded by a man with a metal detector, who frisked people entering and checked their bags.

Given the violence of the recent past, it is scarcely surprising that Belfast, and indeed the whole of Northern Ireland, have an image problem. As

Dawe points out, 'Belfast, more than any other European cities, has been stereotyped to death; its complex history in permafrost; its geo-cultural life as a port, haven, hell-hole, spectacle, dumbed down before the term was invented.'[7] Indeed, according to Allen and Kelly, 'Belfast is commonly understood to be a place familiar precisely because of its unfamiliarity: its representation is supersaturated with images of strangeness, anomaly and deviance.'[8] This is certainly a feature of the construction of a stereotyped Belfast. Yet, as Brown notes, 'the city itself has almost equally often seemed to oblige the literary imagination by running true to type'.[9]

Outsiders may have felt in the past that they knew Northern Ireland but what they knew was precisely what made the place different. Because of that they chose not to visit. Nowadays, however, more and more people appear to be taking city breaks in Belfast, or so the proliferation of city-centre hotels would indicate, lured by the city's new image as proclaimed in the tourist guides. But one broader question immediately arises. To what extent have Northern Ireland in general and Belfast in particular undergone a thorough transformation during the period that has elapsed since these dismal observations were made? Secondly, and of central concern to this chapter, if such a transformation has taken place, how far have sport and leisure been involved in the process of change?

To return to the *Lonely Planet* guide, it is immediately apparent that leisure, in the shape of various forms of consumption, is regarded as a major element in Belfast's transformation. According to the authors

> redevelopment continues apace as Victoria Sq, Europe's biggest urban regeneration project, is set to add a massive city-centre shopping mall to a list of tourist attractions that include imposing Victorian architecture, an attractive waterfront lined with modern art, foot-stomping music in packed-out pubs and the UK's second biggest arts festival.[10]

Also mentioned are the city's 'vibrant nightlife and plenty of good places to eat'. There is no reference to sport, however, in this general overview despite the fact that sports tourism has come to play an increasingly significant role in many cities, both elsewhere in the United Kingdom and beyond. As Crawford notes, 'sport venues become tourist attractions, places to be visited and experienced'.[11] This is a particularly salient point in relation to cities such as Cardiff, Liverpool and Manchester, among others. It is true that those charged with the task of improving Northern Ireland's image have certainly had opportunities to make capital out of a number of relatively high-profile sporting events, including the World Cross-country Championships (1999), the World Amateur Boxing Championships (2001), the International Cricket Conference

Trophy (2005) and the European Under-nineteen Football Championships (2005).

However, with the exception of the Odyssey Arena, Northern Ireland has no major sporting venues that can be clearly identified with tourism. Indeed, such is the air of indifference to this subject in the *Lonely Planet* guide that we are informed that 'international rugby and soccer matches take place at Windsor Park'.[12] In fact, although the Northern Ireland international football team undeniably plays its home matches at that stadium, Ireland rugby internationals have not been played in Belfast since 1954 – and then at Ravenhill rather than at Windsor Park.[13] The guide goes on to observe that Belfast Giants ice hockey team draws big crowds to the Odyssey Arena.[14] There is an ongoing debate, however, as to how attractive the Giants actually are and what the future holds for them.[15] What is certain is that, as a tourist attraction, the Odyssey Arena simply cannot be compared with major outdoor stadia in other cities in Ireland – Dublin (Croke Park) – or Britain – Liverpool (Anfield and Goodison Park), Manchester (City of Manchester Stadium and Old Trafford), Glasgow (Celtic Park and Ibrox Stadium) and Cardiff (Millennium Stadium).

The absence of sporting venues from representations of the 'new' Belfast is perhaps not wholly surprising for anyone familiar with the literature on the relationship between sport, politics and society in Northern Ireland. Although some studies have made reference to the integrative potential of sport,[16] the general tendency has been to argue that sport has not only reflected inter-communal division in Northern Ireland but has also contributed to and, in some instances, helped to exacerbate that division.[17] As Coulter contends, 'among the improbable claims that have gained currency within popular discourse is that which portrays sport as an essential site of communal reconciliation'.[18]

The discussion that follows takes account of this ongoing debate. It does so, however, by engaging with issues and with a literature that have not previously been central to analyses of the relationship between sport and politics in Northern Ireland but which have become increasingly significant concerns within the sociological study of sport more generally. The themes that will be explored in an attempt to provide original and arguably more nuanced insights are the symbolic importance of sport and leisure spaces, the relationship between 'national' teams and national identities and the idea of 'new fandom'.

On sport and leisure spaces

As Bale and Vertinsky note, 'the significance of space and place as central dimensions of sport is well recognized by scholars who have addressed questions of sport from philosophical, sociological, geographical and historical perspectives'.[19] In addition, much of the resultant discussion can be linked to wider debates within urban sociology in relation to civic boosterism, consumerism and urban regeneration. Specifically, there is growing concern with the role of public spaces, including sports grounds and leisure centres. For Zukin 'talking about the cultures of cities in purely visual terms does not do justice to the material practices of politics and economics that create a symbolic economy'. 'But,' she continues, 'neither does a strictly political-economic approach suggest the subtle powers of visual and spatial strategies of social differentiation.'[20] Zukin argues that 'linking public culture to commercial cultures has important implications for social identity and social control'.[21] The brutal fact is that 'who occupies public space is often decided by negotiations over physical security, cultural, and social and geographical community'.[22] It is vitally important to bear this in mind when one is considering the social significance of the sporting and leisure spaces of Northern Ireland and, more specifically, of Belfast.

The fact that potential tourists are not invited to visit the city in order to enjoy what its sports venues have to offer can be interpreted in several ways. In the case of Association football it may simply be recognition of the fact that the domestic game cannot compare with what lies in store for visitors to England, Italy, Spain and so on. As for Gaelic games, perhaps there is an implicit assumption that tourists would be unable to understand the basic rules and fundamental skills that are involved in Gaelic football and hurling, although it is worth noting that numerous visitors to Spain attend bullfights with at least as little knowledge. The Northern Ireland international football team, the Ulster rugby team and the Belfast Giants do attract visitors to Northern Ireland – primarily supporters of opposition teams – but still do not feature as major tourist attractions. Why then does sport not enjoy a more high-profile image?

In large part the answer to this question, one suspects, lies in the fact that, whether consciously or unconsciously, most local residents, including those who are employed in marketing the region, are aware of the exclusive character of most sport and leisure facilities in Northern Ireland. These are quasi-public spaces – privately owned perhaps but in theory accessible to all – to which in reality only certain types of people go and from which others are excluded, feel themselves to be excluded or exclude themselves. This has been shown to be the case for leisure centres, with some people deciding that they do not want to use a particular amenity as it would mean mixing with 'the other sort' and others expressing fears that were they to go to certain leisure facilities their lives would be endangered.[23] The same socio-psychological barriers stand in the way of people going to certain sporting venues. Just as the concept of topophilia (or love of place) can be invoked in relation to sporting spaces, so too can that of topophobia (or fear of place).[24]

The two largest football grounds in Belfast, Windsor Park and the Oval, are located at different ends of the city. Both, however, are situated in what have traditionally been regarded as Protestant working-class areas. Admittedly, the population around Windsor Park, home to Linfield Football Club and the Northern Ireland national team, is now less homogeneous than was once the case and than remains true of the east Belfast streets that surround the Oval, home to Glentoran Football Club. Nevertheless, the environs around both grounds are still characterised by loyalist iconography in the form of painted kerbstones, murals and flags. It comes as little surprise, therefore, that many Catholics are unwilling to visit either stadium. As with topophobia in relation to leisure centres, it matters little whether or not these fears are justified. This is equally true of Protestants, who show no desire to visit Casement Park in west Belfast, the major venue for Gaelic games in Northern Ireland. In this instance, the surrounding area is solidly nationalist and Catholic – hence the topophobic response engendered among many unionists. In addition, the Gaelic Athletic Association (GAA), which governs Gaelic games throughout Ireland, has long been seen by many Ulster unionists as a republican organisation.[25] Even the Ravenhill ground where the Ulster rugby team plays its matches has traditionally been seen as a Protestant sporting space and although this has changed to some degree in recent years, the nature of the sport that is played there, at least within an Irish context, ensures that it remains a largely middle-class sporting space. Indeed, the Odyssey Arena, home to the Belfast Giants and frequently cited as an inclusive leisure space, can also be seen as exclusive, as evidenced by warning signs outside the arena itself and in the adjoining pavilion relating to unacceptable dress codes and forms of behaviour. Even the most rudimentary ethnography reveals that the target audience consists of family groups and young professionals.

Problems relating to exclusivity and sporting space were recognised by the advisory group that was set up in 2000 to assist the then Minister for Culture, Arts and Leisure in the recently established and subsequently mothballed Northern Ireland Executive to devise a strategy for the future of Association football in Northern Ireland. The advisory panel recognised that Windsor Park is not regarded as a welcoming venue by nationalists, nor is it deemed to be an acceptable home for the national team by many supporters of Irish League clubs other than Linfield. It was noted in the panel's final report that 'Northern Ireland does not have a sports stadium that meets all the expected standards for hosting international football' and that 'steps should be taken immediately to address this deficiency'.[26] Thus 'a national stadium, which would provide a neutral and welcome environment and meet international standards for football, should be established'.[27] These findings have led to a protracted debate about the viability of a new 'national' stadium which could host major Gaelic and Rugby Union matches as well as Northern Ireland football internationals, concerts and so on. Not surprisingly, the search for a site that is regarded as both viable *and* inclusive has proved difficult and not without controversy.

At the time of writing, although other sites remain under discussion, the British government, supported by many but by no means all of the interested parties in the revived Northern Ireland Executive, has decided that the most appropriate location for a new 35,000-seater stadium is the site of the former Maze Prison – or Long Kesh, as it was known to generations of loyalists and republican prisoners who were housed there from the 1970s until 2000. The choice has caused considerable controversy for a variety of reasons, all of which throw further light on the intimate relationship between sport and politics in Northern Ireland. The government's decision has been prompted in no small measure by the fact that it already owns the land, thereby alleviating the fear of excessive costs which could be associated with building the new stadium closer to Belfast city centre. However, selecting a site which is ten miles outside the city is clearly at odds with strategies aimed at linking sport and leisure with urban regeneration and civic boosterism. An additional complication arises from the fact that the former prison itself has such a significant place in the history of the troubles, not least as the site of the republican hunger strike in 1981 which led to the death of Bobby Sands, followed by nine other prisoners. According to the Amalgamation of Official Northern Ireland Supporters' Clubs:

> although the SIB [Strategic Investment Board] assured us that the site would be a neutral space, it is hard to believe that the site will not be honoured as a place of martyrdom turning into a ghoulish tourist attraction. This is unlikely to endear the site to an average sports fan who is not interested in such controversial and divisive symbolism.[28]

In truth, there are few sports fans in Northern Ireland who are wholly apolitical, and what is likely to please one faction is almost certain to anger another. To date, calls for the preservation of at least one of the prison's so-called H blocks have been partly answered in the preliminary plans for the new stadium. These propose that, in addition to restaurants, offices, a multi-screen cinema and a hotel, the surrounding site should also include an International Conflict Transformation Centre, with one of the old H blocks, H6, where arguably the seeds of the hunger strike were sown,[29] being preserved along with the prison hospital, where the hunger strikers died.[30]

In terms of sport, other problems emerge, regardless of what site is finally chosen. In the first instance the idea of a new stadium was based on the premise that Windsor Park, for reasons already discussed, was inadequate for Association football's needs. Subsequent attempts to include other major team sports inevitably run the risk of being seen as public relations stunts linked with a community relations agenda. Do Gaelic games and Rugby Union genuinely need a new stadium? How often would they use it? Indeed, how often would it be used even for football matches? The question of 'ownership' is also significant. At present the SIB proposes that the stadium operator should retain the majority of associated profits. The Amalgamation of Official Northern Ireland' Supporters' Clubs has objected, arguing that 'with an effective monopoly due to its rural location, any concession operator at the Maze will definitely generate significant income. The IFA must have a cut of this in any proposal.'[31] It argues that because the GAA and the Ulster Branch of the Irish Rugby Football Union (IRFU) would retain alternative venues, the issue of financial return is less important to them. It is unlikely, however, that either body would be happy with a situation in which fans of their respective sports were generating income exclusively for another governing body.

Another, more general, issue arises. Reference has been made throughout this section to plans for a new *national* stadium. But this of course begs the question – which nation and whose? Is Northern Ireland a nation? It is certainly a sporting country within the context of Association football, with the Irish Football Association (IFA) being recognised as a national governing body by FIFA (Fédération Internationale de Football Association). As for rugby and Gaelic games, however, the sporting nation is Ireland. This leads us to another critical topic that needs to be examined more closely.

Nations, nationalities, national identities

The fact that there is a relationship between sport and national identity has been widely recognised but not perhaps always fully understood. Nevertheless, a growing body of literature has sought to conceptualise this relationship in more sophisticated ways.[32] It is important, for example to be precise in the use of concepts such as nation state and nation, nationality and national identity, cultural nationalism and political nationalism.[33] Not all states are nations other than in a formal, civic sense. Some, including the United Kingdom of Great Britain and Northern Ireland, incorporate a number of nations. This in turn provides evidence that not all nations have statehood. The nation state is a legalistic device. It applies to sovereign states that may or may not correspond to nationhood. Nationality is also a constitutional formula. It relates to citizenship – the idea of 'belonging' to a particular nation state. For many people in the world, nationality and national identity coincide. But such is by no means always the case, because so many nations are uncomfortably located within states, whilst others are divided by state frontiers. The nation, therefore, is best understood as a collective unit which may have no constitutional status but which unites people on the basis of certain criteria. These include language, ethnicity, race, spatiality, shared history or, at its vaguest, a sense of shared values and aspirations. Out of such characteristics national identity emerges, representing what we believe ourselves to be, as opposed to what other people designate us as being. As a result, national identity frequently unites people in opposition to the nation state.

In few areas is the fact that Northern Ireland is a divided society more apparent than in the world of sport. Reference has been made above to the 'national' football team, but in what sense is that team truly national? It does not represent a nation state any more than do the national teams of England, Scotland and Wales. Nor does it represent a nation, at least in the eyes of Irish nationalists. Undeniably, what the Northern Irish football team does represent is an existing political entity, although ultimately it owes its continued existence not to that consideration but rather to Britain's pioneering role in the early development of football as a whole, which ensured that the four 'home' nations, including Ireland in its entirety at the outset, would be guaranteed their own distinct identities by football's international governing bodies. In consequence, the football team, together with Northern Ireland's Commonwealth Games representation, speaks to the existence of Northern Ireland as a place apart. In other sports, including Rugby Union, however, Northern Ireland is subsumed within Ireland, the imagined national community, as opposed to the actual nation state of the Irish Republic, at the highest elite level. These various complexities mean that northern nationalists play for Northern Ireland without necessarily recognising the legitimacy of the political entity that the 'national' football team implicitly represents and Ulster unionists play rugby, and other sports, for Ireland whilst viewing their Irishness in very specific ways or even denying its existence outside the sporting realm.

Lovejoy quotes with apparent approval the view expressed by former Northern Ireland player Derek Dougan, and also from time to time by

George Best himself, that the latter's career might have lasted longer had he been in a position to play for a more successful international side.[34] Cynics, and certainly some cynical Ulster unionist observers, might be inclined to argue that as self-confessed advocates of an all-Ireland national soccer side, neither Dougan nor Best was sufficiently committed to the Northern Irish team. Best once observed, 'I have always believed that the two Associations should have got together and formed one national team.'[35] He argues that politics and money have stood in the way of such a development, adding that 'the hangers-on and the officials of the two Associations are too frightened of losing their freebies and their status'.[36] Dougan was also an Ulster Protestant, like Best, with even stronger views on the need for Irish unity, at least at the level of sport.[37]

Organised separately in Northern Ireland and the Republic of Ireland, by the IFA and the Football Association of Ireland respectively, Association football is actually something of an exception in terms of the organisation of sport in Ireland. The overwhelming majority of sports that are played in Ireland are organised on an island-wide basis. This is particularly appropriate, of course, in the case of Gaelic games, with the GAA acting as a national cultural and sporting organisation. The all-Ireland character of other governing bodies is, however, slightly more surprising, given the British origins of so many of the sports involved, combined with the constitutional separation of Northern Ireland and the Irish Republic. The fact is, though, that most of these governing bodies came into existence long before the political division of Ireland – the Irish Lawn Tennis Association (1877), the IRFU (1879), the Golfing Union of Ireland (1891) and the Irish Hockey Union (1893).

Despite recent developments in the world of Ulster rugby,[38] the principal nurseries in Northern Ireland for games such as cricket, men's field hockey and rugby are the state (predominantly Protestant) schools. Although these do not formally bar Catholics from entry, in practice they have been virtually the preserve of the unionist community, in part because of the existence of an alternative grant-maintained Catholic education sector. In addition, the institutions which nurture the British games' players of the future are mainly the grammar schools, which provide an academic education to a minority of children who are typically drawn from more affluent neighbourhoods. The result is that not only are the overwhelming majority of players of British games from Protestant backgrounds, they are also predominantly middle-class. As such, these individuals are more likely to have grown up in areas less directly affected by political violence and the more extreme ideologies which have flourished in such areas and have helped to sustain the conflict. As has been argued elsewhere, this does not mean that the people involved are apolitical or that they eschew sectarian attitudes in their entirety.[39] It is arguable, however, that, in most cases, they are more able than working-class soccer fans to keep their sporting and political interests separate. The sports that they play, administer and watch are organised on an all-Ireland basis and 'national' teams represent the whole of Ireland, frequently with all the symbolic trappings of the Republic of Ireland nation state. This means that northern unionists often end up representing an entity (a thirty-two-county Ireland) which they would not wish to see being given constitutional legitimacy. Their background and upbringing ensure, though, that this is not a problem for most of them and that their unionism remains unaffected by their sporting allegiance, just as the latter is largely unaffected by their political views. If the only way to play international rugby or cricket is to play for an all-Ireland team, then so be it. Thus former Irish international rugby player Willie John McBride asserts:

> I stand for anyone's national anthem and when I pulled on the green shirt I was playing for Ireland. It was about the performance on the field. I want nothing to do with politics. I am not a flag waver and never will be.[40]

In this comment there are clear traces of sporting pragmatism. However, sporting expediency should not be taken as evidence of political uncertainty. For example, Davy Tweed, the former Irish player who went on to become a highly visible member of the Democratic Unionist Party, certainly did not become any less of a unionist as a result of his time with the Irish rugby squad.

> Well, I think everyone wants to play as high a standard as they can. I always was an Ulsterman and got a huge sense of pride playing for Ulster. The pride I got playing in my Ulster jersey and I would have died in it. Not taking anything away from the Ireland jersey that meant a terrible lot, but to answer your question I would say that the Ulster jersey meant more to me.[41]

Willie Anderson similarly sought to minimise the political significance of certain symbols by emphasising the sporting context when he commented:

> For me, coming from a Unionist, Orange background, I didn't have any problems at all. When I hear the Soldier's Song it reminds me of my first cap, one of the greatest days of my life.[42]

However, as was suggested earlier, there is a version of unionism which takes on board the Irishness of Ulster Protestants but which nevertheless stops short of supporting moves towards the establishment of a thirty-two-county Irish Republic. As Nigel Carr expressed it, 'In playing for Ireland I never felt that I compromised my British citizenship.'[43] It is not considered inappropriate to consider oneself to be primarily British and at the same time play for Ireland. As Gary Longwell, another Ulster Protestant who has represented 'his country', remarked:

> I have played for Ireland at schools, under 21, universities and senior levels. Rugby is played nationally. It gets support both north and south. I have grown up supporting Ireland. It's just natural.[44]

This reflects the unionism of those who are British in political terms but are willing to admit to an Irish dimension of their lives – a version of unionist identity that Jennifer Todd has characterised as 'Ulster British'.[45] This hybrid identity makes it perfectly consistent to play rugby, and other sports, for Ireland whilst defending the union between Great Britain and Northern Ireland. Another former international player, Jeremy Davidson, eloquently expressed the various issues involved:

> Even though most rugby players in Ulster come from a Protestant background it's your main goal to play for Ireland because of the tradition. It's the only sport to unify the whole country. I am British. I have a British passport but at the same time I am Irish. It's a strange situation. I am British but I live on the island of Ireland, so I am Irish as well.[46]

Sensitivity to such complex feelings were clearly influential when it was decided in 1995 that for Ireland's home matches a new song, *Ireland's Call*, should be sung along with the Irish national anthem. What seems plausible, though, is that Rugby Union, and other sports which are played on an all-Ireland basis, have helped certain Ulster Protestants to come to terms with issues centred on national identity. It is ironic that most of these sports are identifiably British in origin, whereas Gaelic games, together with the universal pursuit of Association football, have been demonstrably unsuccessful, give or take a few rare exceptions, in encouraging Ulster unionists to recognise their Irishness. The manner in which working-class soccer players negotiate representing Northern Ireland has not been subjected to the same academic scrutiny to date. The identity concerns of soccer fans, on the other hand, have been a subject of considerable debate.

Sports fandom and the consumption of sport

The enduring appeal of Manchester United is merely one example of the influence of cross-channel football in Northern Ireland.[47] Traditional support for the two great Glasgow clubs, Celtic and Rangers, is relatively easy to understand within the context of ethno-sectarian rivalry. The latter also has some relevance in relation to traditional support for Manchester United and Liverpool. Certainly the presence of the Red

Devil pub on the Falls Road is indicative of the continuing affection felt for Manchester United within Northern Ireland's nationalist community. Similar observations could be made about the location of Liverpool supporters' clubs in loyalist areas. However, just as in the cities of Liverpool and Manchester themselves, traditional loyalty centred on religion is all but a thing of the past. As a result, on any given Saturday throughout Northern Ireland, groups of football fans wearing the club colours of a range of English clubs converge on local pubs to watch 'their' teams play. The fact that they can do this highlights one important aspect of contemporary fandom – the access to live coverage of games courtesy of satellite and digital broadcasting. But not all fans rely on television to watch their favourites.

A visit to either of Belfast's airports towards the end of any given week during the football season or a similar trip to Northern Ireland's ferry terminals offers an immediate insight into another important aspect of contemporary sports fandom. Cheap air fares as well as faster ferry crossings have made supporting Celtic, Rangers, Liverpool, Manchester United and the rest in person far easier than in the past.

The impact on the local game of this type of fandom as well as that of those who rely on television is difficult to gauge. Some will argue that one of the main reasons for taking advantage of increased opportunities to watch cross-channel football is the declining standard of Irish League football. On the other hand, it can also be plausibly suggested that the fall in attendance at local games has inevitably had a deleterious effect on the financial health and, consequently, the development of Irish league clubs. What is undeniable, though, is that clubs such as Glentoran and Linfield, which attracted large crowds in the inter-war and immediate post-war era, are now watched by ever decreasing numbers of paying customers. In addition, nationalist west Belfast has had no major team since Belfast Celtic left the Irish League in 1949, a situation now altered by the promotion of Donegal Celtic to the Irish League Premier Division.[48]

The Setanta Cup, which was first contested in 2005 and involves four teams from Northern Ireland's Irish League and four from the League of Ireland in the Irish Republic, represents an interesting attempt to infuse much-needed life into domestic football on both sides of the border. Despite such an innovation, however, and the more distant prospect of an all-Ireland league, the fact remains that, for the foreseeable future, the level of interest in the English game is unlikely to subside. Indeed, it is inextricably linked with the commodification of the game which itself is part of the wider incorporation of sport and leisure into the dynamics of consumer capitalism.

None of the underlying trends that explain these developments is unique to Northern Ireland. As Crawford notes, 'being a sports fan has always involved elements of consumption, be this simply attending "live" games or reading sports-related stories and results in the local and national press'.[49] However, 'changes within the nature of wider society and moves towards a post-industrial, post-Fordist, disorganized-capitalist consumer culture have increased the opportunities for fans to connect with sport via ever expanding mass-media resources and the growing market of consumer goods'.[50] The result is the emergence of what King describes as 'new consumer fandom'.[51]

Two specific points are worth making in relation to Northern Ireland. Firstly, people were supporting Celtic, Rangers and major English clubs long before the advent of this new category of football fandom, although undeniably the ways in which cross-channel teams are now supported can usefully be linked with 'consumer fandom'. Secondly, it would be a mistake to think that new forms of fandom inevitably transcend sectarian difference. Whilst this may be the case in relation to English clubs, it is largely irrelevant with regard to support for Celtic and Rangers, which in itself often operates alongside following an English club but only occasionally serves as a absolute alternative.

Conclusion: continuity and change in Northern Irish sport

This chapter has looked at the social significance of sport and leisure in Northern Ireland from a number of perspectives that have previously been used only to a limited extent in this particular context. The chapter's findings suggest, however, that, regardless of what themes one chooses to focus on, there is still a large measure of continuity in terms of the ways in which sport reflects and helps to maintain certain divisions within Northern Irish society. This is clearly apparent with reference to sporting spaces despite the ongoing debate about a more inclusive 'national' stadium. The very fact that the idea of Northern Ireland as a nation is itself contested presents a considerable obstacle to this initiative. In other respects, it is true, there has been evidence of change. One recognises, for example, that athletes themselves often make pragmatic decisions concerning nationality and national identity and that more and more of these athletes are female. They are largely willing to represent their sporting country regardless of their political beliefs. However, this has long been the case and owes little or nothing to the peace process. In fact, it is only in relatively recent times that young nationalists born in Northern Ireland have expressed a preference to play international football for the Irish Republic. This can be partially explained by reference to the relative fortunes of the two senior sides. It is also likely, however, to reflect an increase in sectarian attitudes, especially amongst the young, that has been discerned despite, or perhaps because of, the peace process.[52]

Some media sports stars, such as George Best, have appeared capable of transcending the political divide almost completely, as evidenced perhaps by Best's funeral on 3 December 2005. They have done so, however, by representing different things to different constituencies.[53] Similarly, fans are able to enter into cross-community, and therefore, in the general context of Northern Ireland, transgressive, relationships, particularly in relation to English Premiership football and aided by the global media and cheap flights. Beneath the veneer of communality, though, it is obvious that these fans remain divided in relation to the Celtic–Rangers rivalry in Scotland and also in terms of the rival attractions of Northern Ireland and the Republic of Ireland and, within the context of the Irish League, of Cliftonville on the one hand and teams such as Linfield and Glentoran on the other. Belfast has certainly changed since the 1970s. Northern Ireland as whole has also changed. With specific reference to sport and leisure, however, many of the changes have been superficial, with people continuing to take sides in their sporting practices.

Notes

1 F. Davenport, T. Downs, D. Hannigan, F. Parnell and N.Wilson, *Ireland* (London: Lonely Planet Publications, 2006), p. 554.
2 *Ibid.*, p. 652.
3 *Ibid.*, p. 609.
4 T. Paulin, 'The vernacular city', *Guardian* Saturday Review, 23 February 2002, p. 2.
5 G. Patterson, 'I'm a stranger here myself', *Guardian* Travel, 6 August 2005, p. 2.
6 P. Theroux, *The Kingdom by the Sea* (London: Penguin Books, 1984), p. 230.
7 G. Dawe, 'The revenges of the heart: Belfast and the poetics of space', in N. Allen and A. Kelly (eds), *The Cities of Belfast* (Dublin: Four Courts Press, 2004), p. 207.
8 N. Allen and A. Kelly, 'Introduction', in Allen and Kelly, *The Cities of Belfast*, p. 8.
9 T. Brown. (2004) ' "Let's go to Graceland": the drama of Stewart Parker', in Allen and Kelly, *The Cities of Belfast*, p. 117.
10 Davenport *et al.*, *Ireland*, p. 554.
11 G. Crawford, *Consuming Sport: Fans, Sport and Culture* (London: Routledge, 2004), p. 81.

12 Davenport *et al.*, *Ireland*, p. 588.
13 Ireland were, however, scheduled to play Italy in a Rugby World Cup warm-up game at Ravenhill on 24 August 2007.
14 Davenport *et al.*, *Ireland*, p. 588.
15 See A. Bairner, 'On thin ice? The Odyssey, the Giants, and the sporting transformation of Belfast', *American Behavioral Scientist* 46:11 (2003), pp. 1519–32; D. Hassan, 'From Kings to Giants: a history of ice hockey in Belfast, 1930–2002', *Sport in History* 24:1 (2004), pp. 77–93.
16 See, for example, J. Sugden and S. Harvie, *Sport and Community Relations in Northern Ireland* (Coleraine: Centre for the Study of Conflict, University of Ulster, 1995); A. Bairner and P. Darby, 'Divided sport in a divided society: Northern Ireland', in J. Sugden and A. Bairner (eds), *Sport in Divided Societies* (Aachen: Meyer & Meyer, 1999), pp. 51–72; J. Sugden, 'Sport and community relations in Northern Ireland and Israel', in A. Bairner (ed.), *Sport and the Irish: Histories, Identities, Issues* (Dublin: University College Dublin Press, 2005), pp. 238–51.
17 See, for example, A. Bairner, 'Soccer, masculinity, and violence in Northern Ireland: between hooliganism and terrorism', *Men and Masculinities* 1:3 (1999), pp. 284–301; A. Bairner, 'Sport, Sectarianism and Society in a Divided Ireland revisited', in J. Sugden and A. Tomlinson (eds), *Power Games: A Critical Sociology of Sport* (London: Routledge, 2002), pp. 181–95; A. Bairner and P. Shirlow, 'Loyalism, Linfield and the territorial politics of soccer fandom in Northern Ireland', *Space and Polity* 2:2 (1998), pp. 163–77; A. Bairner and P. Shirlow, 'When leisure turns to fear: fear, mobility, and ethno-sectarianism in Belfast', *Leisure Studies* 22:3 (2003), pp. 203–21; J. Sugden and A. Bairner, *Sport, Sectarianism and Society in a Divided Ireland* (Leicester: Leicester University Press, 1993).
18 C. Coulter, *Contemporary Northern Irish Society: An Introduction* (London: Pluto Press, 1999), p. 29.
19 J. Bale and P. Vertinsky, 'Introduction', in P. Vertinsky and J. Bale (eds), *Sites of Sport: Space, Place, Experience* (London: Routledge, 2004), p. 1.
20 S. Zukin, *The Cultures of Cities* (Malden MA: Blackwell, 1995), p. 1.
21 *Ibid.*, p. 19.
22 *Ibid.*
23 See Bairner and Shirlow, 'When leisure turns to fear'.
24 For detailed discussion of these concepts see Y-F. Tuan, *Landscapes of Fear* (Oxford: Blackwell, 1979); J. Bale, *Landscapes of Modern Sport* (Leicester: Leicester University Press, 1994).
25 See Bairner and Darby, 'Divided sport in a divided society'; Sugden and Bairner, *Sport, Sectarianism and Society*.
26 B. Hamilton *et al.*, *Creating a Soccer Strategy for Northern Ireland: Report from the Advisory Panel to the Minister for Culture, Arts and Leisure* (Belfast: Department of Culture, Arts and Leisure, 2001), p. 73.
27 *Ibid.*, p. 74.

28 Amalgamation of Official Northern Ireland Supporters' Clubs, *The Future of International Football in Northern Ireland* (Belfast: Amalgamation of Official Northern Ireland Supporters' Clubs, 2006), p. 25.

29 D. O'Hearn, *Nothing but an Unfinished Song: Bobby Sands, the Irish Hunger Striker who ignited a Generation* (New York: Nation Books, 2006).

30 For more details see http://news.bbc.co.uk/1/hi/northern_ireland/4663512.stm (accessed 31 January 2006).

31 Amalgamation, *The Future of International Football*, p. 21.

32 See, for example, M. Cronin and D. Mayall (eds), *Sporting Nationalisms: Identity, Ethnicity, Immigration and Assimilation* (London: Frank Cass, 1998); A. Bairner, *Sport, Nationalism, and Globalization: European and North American Perspectives* (Albany NY: State University of New York Press, 2001); M. L. Silk, D. L. Andrews and C. L. Cole (eds), *Sport and Corporate Nationalisms* (Oxford: Berg, 2005); A. Smith and D. Porter, *Sport and National Identity in the Post-war World* (London: Routledge, 2004).

33 See Bairner, *Sport, Nationalism, and Globalization*.

34 J. Lovejoy, *Bestie: a Portrait of a Legend* (London: Pan Macmillan, 1999).

35 G. Best, *Blessed: The Autobiography* (London: Ebury Press, 2002).

36 *Ibid.*

37 See D. Dougan, *The Sash he never Wore . . . Twenty-five Years on* (Newtownabbey: Lagan Books, 1997).

38 See D. Hassan, 'Sport, identity and Irish nationalism in Northern Ireland', in A. Bairner (ed.), *Sport and the Irish: Histories, Identities, Issues* (Dublin, University College Dublin Press, 2005), pp. 123–39.

39 A. Bairner, 'Sport, Irishness and Ulster Unionism', in Bairner, *Sport and the Irish*, pp. 157–71.

40 Interviewed by Simon Mason, 6 February 2000. See S. Mason, 'The History of Irish Rugby: A Transition from Amateurism to Professionalism', unpublished M.Sc. (Sport and Exercise) thesis (Newtownabbey: University of Ulster at Jordanstown, 2000).

41 Interviewed by Andrew Gibson, 18 December 2001. See A. Gibson, 'Irish when it Suits? An Examination into Identity Issues within Rugby in Northern Ireland', unpublished B.Sc. (Hons) dissertation (Sport, Exercise and Leisure) (Newtownabbey: University of Ulster at Jordanstown, 2002).

42 Interviewed by Simon Mason, 29 January 2000. See Mason, 'The History of Irish Rugby'.

43 Interviewed by Andrew Gibson, 18 February 2002. See Gibson, 'Irish when it Suits?'

44 *Ibid.*

45 See J. Todd, 'Two traditions in Unionist political culture', *Irish Political Studies* 2 (1987), pp. 1–26.

46 Interviewed by Andrew Gibson, 20 December 2001. See Gibson, 'Irish when it Suits?'

47 See A. Bairner, 'Football in Northern Ireland: the cross-channel dimension', in *Soccer Review 2003* (Houghton on the Hill: Patrick Murphy & Ivan Waddington), pp. 33–7.

48 For detailed information about the rise and fall of the Belfast Celtic club see P. Coyle, *Paradise Lost and Found: The Story of Belfast Celtic* (Edinburgh: Mainstream, 1999).

49 Crawford, *Consuming Sport*, p. 11.

50 *Ibid.*

51 A. King, *The End of the Terraces: The Transformation of English Football in the 1990s*, revised paperback edition (Leicester: Leicester University Press, 2002).

52 See, for example, P. Shirlow 'Northern Ireland: a reminder from the present', in C. Coulter and S. Coleman (eds), *The End of Irish History? Critical Reflections on the Celtic Tiger* (Manchester: Manchester University Press, 2003), pp. 192–207; S. McGrellis (2004) *Pushing the Boundaries in Northern Ireland: Young People, Violence and Sectarianism*, Families and Social Capital ESRC Research Group Working Paper 8 (London: South Bank University, 2004).

53 See A. Bairner, 'Where did it all go right? George Best, Manchester United and Northern Ireland', in D. L. Andrews (ed.), *Manchester United: a Thematic Study* (London: Routledge, 2004), pp. 133–46.

12

From shellshock rock to ceasefire sounds: popular music

Sean Campbell and Gerry Smyth

In recent years a number of authors have sought to establish popular music as an important element within the Irish critical imagination. They have done so because among the many achievements of international popular music studies has been an appreciation that this kind of cultural practice provides one of the key means for subjects to understand the world and themselves in relation to it. As Martin Stokes explains (in a book that coincidentally appeared in the year of the first ceasefires): 'Music is not just a thing that happens "in" society. A society . . . might also be usefully conceived as something which happens "in" music.'[1]

When a particular society comes to be dominated by widespread, long-term conflict – as has been the case in Northern Ireland since the late 1960s – the question of popular music becomes even more significant, for the field provides for a wide range of values, practices and attitudes which are themselves attuned in sensitive ways to the society's wider cultural state. It might reasonably be claimed that people everywhere identify themselves in relation to cultural discourses, and one of the most potent and widely disseminated of such discourses since the middle of the last century has been popular music. We cannot, therefore, afford to ignore popular music in the context of Northern Ireland. In both its creation and its consumption, in the ways in which it directs and enables a range of identities, popular music provides some key insights into life in that particular place.

It is not possible to fully appreciate the changes that have impacted upon Northern Irish society since the various ceasefires came into force without first understanding what life was like there during the preceding quarter of a century of conflict. The popular music produced in Northern Ireland since the 1960s offers a key means of understanding the wider cultural and political fate of its people. This chapter offers a survey of that tradition, stopping off at various key moments to try to hear some of the ways in which this particular society has articulated a sense of crisis (and resolution) through the medium of popular music.

Pre-'troubles' pop: from the showbands to Van Morrison

In the 1960s the showbands ruled supreme throughout the length and breadth of Ireland. The scene began to develop in the north in the immediate post-war years, at a time when dance orchestras were still the dominant form of live popular entertainment. The Clipper Carlton formed in Strabane in the late 1940s, and they were typical of the early showband style. The band's musical range was extremely wide: they played jazz instrumentals, novelty pop, calypso, rock 'n' roll, show tunes, Irish ballads, Country 'n' Western – any form of music, in fact, that would elicit a response from their audience. They introduced glamour and personality into a practice that encouraged reticence, if not outright anonymity. They broadened the age range of the audience for live music consumption, making it an attractive form of leisure practice for everyone, from teenagers to pensioners. Primarily, however, The Clipper Carlton were a *dance* band: their job was to fill the floors of the venues they played year after year, up and down the island.

The popularity of The Clipper Carlton throughout the 1950s was envied by many, and their example was developed by the younger musicians who helped to generate the incredibly vibrant showband scene of the early 1960s. Although Northern Ireland failed to produce any of the scene's high-profile acts (such as The Royal, The Miami, or The Capitol) it was a hotbed of showband activity, producing many minor outfits as well as providing a large pool of individual musicians. So long as the music itself remained the preferred leisure option for a significant audience, the job of showband musician would remain viable for many, and lucrative for some.

The most important thing about the showband scene from our perspective here, however, is that it was manifestly cross-border. This introduces three issues that have become highly significant in theories developed under the auspices of popular music studies generally, and in considerations of Irish cultural history particularly: firstly, its primary function as 'noise' renders music a radically unrestricted discourse that is impossible to contain within cultural (that is to say, human-made) boundaries. Secondly, and related to the previous point, the 'scenes' to which various kinds of musical practice give rise are similarly resistant to established territorial protocols – as Mark Olson writes, 'the place of the scene itself does not necessarily correlate with the boundaries of its geographical referent, for the reach of its effects does not respect geographic borders'.[2] Thirdly, music anticipates the inclusive dispensation towards which the wider politico-cultural formation is tending; music is enabled to do this because of the way in which it blurs the boundaries between commercial and aesthetic discourses of value.[3] The more optimistic among us might claim that, in all these ways, pre-'troubles' popular music already adumbrated – in its assumptions, practices and consumption – the seeds of a post-'troubles' settlement.

This may seem to be over-analysing what was in essence a simple form of music. The fact is, however, that the showband phenomenon was far from simple in any of its features. Musically, sociologically, economically, politically the showband scene raised many interesting questions about identities on either side of the border and about the institutions which invested in them.

It is instructive to recall that the most significant popular music artist to have emerged from Northern Ireland over the last half-century started his career as a showband musician. Van Morrison may not have been as commercially successful as some, but his influence upon Irish popular music has been pervasive, even if much of the time that influence has been filtered through a variety of other sources. Over the course of his near half-century career he has witnessed the 'troubles' come and go. During the same period he has forged a distinctive profile within the popular music world. It would be remarkable indeed if the two phenomena were not linked.

Morrison remains a consummate performer in the idiom of modern popular music precisely because his career straddles the many different historical phases of the discourse, and because the different practices pertaining to these phases are always active in his work. Thus the smiling saxophone player with The Monarchs became the scowling blues shouter of Them, who in turn became the mature solo artist of *Astral Weeks* (1969), the now celebrated 'cycle of songs about Belfast' that remains, for Martin McLoone, 'one of the most evocative portraits' of that city 'produced in any art form'.[4] The singer's achievement (one he shares with all those artists history is wont to classify as 'significant') has been to develop an integrated, discrete vision of the times and places in which he fetched up. That vision stretches beyond the location from which the artist emerged, but like all significant art it returns to that location to report on what Northern Ireland has brought to the world and to consider what the world has brought to Northern Ireland. As McLaughlin and McLoone explain, '[Morrison's] is an art of the periphery, soaking up the influences of the centre, adapting them to its own designs and then offering them back to the centre in a wholly unique form.'[5] Or, to adopt a more appropriate idiom, Morrison's restive journey since the late 1950s has been nothing less than a search for a musical style (blending elements of pop, blues, rock, jazz and country) to which the composite identity he represents (Northern Irish, Irish, British, American) can dance.[6]

And though an experiment such as *Astral Weeks* – which was released on the eve of the 'troubles' – evoked 'a parallel Belfast of the imagination, insulated and isolated from the grim and gruesome realities' of its context,[7] there can be little doubt that popular music in Northern Ireland – as much as any other cultural activity – was profoundly affected by the onset of the 'troubles' in 1969, and by the ensuing escalation in sectarianism. The international forms which had come to predominate in the mid to late 1960s (rock, soul, rhythm 'n' blues) all made a significant impact upon popular consciousness in the region. All, moreover, stressed to some degree or other the values of individuality, love and respect, such values subsisting both 'inside' the music, as it were – as lyrical and musical themes – but 'outside' it as well, among those who, whatever their creed, cast or colour, actually made the music. These values emerged as a reaction to the political dogma which had come to dominate the United States during the Vietnam War, and to the bourgeois complacency that had come to characterise life in post-war Britain. Popular music demanded a vital, energetic and transformative engagement with reality to be instigated at the level of the subject – a revolution in the head, no less. Nowhere was this call answered with greater enthusiasm than in Northern Ireland, where each sub-genre had its cadre of passionate devotees, and where the music appeared to offer genuine alternatives to those available in the 'real' world.

Unfortunately the 'troubles' ushered in an era in which dogma and ideology dominated the cultural landscape in Northern Ireland, and in which the validity of popular music as a medium for the individual's engagement with the world was thoroughly compromised. Other voices – supposedly more 'authentic', certainly more insistent – began to demand the listener's attention; popular music's message – now exposed as hopelessly optimistic if not entirely vainglorious – of 'peace and love' was remorselessly eroded. When it came, however, the blow fell most heavily not upon the consumers but on the producers – the music makers themselves – and not upon the rock or soul variants which espoused the message most assiduously but upon the showbands which had continued to ply their trade up and down the island despite the onset of violence.

The UVF murder of three musicians from the Miami Showband on 31 July 1975 was a watershed in popular music making in Northern Ireland. The observable effects of the massacre have been noted before: the cessation of the cross-border showband scene, and the stigmatisation of Northern Ireland as a dangerous location for touring acts. Both these effects were temporary, as it turned out, although it is true to say that the showband scene – already waning in 1975 – was never the same again. Other, longer-lasting implications emerged only with time. One such implication was the realisation that music cannot be removed from the wider socio-political context in which it is produced and consumed, and that in a highly charged culture where every form of signification is liable to co-option the musical statement – no less than any kind of artistic statement – is always and everywhere a political statement.

A second, related implication is that popular music is not necessarily the most appropriate means with which to address political issues arising from complex historical contexts. As Bill Rolston suggests, in an essay that goes to the heart of this matter, most rock and pop musicians inhabit milieux that are 'far above the day-to-day political concerns and struggles of race and class' and are thus not entirely 'organic to the communities of resistance' that provide 'collective, communal response[s]' to political crises. Or, 'if they are, they are quickly incorporated into the music industry and its concerns'. From within the ostensible 'monolith' of this 'major global industry', then, 'there are rigid limits' (institutional 'structures', 'ideological imperatives') that constrain 'what [musicians] can say and how it can be said'.[8]

Notwithstanding such restrictions, however, the late 1970s witnessed a marked increase in popular music-making activities across Northern Ireland. An unforeseen consequence of the Miami Showband massacre had been an expansion of domestic music making, with local bands filling the vacuum left by the *de facto* touring boycott of more established international acts.[9] At precisely the same time, moreover, the empowering 'do it yourself' ethos of punk was convincing many youngsters in Northern Ireland to write songs that engaged with their own everyday lives.

Punk in Northern Ireland: from 'Alternative Ulster' to 'utter escapism'

The emergence of the punk subculture in Northern Ireland is usually traced to the visit of The Clash to Belfast in 1977.[10] Notwithstanding the actuality of this event as a point of origin, it's clear that the visit had a measurable impact on the local music-making scene, serving – in the words of one contemporary observer – as a 'catalyst' that 'ignited the whole punk movement in Ulster'.[11]

The presence of The Clash in the city precipitated a raft of Northern Irish punk acts whilst consolidating the efforts of others. A range of socio-political factors have been cited to explain the unique 'stronghold' that punk enjoyed in Ulster.[12] The late Clash front man, Joe Strummer, for example, would maintain that punk supplied 'the perfect soundtrack' to what he called the north's 'ravaged cities'.[13] In similar vein McLoone has claimed that Belfast and punk were effectively 'made for one

another', suggesting, 'If there was an element of "the abject" about punk
. . . there was no more abject place in the Western world than Northern
Ireland, specifically Belfast, in 1977.'[14]

As McLoone goes on to explain, however, while punks in the metropolitan centres of London and New York had the comparatively simple
task of 'establishing an alternative' to the conservative 'parent culture',
their Belfast contemporaries had the additional – and rather more perilous – job of defying the existing 'culture of dissent that was represented
by republican and loyalist paramilitaries', assailing not only the 'status
quo' but also 'those aggressive and violent opponents of the status quo
who had reduced daily life to the abject'.[15] In this regard, punk in
Northern Ireland – according to its early observers – supplied 'a two-
fingered salute' to the 'politicians', the 'authorities', and the 'paramilitaries' too.[16]

In the context of this complex ethical matrix, what punk arguably
offered was what McLoone has called 'an imagining beyond . . . sectarian politics', staging 'a rebellion against the complacent certainties of a
sectarian political culture that had delivered nothing but social dishar-
mony and communal breakdown' and pointing to 'the substance of a
new politics' predicated on a 'positive' – indeed, a 'utopian' – message
that deviated sharply from the nihilism of English punk.[17] Contemporary
observers of Belfast punk have also laid stress on the scene's 'positive
force', recalling that it brought together 'for the first time, large numbers
of young people from different backgrounds . . . with kids from Catholic
and Protestant areas mixing together freely . . . without fear or intimidation'.[18] Such reminiscences at least appear to be corroborated by a
famous Belfast graffito from 1977 that declared, 'The Clash unite
Protestant and Catholic Youth in Northern Ireland with punk rock'.[19]

The band that most embodied this 'utopian' project was Belfast outfit
Stiff Little Fingers (SLF). Led by vocalist/guitarist Jake Burns, the group's
early live shows were based (in a curious echo of the showband era)
around 'cover' versions, albeit of contemporary punk standards. One
such formative concert was watched by a visiting English journalist,
Gordon Ogilvie, who at the time was Belfast correspondent for London's
Daily Express. The reporter later approached Burns and the other band
members and 'urged' them – in the words of O'Neill and Trelford – 'to
write their own songs based on life in Northern Ireland.'[20] To assist in
this new project, Ogilvie would co-write their 'troubles'-based song
lyrics. In the face of punk's 'for real' rhetoric, however, this unlikely
press–pop partnership inevitably sparked accusations that the band had
'exploited the situation in Northern Ireland for commercial gain', with a
generically British – rather than a specifically local – audience in mind.[21]

Nevertheless, the band's Belfast live shows would appeal to a 'mixed' demographic audience, with both Catholic and Protestant youngsters in attendance.[22] The band's best-known song, 'Alternative Ulster' (1978), served to register the sentiments of disenfranchised youth in both communities, expressing frustration at the futility of the 'troubles', and assailing militant factions on all sides. The poet Paul Muldoon would later commend the song's 'well-judged, and justifiable, rage', suggesting that it constituted 'a key moment in the artistic life of Northern Ireland', with its song lyrics staging 'an appeal' to 'the power of imagination over nation'.[23] The track consequently came to 'symbolise', as McLoone explains, 'the attempt to forge an alternative politics by the province's severely bored, annoyed and disaffected youth', with the band 'championing an alternative cultural space beyond the clutches of both the political mainstream and the political opposition represented by republicanism and loyalism'.[24]

In stark contrast to the efforts of (the Protestant, Belfast-based) SLF, the (Catholic, Derry-based) Undertones offered little in the way of political address. This band was led by guitar-player/songwriter John O'Neill, alongside vocalist Feargal Sharkey. With their background in Derry's Bogside, The Undertones were not unfamiliar with the idea of crisis that impelled punk's London-based vanguard. However, while Joe Strummer and Johnny Rotten addressed the social realities of life in 1970s Britain, The Undertones were more concerned with the politics of everyday life, offering light-hearted meditations on male adolescence. Thus, while SLF pursued a sort of 'Belfast social realism',[25] The Undertones opted for 'More Songs about Chocolate and Girls' (1980), staging witty allusions to schoolboy pastimes such as Subbuteo ('My Perfect Cousin', 1980), and exalting the pleasures of teenage treats ('Mars Bars', 1979). Even more salient in this regard was the title of the band's paean to youthful thrills that served as lead-off track on their (now celebrated) debut EP 'Teenage Kicks' (1978).

The group's refusal to engage with the 'troubles' generated a considerable amount of debate among critics and fans alike. In early press interviews, for example, the band would stress that their work had 'nothing to do with the troubles', but only for the bulk of media coverage to present them as 'barbed-wire boys'.[26] More than twenty years later Sharkey (who had taken part in a People's Democracy march in 1970)[27] outlined the group's position in clear-cut terms. Notwithstanding the fact that it had been – in the singer's words – 'outrageously dangerous' to signal 'any sort of allegiance one way or another', Sharkey stressed that all The Undertones had 'lived and breathed' the 'troubles' throughout their entire young adulthood, and thus had been forced to confront the effects of the crisis 'every single day'. From this particular perspective, then, what The Undertones' upbeat oeuvre afforded the individual group members – as well as their local fan base – was what Sharkey calls 'utter escapism'.[28]

This escapist ethos would conceivably have been taken in certain quarters as an apolitical betrayal of the band's immediate milieu, with their songs being cast – from such a critical perspective – in a somewhat conservative light. As Sharkey has cogently claimed, however, the band's early audience – who like the group had first-hand experience of the 'troubles' in their everyday lives – 'didn't really need [The Undertones] to get up in front of them . . . and start lecturing them about what was politically and socially going on around them'.[29]

Nevertheless, as Eamonn McCann points out, the group were viewed with a degree of 'suspicion' and 'hostility' by sections of 1970s Derry, not least for their perceived refusal to conform to 'what was expected and what was imposed upon them almost as a sort of communal duty to be part of the Bogside and the Bogside struggle'. McCann thus makes it clear that the band's environs were not merely 'oppressed' but also 'oppressive', elaborating that the 'sweet' and 'beautiful' sounds of Undertones songs – despite being at odds with the 'angry', 'aggressive' codes of punk – were actually 'far from mainstream' sensibilities in the band's immediate milieu. When viewed in the light of such 'oppressive' factors, the group's oeuvre takes on a more progressive character. For if, as McCann explains, punk was about 'revolting against the things around you', then The Undertones quite understandably 'revolted against anger', assembling an aesthetic that arguably constituted – in the climate of 1970s Derry – an 'oppositional statement'.[30] Accordingly, while SLF, as McLoone points out, merely 'preached about an alternative Ulster', The Undertones actually 'lived the alternative and wrote about it by ignoring the political situation completely', with their interest in 'the ordinary' serving as 'an extremely political statement in the highly charged, extraordinary atmosphere of Northern Ireland at the time'.[31]

The view that Northern Ireland's punk musicians might be 'harbingers of a new cross-community youth culture that would lead to an end of the conflict' was, as Rolston explains, somewhat 'premature'.[32] Nevertheless, the short-lived subculture of punk enabled Northern Irish rock musicians to engage a diverse range of responses to their complex social milieu, with the irate and earnest SLF 'imagining', in Muldoon's words, 'other ways of living',[33] whilst the playful and cheery Undertones evoked an 'alternative Ulster' through what their singer calls 'utter escapism'. In the increasingly fractious climate of the early 1980s, however – and in the face of various 'troubles'-based songs from non-Northern Irish musicians – the previously reluctant chief Undertones songwriter, John O'Neill, would stage a direct expressive address to the Northern Ireland crisis.

'Crisis of Mine': 'troubles' rock in the 1980s

In a 1983 essay called 'The Artist and the Troubles' Seamus Deane pointed out that writers 'can often be more troubled by the idea that they should be troubled by a crisis than they are by the crisis itself'.[34] It remains unclear whether Deane was au fait with the work of his fellow natives of Derry, The Undertones, but his point may well have been shaped by this group's early 1980s output, with tracks such as 'Crisis of Mine' (1981) exemplifying Deane's observation. With its titular conflation of the personal and political, this song was born – for songwriter John O'Neill – of a niggling obligation to 'at least try and say something' about the 'troubles', allied to an inhibiting artistic inarticulacy, hence the 'kind of crisis' that the song sought to evoke.[35] Notwithstanding such creative obstacles, though, the band persevered with attempts at social commentary, not least in the allusion to the hunger strikes in 'It's Going to Happen!' (1981), which contained, as McLoone explains, 'a vague but nonetheless heart-felt reference to the impasse over the hunger strikes' via 'an appeal to Margaret Thatcher to change her mind'.[36] If such signals seemed somewhat oblique, the band would unveil their increasing political consciousness when they performed the song on *Top of the Pops*, with guitar-player Damian O'Neill sporting a black armband in honour of the recently deceased Bobby Sands.[37]

This gesture would be the extent of the band's engagement with the 'troubles', however, and – perhaps in the absence of more direct commentary – it was left to musicians from elsewhere on the archipelago to address the Northern Ireland crisis. The best-known of such interventions came from groups like The Police ('Invisible Sun', 1981) and U2 ('Sunday, Bloody Sunday', 1983).[38] Perhaps prompted by the interventions of non-Northern Irish musicians, the hitherto reticent former Undertones leader, John O'Neill, launched a forthright address to the issue, under the aegis of That Petrol Emotion. Featuring a US-born singer, Steve Mack, as well as two local Derry musicians, the only residual link to The Undertones was via O'Neill (guitar) and his brother Damian (bass). With their name evoking the sense of frustration of mid-1980s Derry, the group's work would deviate starkly from the escapist Undertones, acting instead as an expressly political platform, and supplying a sort of alternative information service to offset (what they saw as) the media's mishandling of the 'troubles'.

The band's new-found political stance was overtly republican,[39] with their freshly Gaelic nomenclature (their leader was now called Seán Ó'Néill) underlined by record sleeve tracts on British misconduct in Ireland, detailing the use of plastic bullets ('It's a Good Thing', 1986) and assailing the juryless Diplock courts ('Big Decision', 1987). The group's song lyrics, meanwhile, attacked the media's role in depicting the 'troubles' ('Tightlipped', 1986), and accused unionist leaders of endorsing sectarianism ('Circusville', 1986). Meanwhile the band's best-known song, 'Big Decision' (1987), advised prospective emigrants to stay put in Northern Ireland to help resolve what had become an ever more fractious conflict.

This particular migrant message contrasted starkly with that issued two years earlier by a contemporaneous northern band, Ruefrex, whose song 'The Wild Colonial Boy' (1985) called on Ireland's US-based diaspora to withdraw support for republican violence. Emerging from a loyalist area of north Belfast, the band had been formed in the late 1970s by Tom Coulter (bass) and Paul Burgess (drums). The group's persona as (what their singer Allan Clark would call) 'working-class Belfast Prods'[40] led to many of their songs being seen as accounts of 'working-class Protestant life',[41] with Rolston even suggesting that Ruefrex had 'set out to articulate the unionist case'.[42] The group's overarching ethos, however, was ultimately socialist,[43] and – as Clark would later make clear – their 'message' was 'anti-sectarian',[44] a point endorsed by music journalist Colin Irwin, who stressed that Ruefrex went to 'inordinate lengths to bridge the sectarian gap'.[45] The group's apparent goal of 'bringing the two communities together' was evinced not only in songs such as 'Cross the Line' (1979), but also via their policy of performing in both Catholic and Protestant areas.[46] Indeed, by the mid-1980s the band were at the forefront of a fund-raising concert for Lagan Valley College, the first integrated school for Catholic and Protestant youngsters in Northern Ireland.[47] However, Ruefrex's wish to inhabit what chief songwriter Paul Burgess called 'the middle ground' inevitably ran the risk – as he would openly acknowledge – of 'alienating both sides'.[48] Moreover, this well meaning artistic desire to stage the Northern Ireland crisis from what McCann has called 'somewhere . . . mid-way between the two communities' often merely conjures 'a place where no one lives', or 'an experience which nobody actually has'.[49]

Nevertheless, Ruefrex went on to become something of a (short-lived) *cause célèbre* in London media circles in the mid-1980s after the release of their best-known single, 'The Wild Colonial Boy'.[50] Borrowing its title from a well known – and rather sentimental – migrant tune, the track set out to offer, as O'Neill and Trelford explain, 'a scathing attack on (Irish)

Americans, especially groups like Noraid, who were involved in raising funds to help sustain the IRA's campaign of murder and destruction'.[51] Despite – or perhaps because of – its overtly 'anti-Noraid stance'[52] the record was well received,[53] with critics praising its 'progressively power-ful . . . attack upon the "would-be green men" of Irish America, who readily pay for that vicarious thrill of killing from far away'.[54]

Not everyone was receptive to the Ruefrex project, though, and – perhaps in light of Clark's unfashionable 'hard-man' image,[55] as well as songs such as 'The Fightin' 36th' (1987), which 'commemorated the mass sacrifice of the original 1912 Ulster Volunteer Force at the battle of the Somme' and included the unionist slogan 'No surrender' – the band were dismissed by certain figures as 'Orange bastards'.[56] Notwithstanding such abuse, a member of the group would later suggest that Ruefrex's position as what he called 'the "Prod" band' had been 'more politically incorrect and damaging' (from a marketing point of view) than being seen – like That Petrol Emotion – as an 'oppressed' Catholic outfit.[57] This point invokes, of course, an oft remarked obser-vation that has been made by – among others – James Hawthorne (ex-controller of BBC Northern Ireland), who suggested that 'the Catholic case is sometimes more lyrical because it is about change', whilst 'the conservatism of the Protestant ethos, not well articulated, is of less inter-est'.[58] Whether or not this is the case, it's clear that Ruefrex's role as the 'voice' of what McDonald has called 'the least fashionable community in Western Europe'[59] would scarcely have aided their prospects in a rock culture that venerates the marginal, the subordinate and the subaltern.[60]

The question of rock's relation to working-class Protestantism would continue to be a concern for Northern Ireland's popular music culture. In this context, Burgess would go on to register his unease about what he saw as the post-ceasefire 'alienation of Protestant working-class loyal-ists', explaining that this constituency had been 'left behind in the peace process', pointing out that this could be 'a very dangerous thing'. In 2005 Burgess averred that there was 'more of a need' than 'ever before' to 'give [this] community an articulate voice through music . . . because they feel no one is listening to them', arguing that 'this voice doesn't have to be triumphalist or sectarian' but is at least worthy of 'a place in the world'.[61]

Ceasefire sounds: the 1990s and beyond

In this final section we turn to consider the course that popular music has taken in Northern Ireland during the period of the peace process. Because of the relative proximity of events, it is difficult to say if any enduring 'post-ceasefire' trends in popular music have yet emerged; but if there is one area that has emerged in force since 1994 it is the great variety of electronic dance styles. It's clear that in Northern Ireland, as elsewhere, this kind of music is shared by those who use it merely as an aural accompaniment to a particular form of social activity (clubbing), and those (producers, musicians, DJs, as well as enthusiastic consumers) who have made some form of investment – cultural, emotional or commercial – in one or other particular sub-genre. Given the history of the region before 1994 and the various dangers and difficulties attending 'normal' socialising activities before that time, it's perhaps understandable why 'clubbing' has proved to be so popular in Northern Ireland, and why 'House' and 'Techno' – the parental forms of modern dance music – as well as their innumerable progeny have been welcomed there with such enthusiasm. Not only in the urban centres such as Belfast and Derry, moreover: like the rest of Ireland, clubbing in the north has emerged as an important feature of small-town – even village – life as people look to engage with this international cultural phenomenon in their own back yard, so to speak.

David Holmes was already working as a DJ in and around Belfast when House music and the clubbing subculture it supported began to emerge towards the end of the 1980s. Holmes took to the music enthusiastically, and in many ways his subsequent career has been exemplary: he promoted the new music at events in his native Belfast, as well as running a successful club night there in the early to mid-1990s, attracting an audience of bright young things who were only too happy to turn their backs on the violence of previous generations. Moving from the DJ box to the studio, he began to develop a reputation as an imaginative remixer of other people's material, including Northern Irish bands such as Therapy?. As the 1990s progressed, he began to produce music that was less oriented to the dance floor and more influenced by mixed media events. He became a much sought after writer of film music, first in the United Kingdom and then in the United States, culminating in the soundtrack for *Ocean's Eleven* (2001). He became a 'proper' collaborative musician, including touring a live show, after the release of *David Holmes presents the Free Association* (2003). As a high-profile 'name' within the world of modern electronic music he continues to combine, so far as possible, the different demands of DJ, promoter, remixer, musician and writer-producer.

The other significant product of the Northern Irish dance scene has been Robert 'Fergie' Ferguson, who won an international reputation as a DJ/producer while barely out of his teens. Both Holmes and Ferguson were born into the Ulster Protestant tradition, although it's clearly the case that the kind of music with which they are associated has developed, like punk in the 1970s,[62] a strong anti-sectarian ethos. Above and beyond sociological considerations such as education and class, clubbing, especially, aspires to a kind of existential egalitarianism as its adherents are invited to lose their everyday identity in the neutral space of the dance floor. The power in dance music belongs to the DJ, and resides in the ability to manipulate the body through a variety of physical-emotional responses; the dance floor is in this respect a kind of heterotopian space, a place where the normal parameters of society are suspended (especially those associated with cognition and intellect) and a new dispensation – founded on the radically liberated body – holds sway.

This possibility certainly appeared to be the case with dance culture in Northern Ireland. As Holmes would explain, the club nights that he convened in Belfast in the 1990s attracted youngsters from both Catholic and Protestant areas, who engaged in the act of 'dancing alongside' one another in defiance of what Holmes has termed 'the nonsense' of sectarian life.[63] In this regard, the dance scene in Northern Ireland would, as McLaughlin suggests, be 'instrumental in extending non-sectarian spaces', offering 'an alternative reality to "the Troubles"', and a 'response to the peace process'.[64]

At the same time, however, it could be argued that the 'liberatory jouissance' that Gilbert and Pearson detect in dance music might – as the latter concede – offer 'nothing but an empty space from which no political position as such can possibly be articulated'. The 'tremendously liberating experience' afforded by the act of dancing is thus 'not the same as transformation', hence Gilbert and Pearson's suggestion that '[e]scape – especially if only temporary – is not the same thing as political change': 'when we get back from the party, have we left all those structures as intact as they were before?'[65]

Notwithstanding the fact that dance music, as McLaughlin points out, 'offers no guarantee of how people will behave once the party is over', it may nevertheless be argued that this 'loved-up, pharmaceutically driven culture' (whose participants could be seen embracing 'strangers across the divide'), was at the very least preferable to sectarian violence.[66] So, while the notion of 'a unified dance culture' became 'increasingly difficult to sustain',[67] it would certainly seem that the non-denominational character of this subculture was a major reason why dance music and the associated practice of clubbing flourished in Northern Ireland in the period after the ceasefire.

It is also worth stressing, however, that the same period also witnessed a resurgence of interest in older, more established popular styles. The Larne-raised rock group Therapy?, for example, worked to restore – in the 1990s – the hard-edged guitar-based styles of Northern Irish punk acts such as SLF. Rather than an exercise in reactionary retro, however, Therapy? updated this template so as to make it relevant to contemporary concerns. A song such as 'Screamager' (1993) – which reached the UK top five – can therefore sit alongside a classic such as Nirvana's 'Smells like Teen Spirit' (1991) as one of the key anthems of the 'slacker' generation; the fact that it spoke to such a wide audience perhaps reveals something about the internationalist ambitions of at least some people from Northern Ireland following the years of 'local' fixation.

While the high-octane power pop of Therapy? recalled the efforts of earlier northern rock musicians, it at the same time prefaced the sound of Downpatrick group Ash, whose music and career bear comparison with Therapy? on a number of levels. Like their slightly older, slightly heavier-rocking compatriots, Ash cross-pollinated a number of sub-genres to produce an original hybrid which won them an audience far beyond the soil on which it had been nurtured. Developing a fast-paced variety of guitar-driven punk pop, the band's aesthetic was perhaps not as 'dark' as that of Therapy?, though it was certainly no less vigorous. Tim Wheeler, Ash's front man and chief songwriter, is both charismatic and diffident – an unusual mixture in contemporary popular music. The other characteristic shared by these bands is a respectful, intelligent response to the music which forms their own pre-history. Popular music, no less than any art form, always involves a dual process of remembering and forgetting, of learning from the past and responding to the present; just so, as echoes of Hüsker Dü and SLF suffuse the music of Therapy?, shades of The Beach Boys and The Undertones can be discerned in Ash's oeuvre.

The latter made a significant – and highly celebrated – address to the peace process in May 1998, when the group joined forces with Dublin band U2 to stage a concert at Belfast's Waterfront Hall. This event took place to encourage young people in particular to endorse the recently signed Good Friday Agreement in the forthcoming referendum. The 'yes' campaign, supported by moderates on all sides of the political divide, was faltering; opponents of different ideological hues considered a power-sharing government for Northern Ireland to be unfeasible, an inevitable retreat from the ideals to which they had irrevocably subscribed. Hard-line unionists, especially, regarded the whole peace process (beginning with the IRA ceasefire) with suspicion – a US-driven conspiracy to achieve by political stealth what could not be achieved by persuasion or force of arms. The *status quo ante* might have been an unfortunate situation, but it was, unionist fundamentalists insisted, better than power sharing with those deemed to be murderers and gangsters. From such a perspective a 'no' vote was the only credible response.

Rock had claimed a political consciousness since its somewhat oppor-
tunistic alliance with the counter-culture in the 1960s, and especially the
anti-war stance of a number of high-profile artists. But the fact is that
precedents for focused interventions in the political arena from the world
of popular music were few and far between by the time Ash stepped on
stage in Belfast in May 1998. If one was seeking a parallel, however, it
would have to be Bob Marley's participation in a peace concert in
Jamaica in 1978, at which the singer sought to assuage tensions between
the country's political factions (led by Michael Manley and Edward
Seaga), rather than to support one or another side.[68]

Whether the Waterfront concert helped to sway the vote is debateable;
whether the gesture represented a victory for popular culture over hide-
bound, institutionalised politics is likewise so. Rolston appeared to have
no doubt when he claimed that the concert was 'a government-sponsored
public relations exercise, not the symbol of a truce between rivals', before
going on to argue, apropos the Marley comparison, that '[the] political
power of reggae at a particular conjuncture in Jamaican history stands
in stark contrast to the political subservience of pop at a key point in Irish
history'.[69] On the other hand, there should be no doubt about the powerful image presented by the sight of U2's Bono holding aloft the hands
of John Hume and David Trimble. Certainly, also, the 'no' campaign was
irritated (Bob McCartney, one of its leading voices, dismissed the event
as 'silly and superficial')[70] and may have wished, despite accusing the
opposition of being populist and patronising, for a roster of equally fashionable, high-profile artists to perform for their cause. One thing it did
reveal, however, was the continuing appeal of popular music as an accessible contemporary medium for the 'performance' of powerful emotions,
whether they be private or, as in this case, public.

Despite the fact that Ash had acted as the voice of northern rock at the
Waterfront 'yes' concert, it was arguably The Divine Comedy that
became Northern Ireland's most high-profile act during the mid to late
1990s. This rather chintzy cabaret rock ensemble was led by singer Neil
Hannon, the Enniskillen-raised son of an Anglican clergyman. Unlike
most northern rock musicians – who favoured fast-paced, guitar-based
styles – the singer drew on the rather more refined sources of Noel
Coward, Scott Walker and Jacques Brel, using strings, brass and orches-
tral layers. At the same time, Hannon took on a somewhat foppish
persona, with signature dandy-style suits and urbanely witty song
lyrics.[71] The band's idiosyncratic style reached its commercial zenith on
Fin de Siecle (1998), which included tracks such as 'National Express',
an ironic eulogy of Britain's best-known coach company, and the group's
first UK top ten single.

Fin de Siecle also comprised rather more serious material, not least 'Sunrise', Hannon's most overt address to 'troubles' and the record's reflective finale. Recorded in the context of the peace process, the song supplied a tender meditation on the preceding years of crisis, alluding to the vicious IRA bombing of Enniskillen in 1987, and issuing an implied critique of political extremism on all sides, before pointing – in the song's moving coda – to a 'sunrise' that served as a 'ray of hope' and 'a beam of light', offering an 'end' to 'thirty years of night'. With the noted success of the 'yes' campaign in May 1998, Hannon could scarcely have antici-pated that when 'Sunrise' was released (as part of the *Fin de Siecle* album) in August of that same year, it would coincide with Northern Ireland's most violent episode, a Real IRA bomb attack on the market town of Omagh, which claimed the lives of twenty-nine people, and injured 300 others. In this brutally tragic context, the song accrued an unsettling res-onance, affording the band a gravitas that was ostensibly at odds with Hannon's foppish facade.

If The Divine Comedy had offered a form of light entertainment for the postmodern age, then the pop-cultural values of lightness and style would go on to imbue some of the best-known musical efforts from Northern Irish acts at the start of the twenty-first century. Snow Patrol, the most high-profile band of this period, renewed the spiky guitar aes-thetics that had shaped their Ulster rock antecedents, but with more com-mercial success than their harder-edged predecessors: the group's third album, *Final Straw* (2003), sold more than two million copies (leading to a prestigious slot at the 'Live8' event in 2005), before the follow-up, *Eyes Open* (2006), became the United Kingdom's best-selling album of 2006.[72] Led by the Bangor-born singer/lyricist Gary Lightbody, the group drew on an alternative rock template, displaying an easy-going – and highly accessible – sensibility that was of a piece with contemporary British guitar bands such as Coldplay and Travis. Lightbody, who attended Belfast's Campbell College (*alma mater* of C. S. Lewis), recalls knowing people who were injured or killed during the 'troubles' but explains that an 'open-minded and tolerant' upbringing ensured that he eschewed any 'fundamentalist' ethos.[73] Thus, while Snow Patrol were described by the *Guardian* as a 'politically committed' act, this engage-ment pertained to the more global concerns of Amnesty International and Make Poverty History.[74] Despite their occasional denunciations of violence, then, there is little in the band's 'inward-looking'[75] oeuvre that evoked Ulster's social milieu.

It is also worth noting, here, that while earlier generations of northern rock musicians were framed incessantly – in British media discourse – by their geographical origins, a great deal of Snow Patrol's press has overlooked their northern provenance.[76] This is perhaps symptomatic of the band's long-term residence in Glasgow, but it arguably also pertains to the effects of the ceasefire and peace process, with this changing context offering journalists a less dramatic backdrop than that supplied by the 'troubles'. With this in mind, it may also be suggested that Snow Patrol evoke the sentiments of a certain post-ceasefire youth, troubled mostly by their own adolescent crises. If an unforeseen outcome of an event such as the Miami Showband massacre had been an upsurge in the domestic music-making scene, then an equally unanticipated upshot of the ongoing peace process may be an increasing weightlessness in northern rock. In this regard, it was perhaps appropriate that Snow Patrol acted as ambassadors of northern rock at the 'Rediscover Northern Ireland' event – a promotional showcase (led by the Department of Culture, Arts and Leisure and co-sponsored by the Ulster Bank) to attract tourism and business to Northern Ireland – in Washington DC in 2007.[77] The band also have their own interest in cultural regeneration: in 2007 Lightbody announced plans to launch a record label to showcase talent from Northern Ireland.[78]

Nothing bespeaks the confidence of a scene more than the willingness of musicians to remain located in, and identified with, it. Such is the case with Lisburn-born Peter Wilson, who operates under the name of Duke Special and who has produced two albums of quirky pop rock while resisting the logic which demands relocation to the industry centre in London. Not since the emergence of Scottish band The Proclaimers has a singer insisted on the validity of his own accent with such charming insouciance. So, on *Songs from the Deep Forest* (2006), 'down' becomes 'dine' ('Wake up Scarlett'), 'brown' becomes 'brine' ('Brixton Leaves'), 'tower' becomes 'tar' ('Salvation Tambourine'), and so on. On the other hand, one may suspect an element of calculation here: with so little to distinguish one artist from another in a saturated market, any 'unusual' element (such as a charmingly accented singing voice) may represent an advantage worth stressing. The Northern Irish artist, in other words, is still obliged to negotiate a balance between finding a form of valid self-expression and the temptation of playing to the metropolitan audience in search of exotica.

Wilson's songs are resolutely 'post-ceasefire' in as much as they occasionally cast a glance back towards the 'troubles' from which the community has emerged ('curse those fifes and damn those drums' he sings in 'Brixton Leaves'); for the most part, however, they focus on 'universal' human issues of love, commitment, disappointment, etc. The music itself is significantly removed from the guitar-dominated sound which has traditionally characterised Northern Irish rock. For one thing,

Wilson plays and writes on the piano, and this has clearly influenced the kind of music he is interested in producing. Inspired to some extent by The Divine Comedy (whom he has supported on tour), Wilson's characteristic sound is 'unusual' in popular music terms, featuring odd keys and time signatures, ambitious arrangements, and clever, multi-layered lyrics. The effect is topped off by a 'unique' image featuring eyeliner, dreadlocks and 'distressed' clothing. Societies tend to get the pop stars they deserve; with his curious mixture of sound and image, Duke Special is an aspiring pop star who perfectly mirrors post-ceasefire Northern Ireland's delicate cultural economy of dependence and independence.

Regardless of how the Duke Special project develops, it's clear that with acts as diverse as Ash, David Holmes, The Divine Comedy and Therapy? continuing to record and perform, and The Undertones, SLF and Ruefrex engaging in 're-union' activities – all alongside the enduring presence of Van Morrison – popular music in Northern Ireland has shown sufficient variation and longevity to adapt to the shifting conditions of the region's evolving milieu.

Notes

1 M. Stokes (ed.), *Ethnicity, Identity and Music: The Musical Construction of Place* (Oxford: Berg, 1994), p. 2.
2 M. J. V. Olson, ' "Everybody loves our town": scenes, spatiality, migrancy', in T. Swiss, J. Sloop and A. Herman (eds), *Mapping the Beat: Popular Music and Contemporary Theory* (Oxford: Blackwell, 1998), p. 275.
3 As Jacques Attali writes: 'Music is prophecy. Its styles and economic organization are ahead of the rest of society because it explores, much faster than material reality can, the entire range of possibilities in a given code' (Attali, *Noise: The Political Economy of Music*, 1977, trans. Brian Massumi, (Manchester: Manchester University Press, 1985), p. 11).
4 M. McLoone, 'Madam George and Cyprus Avenue: Van Morrison', in S. Hackett and R. West (eds), *Belfast Songs* (Belfast: Factotum, 2003), p. 52.
5 N. McLaughlin and M. McLoone, 'Hybridity and national musics: the case of Irish rock music', *Popular Music* 19:2 (2000), p. 184.
6 For the view that Morrison's persona has been shaped by a specifically Ulster Protestant sensibility see J. Rogan, *Van Morrison: No Surrender* (London: Secker & Warburg, 2005).
7 McLoone, 'Madam George and Cyprus Avenue', p. 52
8 B. Rolston, ' "This is not a rebel song": the Irish conflict and popular music', *Race and Class* 42:3 (2001), p. 65.
9 T. Clayton-Lea and R. Taylor, *Irish Rock: Where it's come from, Where it's at, Where it's going* (Dublin: Gill & Macmillan, 1992), pp. 55–6.
10 M. McLoone, 'Punk music in Northern Ireland: the political power of "what might have been" ', *Irish Studies Review* 12:1 (2004), p. 30.

11 S. O'Neill and G. Trelford, *It Makes You Want To Spit! The Definitive Guide to Punk in Northern Ireland* (Dublin: Reekus Music, 2003), p. 47.
12 *Ibid.*, p. v.
13 *Ibid.*, p. 50.
14 McLoone, 'Punk music in Northern Ireland', p. 32.
15 *Ibid.*, pp. 35–6, 38.
16 O'Neill and Trelford, *It Makes You Want To Spit!*, p. v.
17 McLoone, 'Punk music in Northern Ireland', pp. 32, 38, 35. This point has been confirmed by many of the scene's participants, not least the former Ruefrex drummer, Paul Burgess, who maintains that a crucial difference between London punks and their Belfast counterparts was the latter's 'sheer belief and commitment in the political force for change' (A. Ogg, sleeve notes for Ruefrex, *Capital Letters: The Best of . . .* , Cherry Red, 2005).
18 O'Neill and Trelford, *It Makes You Want To Spit!*, p. v.
19 *Ibid.*, p. 49.
20 *Ibid.*, p. 206.
21 McLoone, 'Punk music in Northern Ireland', p. 36.
22 R. Denselow, *When the Music's Over: The Story of Political Pop* (London: Faber, 1989), p. 159.
23 P. Muldoon, 'Alternative Ulster: stiff little fingers', in S. Hackett and R. West (eds), *Belfast Songs* (Belfast: Factotum, 2003), pp. 8–9.
24 McLoone, 'Punk music in Northern Ireland', p. 36.
25 J. Savage, *England's Dreaming: Sex Pistols and Punk Rock* (London: Faber, 1991), p. 596.
26 S. Prophet, 'Overtones of the Undertones', *Record Mirror*, 11 November 1978, p. 13.
27 Denselow, *When the Music's Over*, p. 160.
28 T. Collins, *Teenage Kicks: The Story of The Undertones* (DVD, 2001).
29 *Ibid.*
30 *Ibid.*
31 McLoone, 'Punk music in Northern Ireland', pp. 36–7.
32 Rolston, ' "This is not a rebel song" ', p. 59.
33 Muldoon, 'Alternative Ulster', p. 8.
34 S. Deane, 'The artist and the troubles', in T. Coogan (ed.), *Ireland and the Arts*, special issue of *Literary Review* (London: Namara Press, 1983), p. 42).
35 Collins, *Teenage Kicks*.
36 McLoone, 'Punk music in Northern Ireland', p. 37.
37 See Collins, *Teenage Kicks*.
38 See also Spandau Ballet, 'Through the Barricades' (1986) and Simple Minds, 'Belfast Child' (1989). While the song lyrics of such tracks offered vaguely liberal (and clearly well-meaning) accounts of the North, other (less mainstream) acts, such as Manchester 'indie' outfit Easterhouse, took a more radical stance, with songs such as 'Easter Rising' (1986) and 'Nineteen Sixty-Nine' (1986), espousing republican views, and 'Inspiration' (1986) – a eulogy for the hunger strikes – including an image of Bobby Sands on the

record sleeve. Among the Irish diaspora, meanwhile, musicians such as Morrissey and Shane MacGowan were staging their own responses to the 'Troubles', with the former endorsing an IRA bomb attack on the British Conservative government (at Brighton in 1984), whilst the latter composed a song for The Pogues entitled 'Birmingham Six' (1988). For Morrissey's response to the bombing see I. Pye, 'A Hard Day's Misery', *Melody Maker*, 3 November 1984, p. 39. For an account of diaspora musicians see S. Campbell, ' "What's the story?" Rock biography, musical "routes" and the second-generation Irish in England', *Irish Studies Review* 12:1 (2004), pp. 63–75.

39 Rolston, ' "This is not a rebel song" ', p. 59.
40 H. McDonald, 'Return of the angry young prods', *Observer*, 2 October 2005, www.guardian.co.uk/Northern_Ireland/Story/0,1583132,00.html.
41 M. J. Prendergast, *Irish Rock: Roots, Personalities, Directions* (Dublin: O'Brien Press, 1987), p. 255.
42 Rolston, ' "This is not a rebel song" ', p. 59.
43 C. Irwin, 'Look back in anger', *Melody Maker*, 15 March 1986, p. 25; Denselow, *When the Music's Over*, p. 160.
44 McDonald, 'Return of the angry young prods'.
45 Irwin, 'Look back in anger', p. 25.
46 Denselow, *When the Music's Over*, p. 160; O'Neill and Trelford, *It Makes You Want To Spit!*, p. 175; McDonald, 'Return of the angry young prods'.
47 O'Neill and Trelford, *It Makes You Want To Spit!*, p. 176.
48 Irwin, 'Look back in anger', p. 25.
49 *The Late Show*, BBC2, 21 September 1993.
50 O'Neill and Trelford, *It Makes You Want To Spit!*, p. 176; Ogg, sleeve notes.
51 O'Neill and Trelford, *It Makes You Want To Spit!*, p. 176.
52 Irwin, 'Look back in anger', p. 25.
53 Denselow, *When the Music's Over*, p. 160.
54 R. Holland, 'Rue Fuss', *Sounds*, 14 December 1985, p. 30.
55 Irwin, 'Look back in anger', p. 24.
56 Cited in McDonald, 'Return of the angry young prods'; O'Neill and Trelford, *It Makes You Want To Spit!*, p. 179.
57 Ogg, sleeve notes.
58 *The Late Show*, BBC2, 21 September 1993.
59 McDonald, 'Return of the angry young prods'.
60 S. Frith, 'Music and identity', in S. Hall and P. du Gay (eds), *Questions of Cultural Identity* (London: Sage, 1996), p. 122.
61 McDonald, 'Return of the angry young prods'.
62 The claims with regard to the non-denominational status of punk and dance music replicate those made a generation earlier in respect of the folk revival in Northern Ireland in the 1960s, a movement which, as May McCann suggests, 'provided a social context in which young Catholics and Protestants could interact within a shared cultural framework . . . [The] apparent apolitical nature of folk song enabled [an] oasis of music-making in Belfast,

mirroring as it did the fundamental social strategy of avoidance of sensitive political issues which facilitated the peaceful operation of sectarian practice in Northern Ireland prior to 1969' ('Music and politics in Ireland: the specificity of the folk revival in Belfast', *British Journal of Ethnomusicology* 4, 1995, pp. 51–3).

63 D. Holmes, *Gritty Shaker*, BBC Northern Ireland, 1996.
64 N. McLaughlin, 'Bodies swayed to music: dance culture in Ireland', *Irish Studies Review* 12:1 (2004), pp. 82, 83–4.
65 J. Gilbert and E. Pearson, *Discographies: Dance Music, Culture and the Politics of Sound* (London: Routledge, 1999), p. 164.
66 McLaughlin, 'Bodies swayed to music', p. 82.
67 *Ibid.*, p. 83.
68 Denselow, *When the Music's Over*, pp. 127–34.
69 Rolston, ' "This is not a rebel song" ', p. 50.
70 S. O'Hagan, 'I was there helping to make history', *Observer* Review, 24 May 1998, p. 2.
71 In this context it is worth noting that many observers assumed that Hannon was English. See K. Kallioniemi, ' "Put the Needle on the Record and Think of England": Notions of Englishness in the Post-war Debate on British Pop Music', unpublished Ph.D. thesis (Turku: University of Turku, 1998), p. 91.
72 See B. Marshall, 'In from the cold', *Guardian* Guide, 29 April 2006, p. 8; M. Odell, 'The Q interview. Gary Lightbody', *Q*, April 2007, p. 98.
73 Odel, 'The Q interview', p. 100.
74 Marshall, 'In from the cold', p. 8.
75 *Ibid.*, pp. 8, 10.
76 For an example of Snow Patrol's reception see Marshall, 'In from the cold', pp. 8–10. For a discussion of the reception of Northern Irish rock musicians more generally see McLaughlin and McLoone, 'Hybridity and national musics', p. 181.
77 'Northern Ireland rocks Washington', http://archive.nics.gov.uk/cal/070322f-cal.htm.
78 Odel, 'The Q interview', p. 102.

13

House training the paramilitaries: the media and the propaganda of peace

Stephen Baker and Greg McLaughlin

Since its beginnings in the late 1960s the conflict in Northern Ireland has been understood by the media in terms of changing interpretative frameworks, from civil rights to anti-terrorism to conflict resolution.[1] These media representations of the conflict have been thoroughly researched and debated, with the emphasis being on issues of propaganda and censorship.[2] Of particular interest to this chapter is the way in which the media have responded to the new dispensation of the peace process and Good Friday Agreement. So far, research into the reporting and representation of the peace process has focused almost exclusively on news and current affairs, with the assumption that these forms provide the most authoritative accounts and play a crucial part in the formation of public opinion.[3] While this is not entirely unreasonable, it is still a limited approach. News, after all, is not produced in a cultural vacuum but is itself a manufactured 'cultural artefact'.[4] It both informs and is informed by cultural and ideological assumptions in society that are reproduced by a range of communicative sources. It is important, therefore, to move beyond an analysis of news accounts of the conflict in Northern Ireland and examine a much broader spectrum of media representation – film, television drama and comedy, public service broadcasting and official propaganda. This chapter is by no means comprehensive – time and space do not allow that – but it does highlight the way in which at key moments, and in important places, the mainstream media have embraced the peace but, frankly, run scared of the politics.

Political context

Two years after the signing of the Good Friday Agreement, David Trimble, then leader of the Ulster Unionist Party (UUP), remarked that republicans would need to be 'house trained' before they could enter the Northern Ireland Executive.[5] While the jibe offended Sinn Féin, in reality a process of domesticating the paramilitaries in public perception had already been initiated some time before by the British government. In 1994, during the initial phase of the peace process, it gave Sinn Féin some interesting public relations advice in a secret communiqué, specifically that the party should publicly challenge the British government to sit down to talks. In fact it was suggested that Sinn Féin should use the analogy of marriage and say, 'We are standing at the altar. Why won't (the British) come and join us?' Just days later Martin McGuinness made the proposal in an interview with *The Guardian* newspaper.[6] In the same period the government commissioned a new series of public films for its confidential telephone service which portrayed paramilitary figures as ordinary family men with a choice to make between war and peace. This marked a shift in government propaganda that, up until then, had portrayed the paramilitaries, especially republicans, as psychopathic monsters, outside society and with nothing to offer but 'murder and mayhem'. McLoone argues that the shift prepared public opinion for the disclosure of lines of communication between government representatives and Irish republicanism. But it also prepared the ground for the day when republican and loyalist paramilitaries might sit down at the negotiating table and play a constructive, political role in the future of Northern Ireland.[7]

There is no question that the peace process and the multi-party negotiations that accompanied it were changing the political and cultural atmosphere in Northern Ireland. Certainly the media generally began to revise their own interpretative and representational frameworks in response to the new political dispensation, promoting a version of privatised citizenship that is inimical to political engagement. In many ways the domesticated representation of the paramilitaries during the peace process seems extraordinary in the historical context of the conflict in Northern Ireland. In the 1970s and 1980s government policy sought to criminalise paramilitary violence and empty it of political content. Censorship and propaganda were key functions of this policy and had a deadening impact on how the media were able to report the conflict. The 1980s, in particular, saw public service broadcasting in direct confrontation with the British government over a number of current affairs programmes and documentaries that appeared to be insufficiently critical of, or even sympathetic to, terrorists. A notable example here is a programme in the BBC's 1985 documentary series *Real Lives*, 'At the Edge of the Union'.

'Lovable people with babies': the *Real Lives* controversy

'At the Edge of the Union' caused controversy, not because it gave voice to a prominent republican, Martin McGuinness, who was widely regarded as an IRA leader in Derry, but because it showed him in a domestic setting with his wife and children. Ironically, there appeared to be no objection to scenes of Gregory Campbell loading a handgun at home. The weapon was issued to him by the police for defensive purposes and seemed to underscore his extraordinary domestic environment, fortified by armoured doors, steel window grilles and security cameras. In contrast, McGuinness's home looked 'normal', which was exactly what aroused such political controversy about the programme. Some BBC governors objected to the 'domestication of the IRA' and their portrayal as 'lovable people with babies'.[8]

The British government initially opposed the broadcast of the documentary and relented only when the producers agreed to re-edit it to include images of IRA violence. The *Real Lives* controversy highlights how difficult it was at this time for media producers to work outside of the very restrictive anti-terrorist propaganda framework. In this context, depicting the paramilitary as a family man was strongly discouraged. However, the peace process demanded a shift in the official propaganda, away from an anti-terrorist discourse and towards the possibility that paramilitaries could be brought to the negotiating table. The first sign of this change of direction became apparent in the British government's films advertising the confidential telephone line.

Confidential telephone films

The confidential telephone service was set up by the Northern Ireland Office (NIO) in the 1970s to appeal for anonymous information from the public regarding paramilitary activity. It was publicised through a variety of media, but of most interest here are the television advertisement campaigns. The early campaigns were strictly anti-terrorist in orientation and fitted into the wider British propaganda framework. Terrorism was held to have no political content or context and the terrorists themselves were portrayed as ruthless, psychotic criminals. For example, *A Future* (1988) features a young man reflecting on the future for his wife and child in a community dominated by paramilitary violence. What, he asks on his odyssey around his troubled city, have these 'hard men' ever done for him? 'They've left me with no job and no hope, they've wrecked where I live, they've hijacked our cars, they've fed off our backs, and when I saw their kind of justice I thought, there's gotta be something better than this.' This voiceover accompanies images of a war-torn urban environment that evidently stands in for Northern Ireland: bombs exploding, punishment shootings in back alleys, paramilitaries collecting funds in local pubs. The lighting is dark and the atmosphere foreboding, an effect heightened by a crime thriller score. However, the film ends with our 'everyman' returning home to his wife and child and deciding to use the confidential telephone number. He is determined to defend the assumed sanctity and security of his family in the face of the violence beyond his door. In the final scene the family are assembled happily on the settee – the father, baby in arms, and his wife – as if to emphasise what is at stake in the decision to call the confidential telephone number.

The NIO continued the service into the 1990s and the period of the peace process. But the new circumstances brought a perceptible shift in emphasis in the advertisement campaigns. In *A New Era* (1994) the traditional symbols of conflict and division are transformed before our eyes into images of peace and prosperity. A paramilitary gun morphs into a starting pistol for the Belfast marathon; security bollards turn into flower displays; a police cordon turns into ceremonial tape for the opening of a new motorway; and two RUC constables reunite a lost child with its mother, confounding the controversial history of the force. Two adverts from 1993, *Lady* and *I Wanna Be Like You*, specifically changed the portrayal of paramilitaries. Whereas *A Future* drew clear boundaries between the psychotic paramilitary and the family, these new adverts begin to situate the paramilitary in a more ambiguous position in the domestic sphere.

Lady tells the story of two women whose lives are blighted by violence. The ethno-religious identity of the women is not made explicit: they are both portrayed as victims. One of the women is a widow whose husband is murdered by a paramilitary. The other woman is married to the paramilitary, who is imprisoned for the murder. A female narrator intones, 'Two women, two traditions, two tragedies. One married to the victim of violence, one married to the prisoner of violence. Both scarred, both suffering, both desperately wanting it to stop.' As with *A Future*, *Lady* is about the impact of violence on private and domestic relations except that, in this instance, violence is presented as equally tragic for paramilitaries and their victims.

I Wanna Be Like You also reflects upon the cost of paramilitary violence to family relations, specifically those of father and son. There is no voiceover narrative in this film. Instead it is accompanied by a version of the Harry Chapin song *Cat in the Cradle*. It presents a man's journey over a number of years from paramilitarism to recognition of the futility of violence. In the beginning he neglects his family, ends up in prison and eventually sees his son follow in his footsteps as a paramilitary. The son in turn becomes remote from the father and is shown gunning a man down in front of his child. He himself loses his life to violence and the advert closes with the image of the father grieving at his son's grave.

The underlying assumption of these ads is that a solution to the conflict can be reached through security measures rather than through political dialogue. However, they mark a significant departure from the ads broadcast before 1993. Whereas the earlier campaigns sought to depict paramilitaries as isolated from those around them, the more recent campaign acknowledged that they were in fact part of the wider community. Suddenly the paramilitary is shown in a domestic context, with family relations, but his violence is a continuing threat to the stability and normality predominantly associated with family life – his own and other people's.

After the paramilitary ceasefires in 1994 the NIO commissioned a very different series of public films that moved away from the anti-terrorist message altogether. Broadcast during the summer of 1995, they showed Northern Ireland as a place where people enjoyed life without fear of violence, and they were also scored with some of the best-known songs of Van Morrison, such as *Brown Eyed Girl, Days Like This* and *Have I Told You Lately*. The four films have the glossy look of tourist advertisements, marketing peace in Northern Ireland as consumer commodity. In one, *Northern Irish Difference*, babies and toddlers play at a crèche, oblivious to sectarian or cultural difference; in another, *Northern Irish Life*, two boys from both traditions play on a beach and innocently exchange what would, in the conflict of the past, have been seen as sectarian badges of identity – King Billy for Glasgow Celtic Football Club! *Northern Irish Quality* celebrates the sporting and cultural achievements of people like Mary Peters, George Best and Liam Neeson, while *Northern Irish Spirit* reminds the people of the stunning coastal and rural scenery.

All the films end with Van Morrison's closing epithet from *Coney Island*, 'Wouldn't it be great if it was like this all the time?' and the on-screen slogan 'Time for the bright side'. The use of Morrison's music in this series of films came with his explicit permission and blessing and reveals much about the heady, optimistic mood that gripped Northern Ireland in the hot summer of 1995. When the IRA ended its ceasefire in 1996, with bombs in London and Manchester, the NIO returned to the violent imagery of the early confidential telephone advertisements. However, the restoration of the ceasefires and the negotiations towards the Good Friday Agreement in 1998 brought a return to optimism. During the referendum campaign, in May that year, the NIO distributed to every home a copy of the Agreement document, its cover showing the archetypal nuclear family silhouetted against a rising sun, symbolising the Agreement as a new dawn for the people of Northern Ireland. It was revealed later that the picture was actually of a sunset and was taken in

South Africa, perfect dawns being difficult to catch in Northern Ireland. Still, these idealised, post-ceasefire images marked a radical departure from the violent imagery of *A Future*, even from the more positive confidential telephone ads of the early 1990s, for they dispensed with the anti-terrorist message altogether and held out the prospect of real peace and a final settlement of the conflict.[9]

Film and television drama also responded to the new circumstances of the peace process with their own revisions of the conflict narrative. Very few went so far as the idealised depictions of the NIO's 'Time for the bright side' campaign but they changed old visual and narrative conventions in new and sometimes unexpected ways.

Film and television drama

The dramatic contrast in imagery between 'strife-torn maelstrom' and 'blissful, rural idyll', typifies two of the most prevalent visual representations of Ireland in the twentieth century and, as John Hill has shown, it is the former image that has dominated cinematic portrayals of the north.[10] The Carol Reed film *Odd Man Out* (1947) is an antecedent of this tradition. The film follows Johnny McQueen, a leader of the 'organisation' (a euphemism for the IRA), who is wounded in an armed robbery and escapes into the city before he and his sweetheart, Kathleen, are shot by the police, their romantic intentions unfulfilled. While Hill acknowledges the film's very distinctive visual style, he argues that its narrative is typical of cinematic representations of the Irish conflict, in that it ignores political and historical context, reducing violence to 'a manifestation of the Irish "national" character'.[11] Not only are the 'personal and political assumed to be separate but they are also set in opposition. It is romantic love and domestic stability which political violence inevitably damages; and it is only through an acceptance of love and domesticity that divisions wrought by violence may be avoided or overcome.'[12]

In some significant ways, films in the period of the peace process draw upon this tradition and its conventions: *Nothing Personal* (1996), *Some Mother's Son* (1996), *Titanic Town* (1998), *Resurrection Man* (1998), *The Boxer* (1998) and *Divorcing Jack* (1998) all portray political violence as antipathetic to romantic success and domestic life. However, they also represent the state as largely ineffectual or pernicious, and, in some instances, the role of enforcing the social order is entirely usurped by paramilitaries.

For example, *Titanic Town*, set in the early 1970s, focuses on Bernie McPhelimy, a housewife who is concerned to protect her home and family from the encroaching violence in her neighbourhood. She is the custodian of womanly decorum in the film; a conscientious house-keeper – dignified, humble and selfless in her commitment to her family, and determined to sustain its domestic integrity in the face of growing adversity. When the British army carries out a series of raids on the homes of the district, Bernie frets that the soldiers may enter her home to find the beds unmade and the children still in their nightclothes. This homely propriety is charming and comic, and is designed to elicit the empathy of the audience for the character of Bernie. Meanwhile, her republican neighbour rants in the street, maintaining a barrage of republican rhetoric and abuse as she shakes her fist at the army, an indecorous and charmless characterisation that makes clear the film's aversion to overt and partisan politics and its preference for Bernie's domestic instincts.

Ultimately Bernie's attempts to broker a ceasefire between the IRA and British soldiers are undone by the duplicity and politicking of British representatives and republicans alike; with her own life and those of her family in danger, she is forced to stand down from the peace movement and leave her home. *Titanic Town* lauds the domestic virtues and instincts that inspired Bernie's campaign for peace but, because it poses the political sphere as being diametrically opposed and threatening to the domestic, it can find no place for the 'homely' Bernie in public life. Ultimately her righteousness is seemingly dependent upon her political passivity.

A similar retreat from the apparently insensible world of politics is evident in *Some Mother's Son*, a film based upon the republican hunger strikes of 1981. Its characters are mostly fictional but it also portrays historical figures such as Bobby Sands (played by John Lynch), the first of ten prisoners to die in the protest at the Maze prison. The central character is Kathleen Quigley, a politically disinterested middle-class Catholic who is, nevertheless, drawn by necessity into the political sphere when her imprisoned son joins the hunger strike. In the course of the film Kathleen befriends Annie Higgins, whose son is also on hunger strike. The character of Annie contrasts sharply with that of Kathleen. She is working-class and steeped in the republican tradition and her politics are afforded a respect in the film denied to Bernie's neighbour and nemesis in *Titanic Town*. Nevertheless, in an effort to avert the death of their sons, both women travel to London to lobby government officials. The trip is fruitless save for them learning that the fate of their sons lies in their own hands. Farnsworth, a British official, tells the women, 'The law quite clearly states that if your sons should lapse into comas you have the legal right to take them off the strike.' He adds, with mock poignancy, 'Surely no mother would allow her son to die?' This is certainly to be read as a piece of arch politicking by the British government, shifting the burden of responsibility to the mothers, irrespective of their sons' political convictions.

In the end, Kathleen is the first to take her son off the hunger strike. He is close to death when the last hope of a compromise between republican and British sources is extinguished. The failure to achieve a settlement of the prison dispute also seems to be the occasion of Kathleen's retreat from a duplicitous political sphere, which she only ever entered to save her son's life. She goes to the hospital and signs the form that sees her son put on a drip. His life is saved as next door Annie's son passes away. The two women meet in the hall and, despite Annie's republican convictions, she does not reproach Kathleen but admits that someone had to act to end the hunger strike. In *Some Mother's Son* the political sphere is peopled by haranguing, obdurate types, and seemingly antipathetic to family ties and private intimacies, as represented by Kathleen's relationship with her son. Even Annie with her republican convictions seems to agree.[13]

Divorcing Jack, based on a novel by Colin Bateman, offers an equally dystopian view of the political sphere in Northern Ireland and advocates avoiding it, once again, in favour of the domestic sphere. This is demonstrated figuratively in an exchange between its protagonist, journalist Dan Starkey, and a colleague from the United States. The American asks what Dan prefers to call Northern Ireland: 'Ulster', 'the occupied six counties', 'the North' or 'the province'. Starkey tells him he just calls it 'home'. Fittingly most of the film is taken up with Starkey's efforts to rescue his home life after an act of infidelity plunges him into the world of political machinations, estranges him from his wife and leads to her being held hostage by a renegade paramilitary. Starkey's attempt to rebuild his marriage is linked with his efforts to extricate himself and his wife from the chaotic world of politics.

While in *Divorcing Jack* the achievement and maintenance of heterosexual domesticity are a mark of virtue and normality, in films such as *Nothing Personal* (1996) and *Resurrection Man* (1998) loyalist paramilitaries are distinguished by apparently dysfunctional sexualities. In *Resurrection Man* loyalist gang leader Victor Kelly is in the grip of an Oedipal crisis: too enamoured of his indulgent mother and seemingly uninterested in consummating his relationship with his promiscuous girlfriend, Heather. Victor's libido seems to be sated only by the blood of his victims, whom he murders in particularly brutal ways. If that is not enough to signify his social and psychological dysfunction, the film also alludes to his homosexuality and possible paedophilia. In a particularly heavy-handed scene he is shown drinking and taking drugs with a senior loyalist, McClure. The two get intimate and, as McClure fingers the features of Victor's face, Victor asks to see again a set of photographs depicting 'English boys in bed together'.[14]

In the film *Nothing Personal* homosexuality also lies beneath the surface of the homosocial world of gang membership, in particular the relationship between Kenny, the loyalist gang leader, and his right-hand man, Ginger. Initiation into the gang takes the form of a perverse marriage ceremony with its oaths of loyalty and fidelity. The sexual tensions underlying this process and gang membership generally are emphasised by the violent and apparently jealous reaction of Ginger to the initiation of a new recruit. And as if to offset anxieties about this underlying homosexuality, the gang frequently indulge in graphic, misogynist banter and jokes about the sexual preferences of rivals.

Kenny's estrangement from heterosexual domesticity is apparent in his separation from his wife, typically on account of his violent convictions, although the film does hold out the possibility of romantic redemption in the chance encounter between Kenny's wife, Anne, and Liam, a single Catholic father. On a night of rioting Liam leaves his children to defend his home and district from encroaching loyalist rioters but gets stranded on the wrong side of the peace line and is beaten up. Anne finds him on the street and brings him into her home to recover, where there is clearly a growing intimacy between the couple. But, when Liam resumes his journey home, he is abducted by Kenny and his gang. They take him to a loyalist drinking den and proceed to torture him until Kenny suddenly recognises his victim as a childhood friend. He orders an end to the torture and sees Liam home safely, beaten but at least alive. When, later in the film, Ginger threatens to shoot Liam, Kenny wounds his comrade in the leg. Events take a tragic turn when a Catholic youth tries to exact revenge on the loyalist gang but accidentally kill Liam's daughter. Sorry for Liam's loss and revolted by Ginger's pleasure at the girl's death, Kenny shoots Ginger.

Again there are similarities here between *Nothing Personal* and *Resurrection Man*, in that both films suggest that their loyalist protagonists are assassinated at the behest of their superiors. In *Resurrection Man* McClure has Victor Kelly assassinated when his violence escalates beyond control. In *Nothing Personal* Leonard Wilson orders Kenny to shoot his friend Ginger, whose violent behaviour begins to threaten a recently brokered ceasefire between loyalists and republicans. Kenny vacillates at first but resolves to follow orders when he is finally confronted with the depths of Ginger's depravity. His hesitation, however, proves fatal when Wilson sets him and his gang up for an ambush by the British army.

The dark dystopia of loyalism in *Nothing Personal* and *Resurrection Man* stands in sharp contrast to the thoroughly domesticated version of republicanism portrayed in *The Boxer*. Although the film measures the impact of political violence on domestic and private relations, it goes further, to suggest that paramilitaries may have a role in forging rather than destroying such relations. The central character in *The Boxer* is Danny, a republican ex-prisoner who tries to rekindle his affair with former lover Maggie. However, she is already married to an IRA man still serving time in prison and Danny's advances provoke consternation in the republican community. Indeed, it makes him a target for Harry, a hard-line republican, who considers their relationship a betrayal of the incarcerated husband. Harry is further outraged by Danny's rejection of political violence, and the two are set on a collision course, threatening Danny's relationship with Maggie.

Significantly, their relationship is saved not by the forces of law and order but by the violent intervention of Maggie's father, Joe Hamill, himself a senior republican and architect of the peace strategy. Hamill commissions Harry's murder, simultaneously securing the ceasefire and a successful romantic conclusion to Maggie and Danny's affair. The film closes with a scene in which Danny and Maggie are stopped at an RUC checkpoint. An officer asks them where they are going. 'We're going home,' says Maggie. There are no further questions and the police officer waves them on their way. Even the RUC, ostensibly the malevolent foe of northern nationalism, cannot object to such a natural and plainly righteous destination.

McLoone argues that Joe Hamill stands in a cinematic tradition of IRA men who are in many ways 'more sympathetic and more flexible' than some of their hard-line comrades. In this way *The Boxer* confirms a post-ceasefire politics that presents the way forward as being 'through compromise and accommodation'.[15] However, this misses the crucial significance of Harry's assassination. Far from the optimistic conclusion of peace 'through compromise and accommodation', the film alludes to some of the uncomfortable choices that lie ahead for republicans, namely policing dissent within their own ranks – by violent means if necessary.

As with *The Boxer*, *Love Lies Bleeding* ends with the elimination of dissident elements by supporters of the republican peace strategy, but, unlike the former, this violent action destroys the romantic intentions of its protagonist rather than rescuing them. Written by Ronan Bennett, *Love Lies Bleeding* explores the ambiguities, contradictions and compromises inherent in bringing a campaign of political violence to an end. Broadcast in September 1993, the drama was conceived prior to the public admission of the British government that it had been talking to republicans and it pre-dates the initial IRA ceasefire by almost a year. The story is told from the point of view of Conn, an IRA prisoner on day release who is determined to find out the truth about the death of his lover, Layla. His quest coincides with attempts by IRA chief Thomas Macken to initiate a ceasefire, a proposal that is violently opposed by hard-liners in the movement. It transpires that Layla was one such hard-liner and her assassination was carried out on Macken's orders. Further killings ensue, including the slaying of the IRA faction opposed to the peace strategy at the hands of Macken and his supporters. This action clears the way for the announcement of the ceasefire that is greeted with jubilation by republican inmates back at the prison. Meanwhile Conn is left to come to terms with the notion that political imperatives have taken precedence over his private life, specifically his relationship with Layla. As Macken explains, 'Death here isn't just a personal thing.'

The Boxer and *Love Lies Bleeding* stand in sharp contrast to earlier cinematic representations of the conflict, such as *Odd Man Out*. In the latter it is the police, and so by implication the state, that dispatches dissidents such as Johnny McQueen, rather than his superiors in the 'organisation'. As John Hill makes clear, the state in this film is 'not only exempt from political enquiry but, at least implicitly, legitimated as the repository of a divine and absolute justice'.[16]

In many of the films considered here the state is presented as ambivalent, pernicious or lacking. In *Titanic Town* and *Some Mother's Son* the state, represented by British officials and politicians, is duplicitous and conniving. In *Nothing Personal* it arrives belatedly in the shape of the British army to finish off the loyalist gang. In *Resurrection Man* its representative, Herbie Ferguson, a CID man, is conscientious but impotent. In *Love Lies Bleeding* the state is largely usurped by IRA chief Thomas Macken, who acts to secure the peace by luring dissidents into a lethal ambush. In *The Boxer* the state's role is reduced to surveillance, represented by searchlights and the noise of overhead helicopters. In its place stands the IRA leader, Joe Hamill, who defends the social order by policing dissent, securing the peace strategy and defending the new domesticated republicanism represented by Danny, Maggie and her son. Seen in this light, Hamill represents a republicanism shorn of its radical potential and pressed into the service of preserving a social order based on political agnosticism and privatised citizenship.

Situation comedy

While some film and television dramas in the period of the peace process represented paramilitary figures in authoritative and increasingly constitutional roles, television offered images of them as comic grotesques. In 1994, the year following the broadcast of *Love Lies Bleeding*, the BBC aired *The Empire Laughs Back* as part of its 'Twenty-five Bloody Years' season to mark the anniversary of the troubles. This was a one-off special that featured a number of Irish stand-up comedians performing at the Empire Comedy Club in Belfast. Their routines plundered Northern Ireland politics for humour, a risky venture, given that a previous attempt at satire on BBC NI had met with vocal opposition from local politicians and public figures across the community. On that occasion *The Show* (1989–91), which consisted of chat, music and comedy sketches that often lampooned Northern Ireland politics, was eventually forced to water down its content and become a conventional variety show.

The Hole in the Wall Gang, an ensemble of local comedians, featured in both *The Show* and *The Empire Laughs Back*. In 1995 the BBC broadcast their satirical comedy *Two Ceasefires and a Wedding*, which for the first time perhaps on television depicted thoroughly domesticated versions of loyalist and republican paramilitary types. *Two Ceasefires and a Wedding* was in effect the pilot for the sit-com series *Give My Head Peace*, which has run since 1996. Both marked a departure for television comedy in Northern Ireland. Previous sit-coms set in Belfast, such as *Foreign Bodies* (BBC NI, 1986–87) and *So You think You've Got Troubles* (BBC, 1991), were much more reticent about the representation of political militants.

Give My Head Peace contains its belligerents within the domestic context of an extended family, albeit a comically dysfunctional one. Emer, the daughter of an ardent republican, marries Billy, an RUC officer and the nephew of vociferous loyalist Uncle Andy. She moves in with Billy, and together they share a house with Uncle Andy, who is outraged at having a Catholic living in his home. His disdain is mirrored by Emer's father, Da, and her brother, Cal, who abhor their loyalist in-laws. The show's attempts at humour derive from the truculent behaviour of its loyalist and republican characters and their potential to disrupt 'normal' family life. In this respect, Emer's mother, known only as Ma, provides a measure of apolitical and simpleminded domestic probity in contrast to the comically portrayed political passions of the men.

The domestic context of *Give My Head Peace* renders its belligerent characters 'safe', mapping Northern Ireland's unruly politics on to the comfortingly familiar institution of the family. As with all film and television comedy, the spectators' laughter secures them in a position of superiority and power in relation to the text and its characters.[17] Meanwhile the cyclical nature of the sit-com narrative works to ensure that, no matter what comic outrages or upheavals occur in the show each week, relatively normal family life is reinstated by the end of each episode. This means that, despite the sectarian rhetoric and antics of Da,

Uncle Andy and their respective ensemble of republican and loyalist associates, essential family relations are unaffected.

Public service broadcasting and *Talk Back*

Give My Head Peace offers a curiously consequence-free version of sectarianism that risks presenting bigotry and prejudice as relatively harmless. Indeed, it lacks a genuinely critical edge to its satire that would make its viewing more uncomfortable for a society where sectarianism is endemic. As a BBC Northern Ireland production the programme has wider implications for the way in which public service broadcasting has handled the conflict. For the conception of 'family' is one remove from the BBC's imagining of the 'nation', in which there is a constant drive for a common Northern Ireland identity between unionism and nationalism. A good example of the problem is the public access Radio Ulster programme, *Talk Back* and its relationship with its audience.

Talk Back has gained a reputation for being unafraid to broadcast the most uncompromising and bigoted opinions. Each weekday, between noon and 1.30 p.m., its presenter, David Dunseith, encourages and provokes listeners to phone in and comment on the news of the day and other 'burning issues'. In Northern Ireland such an invitation inevitably draws sectarian reaction and bad-tempered political debate on air. It also draws criticism from republicans and loyalists, who regularly target their anger at *Talk Back*'s presenter, as well as the programme itself and, by extension, the BBC. Unionist listeners berate the show for promoting a republican agenda, while nationalists attack its perceived unionist bias. Such criticism is by now routine but it completely misses the point. *Talk Back* is indeed biased but its political preferences are neither loyalist nor republican. As befits a product of the BBC in Northern Ireland, the programme makes room for balanced sectarian comment but its conscience is determinedly centrist. The presenter often consoles himself on air with the notion that if *Talk Back* is attracting flak from 'both sides' in Northern Ireland then it must be 'doing something right', namely demonstrating its impartiality and balance. However, David Dunseith provides the programme with its paternal voice of reason and moderation; he is the personification of the BBC and its preference for consensual politics. Nevertheless, it has to be said that since Dunseith's arrival in the *Talk Back* chair the programme has been one of the few that have aired the sort of fractious voices that are probably more typical of Northern Ireland than the liberal sensibilities of the BBC.

Of course, like *Give My Head Peace*, *Talk Back* proposes family as way of assuaging conflict, which suggests that domesticating political belligerents is an ideological strategy at the BBC NI. When asked about how the programme managed a dispute with the Grand Master of the Orange Order, Robert Saulters, the producer, Seamus Boyd, draws the analogy of a family dispute: '*Talk Back* is a bit like a family. There are fall-outs; people have a little bit of annoyance but then they'll come back some other day because we've annoyed somebody else instead and they like that.'[18] The problem here is that conflict is managed within the ideological constraints of public service broadcasting and the impulse to conceptualise the audience in domestic terms. This tends towards consensus where none in fact exists.

The BBC regularly produces programmes on television and radio that search for the common denominator, a shared sense of identity that can give no offence. But it is Holy Grail broadcasting because the very notion of Northern Ireland as a country or a state has been so violently contested for the past forty years. Essentially, public service broadcasting in Northern Ireland suffers a crisis of legitimacy in which it constantly attempts to forge a national identity and to balance the kind of sectarianism that is endemic in society.[19]

Conclusion

The 'house training' of Northern Ireland's paramilitaries has been paradoxical. Once kept symbolically separate in official discourse from the domestic sphere, state propaganda has since found an ambiguous place for them in family life. In film, paramilitary figures have been afforded a much more sympathetic portrayal than previously, particularly those that police their hot-headed dissidents. There is also a sharp contrast in the portrayals of republicans and loyalists. The loyalists of *Resurrection Man* and *Nothing Personal* are shown stuck in the mire of sectarianism and criminality, their violence arising out of primal bloodlust rather than any political motivation. By contrast, the IRA leaders in *The Boxer* and *Love Lies Bleeding* are shown as authoritative, politically maturing individuals prepared to slay dissident comrades for the greater good. Once reviled by the state, men like these are represented on screen as proxies for the state. As we have shown, Joe Hamill in *The Boxer* is an exemplar of this, stepping in to protect not just the peace strategy but also that cornerstone of social order the heterosexual family, as represented by Danny, Maggie and her son.

However, there is something depressingly conventional about the way in which such visions of bourgeois domesticity in 'ceasefire cinema' act to signify social legitimacy, virtue and integrity. The privileging of the private and the denial of politics is a common position among the media classes in Northern Ireland even when confronted with the stark truth that the conflict is far from over. Terry Cafolla, screenwriter of the BBC drama *Holy Cross*, about one of the darkest episodes of sectarianism in the recent history of Northern Ireland, said the film was not about the politics of the Holy Cross dispute but its impact on the lives of individuals and families in the Ardoyne, as if one can be separated from the other.[20] Pearse Elliott, producer of the BBC film *The Mighty Celt* (2005), makes a similar disavowal of political content. He says he wanted to make a film about life in Belfast with 'a degree of authenticity', a post-conflict film that 'concentrates on the serious things . . . just getting on and living, having a bit of craic, you know, and all the everyday problems as opposed to the political situation'.[21]

In more difficult times than these some film makers were brave enough to project a much more radical vision on screen. For instance, Joe Comerford's *Reefer and the Model* (1988) and *High Boot Benny* (1993), and Thaddeus O'Sullivan's *December Bride* (1990), radically reimagine personal relationships and challenge conservative notions of community and nationhood. The renegades and misfits that people Comerford's films are provocative alternatives to traditional versions of Irish nationalism, while Thaddeus O'Sullivan's *ménage à trois* in *December Bride* offers an affront to patriarchy and religious communal conformity. Martin McLoone argues that their work was typical of 'a cinema of national questioning'.[22]

So how can we explain this ideological shift to the humdrum and apolitical? We propose that it has something to do with the abandonment of politics by a significant section of the middle-class intelligentsia in Northern Ireland, including that which regulates, funds and produces film and television output. This elite section of Northern Irish society conceives the Good Friday Agreement in terms of the 'peace dividend', as a transformation of its own material existence and cultural experience, rather than of political and social conflict, a kind of wish fulfilment that denies the realities on the ground. Indeed, McLoone attacks the way in which public funding for film making in Northern Ireland has become corrupted by commercial imperatives, with films seen as opportunities to promote tourism and the lifestyle of conspicuous consumption rather than say something challenging about society in Northern Ireland.[23] The banal and anodyne sentiment in so much of this output has dumbed down public discourse to such an extent that separating oneself from the political sphere, staying home and sinking into domestic solipsism is presented as an adequate response to political challenges that need to be faced as matter of urgency.

Events in Northern Ireland – most notably the Holy Cross dispute in 2001, continuing interface violence and the so-called loyalist 'uprising' in September 2005 – would suggest that febrile sectarian conflict remains real and unresolved, most nakedly in Belfast. Nationalists and unionists are becoming more, not less, polarised since the signing of the Good Friday Agreement in April 1998, as subsequent elections results would indicate. The drama *Love Lies Bleeding* at least acknowledges this polarisation even if it does not investigate it thoroughly. As the loyalist leader Geordie Wilson tells Conn, 'There's people – so-called well-meaning people – always going on about how really we've more in common than you'd think. But my opinion is that's a load of bollocks!' More typical, in film and television drama, is the tendency to domesticate and privatise the conflict rather than engage with the politics of gender, class or nationalism that structure the private or domestic sphere as much as the public domain. It is simply disingenuous to assume that the domestic sphere offers sanctuary and respite from politics.

Feminists rightly insist that private and domestic spheres are political, but in representations of Northern Ireland domestic relations have been stripped of politics in the interests of ameliorating sectarian conflict. The consequences of this are apparent in the ceasefire depictions of women. In *Give My Head Peace* Ma functions first and foremost as a *bona fide* of the domestic probity within which her belligerent husband and in-laws are contained. Maggie in *The Boxer* is a mere signifier of Danny's growing social legitimacy. Kathleen Quigley in *Some Mother's Son* and Bernie McPhelimy in *Titanic Town* are similarly confined to the ideological prison of domesticity, because the political sphere is presented as alien to them. We therefore reject any notion here that the characters of Bernie McPhelimy or Kathleen Quigley somehow subvert traditional cinematic representations of women and their position in the conflict in Ireland. As Sarah Edge argues, 'Traditional femininity has been remobilised [in these films] to exclude women from debates on the nation, while a new imagining of masculinity, in the figure of the father, has been designed to unite men from different nationalities.'[24] This is more than just an academic argument. The return home of paramilitary prisoners, though integral to the peace process, has raised questions as to the place and role of women in Northern Ireland. Rosemary Sales notes the concerns of women who have made 'substantial moves into the public sphere', especially at community level, but fear they may be ousted from that role when the men return from prison.[25]

While gender politics in the new dispensation are effectively marginalised in media representation, class politics barely register at all – little wonder, perhaps, when it is absent from the script of the Good Friday

Agreement. Colin Coulter writes that 'nation and ethnie have . . . come to represent the principal authors of political allegiance within the six counties', even though 'economic status has an altogether more substantial bearing upon the iniquitous distribution of life chances'. The Agreement, he argues, exudes pluralism but its terms are 'oppressively narrow' and privilege rather than question the designations 'unionist' and 'nationalist'.[26] Of course, it was never government policy to challenge the ethno-nationalism of Northern Irish politics, only to pacify, institutionalise and 'house train' it. The media's domesticated imagery has played its part in this, just as it seems to have dispensed with the politics of gender and class.

Of course, this very local analysis neglects some wider social and political forces at work in the period leading up to and during the peace process. These include the historic 'break-up of Britain',[27] culminating in variable degrees of devolution in Scotland and Wales as well as Northern Ireland; the rise of the so-called 'Celtic Tiger' economy in the Republic of Ireland; British and Irish partnership in Europe; the end of the Cold War, with the collapse of communism and, more crucially still, the apparent triumph of capitalism. Seen in this light, Ulster loyalism and Irish republicanism may appear as anachronisms, spent forces ready to be tamed and pacified. Yet such an assumption ignores their potential to become even more aggressive and virulent, partly in response to those broader social and political forces that threaten their political identity and sense of purpose. This does not seem to have been considered by broadcasters and film makers, who have become all too complacent amid the hype and rhetoric of the peace process, preferring instead a domesticated, unproblematic vision of Northern Ireland. Not only is this considered conducive to a political settlement, as indicated by the British government in its secret communiqué with Sinn Féin and in the confidential telephone ads, it also coincides with the privatised, consumer sovereignty favoured by neo-liberalism. In this respect the British government's often stated position that 'there is no plan B', no alternative to the Agreement, is an echo of neo-liberalism's triumphant 'end of history' thesis.

Media visions of a pacified, domesticated Northern Ireland may seem preferable to those of interminable conflict between unionism and nationalism. But they represent an abandonment of politically engaged public discourse and cultural representation; and they negate the very idea that political struggle is imaginable at the very moment when neo-liberalism, poverty, social exclusion and war make it most necessary, and when the intellectual weaknesses of unionism and nationalism make it most attractive.

Notes

1 G. McLaughlin and S. Baker, 'The Media, Terrorism, and Northern Ireland: Changing Frameworks, Changing Images', paper delivered to conference of Commonwealth Journalists Association, 'Peace or Patriotism: Journalists in Conflict', Belfast, 11–13 February 2004.

2 See, for example, D. Miller, *Don't Mention the War: Northern Ireland, Propaganda and the Media* (London: Pluto Press, 1994); D. Butler, *The Trouble with Reporting Northern Ireland* (Aldershot: Avebury, 1995); B. Rolston and D. Miller (eds), *War and Words* (Belfast: Beyond the Pale Publications, 1996); L. Curtis, *Ireland, the Propaganda War: the British Media and the 'Battle for Hearts and Minds'* (Belfast: Sasta, 1998).

3 See, for example, G. McLaughlin and D. Miller (1996), 'The media politics of the Irish peace process', *International Journal of Press/Politics* 1:4 (1996), pp. 116–34; G. Spencer, 'Keeping the peace? Politics, television news and the Northern Ireland peace process', *Irish Journal of Sociology* 10:2 (2001), pp. 57–76; for a comparative international perspective on media reporting of the peace process see G. Wolfsfeld, *Media and the Path to Peace* (Cambridge: Cambridge University Press, 2004).

4 Glasgow University Media Group, *Bad News* (Milton Keynes: Open University Press, 1975), p. 1.

5 *Guardian*, 29 May 2000.

6 G. McLaughlin and D. Miller, 'The media politics of the Irish peace process', p. 130.

7 M. McLoone, 'Drama out of a crisis: television drama and the Northern Ireland Troubles', in M. McLoone (ed.), *Broadcasting in a Divided Community* (Belfast: Institute of Irish Studies, 1996), pp. 73–104.

8 L. O'Carroll, 'The truth behind *Real Lives*', *Media Guardian*, 12 December 2005, p. 3; see also M. Leapman, 'The *Real Lives* controversy', in Rolston and Miller, *War and Words*, pp. 96–117.

9 See also, M. McLoone, 'What kind of peace?' in *Willie Doherty: Same old Story* (Colchester: Firstsite, 1997), pp. 23–6.

10 J. Hill, 'Images of violence', in K. Rockett, L. Gibbons and J. Hill, *Cinema and Ireland* (London: Croom Helm, 1987), pp. 147–56.

11 *Ibid.*, p. 149.

12 *Ibid.*, pp. 155–6.

13 For a feminist perspective on *Titanic Town* and *Some Mother's Son* see S. Edge, 'Representations of women in films about the Troubles: gender and nationalism in Northern Ireland', in V. Tolz and S. Booth (eds), *Nation and Gender in Contemporary Europe* (Manchester: Manchester University Press, 2005), pp. 149–65.

14 For a detailed analysis of *Resurrection Man* and *Nothing Personal* see S. Baker, 'Vampire troubles: loyalism and resurrection man', in R. Barton and H. O'Brien (eds), *Keeping It Real: Irish Film and Television* (London: Wallflower Press, 2004), pp. 78–86.

15 M. McLoone, *Irish Film: The Emergence of a Contemporary Cinema* (London: BFI, 2000), p. 78.
16 J. Hill, 'Images of violence', p. 160.
17 S. Neale and F. Krutnik, *Popular Film and Television Comedy* (London: Routledge, 1990), p. 80.
18 Interview with the authors, Belfast, 11 August 2004.
19 For a full discussion of these issues see Butler, *The Trouble with Reporting Northern Ireland*, pp. 94–113.
20 *The John Daly Show*, BBC Northern Ireland, 10 November 2003.
21 Taken from an interview with Elliott on: www.bbc.co.uk/films/ukmovies/newmovies/incinemasnow/the_mighty_celt.shtml.
22 M. McLoone, 'National cinema and cultural identity: Ireland and Europe', in J. Hill, M. McLoone and P. Hainsworth (eds), *Border Crossing: Film in Ireland, Britain and Europe* (Belfast: Institute of Irish Studies/British Film Institute, 1994), pp. 146–73. For examples of radical feminist visions of Ireland in cinema see S. Edge, 'Representations of women in films about the Troubles'.
23 M. McLoone, 'Topographies of terror and taste: the re-imagining of Belfast in recent cinema', in R. Barton and H. O'Brien (eds) *Keeping It Real: Irish Film and Television* (London: Wallflower Press, 2004), pp. 134–46.
24 S. Edge, 'Representations of women in films about the Troubles', p. 162.
25 R. Sales, 'Gender and Protestantism in Northern Ireland', in P. Shirlow and M. McGovern (eds), *Who are 'the People'? Unionism, Protestantism and Loyalism in Northern Ireland* (London: Pluto Press, 1997), p. 156.
26 C. Coulter, 'The absence of class politics in Northern Ireland', in P. Stewart and P. Shirlow (eds), *Capital and Class 69* (1999), special issue 'Northern Ireland: Between War and Peace?', pp. 70–100.
27 T. Nairn, *The Break-up of Britain: Crisis and Neo-nationalism* (London: Verso, 1972).

Index